BRANDY

Our Man in Acapulco

Brandy, Our Man in Acapulco

The Life and Times of
Colonel Frank M. Brandstetter

A biography by

Rodney P. Carlisle

and

Dominic J. Monetta

Foreword by
Astronaut James A. Lovell, Jr.,
Captain, U. S. Navy (Ret.)

University of North Texas Press
Denton, Texas

© 1999, Resource Alternatives, Inc.

Printed in the United States of America.
First edition 1999
10 9 8 7 6 5 4 3 2 1

Permissions:
University of North Texas Press
PO Box 311336
Denton TX 76203-1336

The paper used in this book meets the minimum requirements
of the American National Standard for Permanence of Paper for
Printed Library Materials, z39.48.1984. Binding materials
have been chosen for durability.

Library of Congress Cataloging-in-Publication Data

Carlisle, Rodney P.
  Brandy, our man in Acapulco: the life and times of Colonel
Frank M. Brandstetter / by Rodney P. Carlisle and Dominic J.
Monetta.
    p. cm.
  Includes bibliographical references (p.   ) and index.
  ISBN 1-57441-069-5 (cloth : alk. paper)
    1. Brandstetter, Frank M., 1912-   . 2. Intelligence officers—
United States—Biography. 3. Intelligence service—United
States—History. 4. Secret service—United States—History.
I. Monetta, Dominic J. II. Title.
JK468.I6C36   1999
327.1273'0092—dc21   99-22172
                                            CIP

Design by Angela Schmitt

This book is dedicated to the memory of my friend
Dominic A. Paolucci, who introduced me to the
most remarkable man I know, Frank M. Brandstetter.
—DJM

Contents

Acknowledgments

The authors wish to thank numerous people who assisted as we put this work together. Donald Davis served as a dedicated research assisstant, helping to assemble the many boxes of Brandstetter files and memorabilia. William Sparks patiently labored to shepherd the manuscript through its publication travails. The gracious patience and support of our wives, Loretta and Gail, kept us going through this process. And most crucial, we thank Frank M. Brandstetter himself for sharing his memories, his library, his archives, and his home to make the work possible.

The reader will want to understand that this biography is entirely factual. The work is based on Frank Brandstetter's phenomenal memory, verified and substantiated from his collection of primary documents and from published literature on many of the events in which he participated. The precise dates of events are confirmed either from independent sources or from manuscript material in the collection. Conversations in quotation marks are as Brandy remembered them; other, paraphrased conversations, represent his best recollection of the lines of discussion.

Thanks also are due to two invaluable contibutors to the publishing process. Peter Lane, of the University of North Texas History Department, proved himself helpful with insights and suggestions, particularly with regard to the early events in Central and Eastern Europe. Richard Himmel, archivist at UNT, gave the whole manuscript the benefit of meticulous editing and helped pull together the many and varied strands in the concluding chapter. The Frank M. Brandstetter files have been organized and placed on deposit at the library archives of the University of North Texas in Denton, Texas, where Peggy Price and Jane Howard have been of particular service. This collection may serve as the basis for much research into such varied subjects as World War II military interrogation and intelligence methods, hotel management in New York in the 1930s, Havana in the 1950s, Acapulco in the 1960s, and the many personalities who crossed paths with Brandy.

Rodney P. Carlisle
Dominic J. Monetta

Foreword

One of the perks of being an astronaut is the chance to meet hundreds of fascinating people back here on earth. For me, one of the most interesting is Frank M. Brandstetter—"Brandy," as everyone calls him. Over the years, I have never tired of listening to Brandy's adventures, for he has led a fascinating life at the center of some of the major events that shaped the twentieth century. Many of us who know him have been urging him for years to tell his story to the rest of the world. Now, with the help, dedication, and skill of Rodney P. Carlisle and Dominic J. Monetta, he finally has done just that. This book documents with great accuracy so many fresh and previously untold tales that it is hard for me to choose a personal favorite.

One of the top contenders is surely Brandy's work as chief of a paratrooper intelligence unit in Great Britain during World War II. He uncovered and foiled a German plot to free thousands of German POWs in camps throughout Britain who were to create a "third front" or major diversion during the Battle of the Bulge.

Another highlight is Brandy's stint as an aide to Gen. Matthew Ridgway, during which he arrested the infamous Nazi Alfried von Krupp and accepted the surrender of the Germans in Copenhagen. Then he informally occupied Denmark in the name of the United States to the chagrin of the British, who had been assigned to officially occupy the country.

After the war, Brandy undertook one of the first intelligence forays behind the recently fallen iron curtain—a quest both political and personal. Brandy learned that his sister had worked with the resistance, was captured and tortured by the Nazis, and might still be alive and recovering in Czechoslovakia or Austria. After a trip behind the emerging iron curtain, Brandy supplied his superiors with some of the first reliable information about the postwar Communist build-up in Eastern Europe.

The cold war brought new challenges. In January of 1959, Brandy led the harrowing evacuation of hundreds of Americans trapped in Havana when Fidel Castro's rebel army defeated Batista and marched into the city. Working closely with the U.S. Embassy, Brandy, who managed the Havana Hilton at the time, offered the famous Hilton hospitality to Castro and his men. He also prevented a mob from burning down the hotel, and later arranged an interview for Jack Paar with Castro. The interview, considered one of Paar's best, turned out to be an intelligence coup for the Pentagon as well.

In the 1960s and 1970s, Brandy built the Las Brisas resort in Acapulco where he pampered and charmed world leaders like Lyndon Johnson, astronauts like me, and famous writers and actors like Leon Uris, Jimmy Stewart, and Dick Van Dyke.

Whether he was uncovering the schemes of international criminals, saving Americans in Cuba, or charming the powerful and beautiful at Las Brisas, Brandy remained the quintessential patriot, the last of a noble breed. As such, Frank Brandstetter can serve as a role model for every American, whether an astronaut or a hard-hat.

I am delighted that these stories, which Brandy carried in his head for so long, are finally being told. I wish it, and above all Mr. Brandstetter, well. It is fitting that his life story appears at the dawn of the new millennium. Perhaps "Our Man in Acapulco" can help guide our steps into the twenty-first century.

James A. Lovell, Jr.

1

Casa Tranquilidad

The scene has a picture-postcard quality. From the terrace which borders the turquoise colored pool, one looks down a steep precipice crowded with the brilliant white villas of international millionaires, over green papaya trees and palms, over the Las Brisas tennis courts cut into the mountain, to the broad sweep of Acapulco Bay to the north. The beach curves to the rocky cliffs of La Quebrada, famous for its daring divers. The blue bay, white surf, and golden sand stretch like a draftsman's perfect stroke; the line they make in the morning haze lies below the row of white, high-rise hotels.

The sun cuts through the morning fog that blankets the Pacific Coast of central Mexico; in the fog is a constant smoky, blue-gray reminder that inland, a struggling, churning, vibrant economy, poised between the third world and modernity, may come to threaten the tourist paradise below. But here, near the crest that rises above Las Brisas, stands a beautiful villa. It nestles below a towering 170.5-foot white cross that marks the peak; a house called Casa de la Tranquilidad, the home of Colonel Frank M. Brandstetter.

Dressed in his characteristic spotless white Guayabera shirt and white bermuda shorts, Brandstetter rarely pauses in his energetic rounds to drink in the vista spread below his terrace. In the 1990s he is too busy, too devoted to his passions: providing hospitality to the flow of house guests, managing his household staff with the experience of decades in the hotel and restaurant business, sorting his files and mementos of service to his country. That country is the United States. Proudly, above the villa, he flies the Stars and Stripes next to the Mexican flag, together with an emblem of his family crest, the traditional "Don't Tread on Me" banner of the American Revolution, and an assortment of banners brought out in honor of this week's guests.

Behind the pool lies the open-sheltered, onyx-floored entry, in which a ten-foot boulder, splashed with ever-running water, is a centerpiece and fountain. To the left of the patio is his study, lined to the ceiling with books, many inscribed by the authors to Brandstetter himself. And to the right of the patio, another large room, formerly the dining room of the villa, now his museum room, is hung with his "Space" collection: photographs, documents, artifacts, gifts, awards, and plaques.

As visitors browse through the museum, through the framed documents on the office wall, and through the displays in the shaded portions of the outside terrace near the pool, they are charmed, mystified, awed, and sometimes intensely curious. A case of medals in his study catches the eye: the Silver Star, the Bronze Star, and many others including international recognition from Mexico, France, Italy, Belgium, and the Vatican. Among the pictures are familiar figures, some photographed in that very setting. Here one of Lyndon Johnson, posing with Lady Bird and Brandstetter in the museum room itself; another of Henry Kissinger sitting at the table on the terrace; still others of actors and actresses, some barely remembered from old television series, others unforgettable, like Charlton Heston and Jimmy Stewart. His Space collection contains a rich assortment of letters and artifacts from the American astronauts who orbited Earth and landed on the Moon. One section houses documents and materials from the German V-2 rocket program, given to him by the widow of General Walter Dornberger, German commanding general at Peenemünde, the test center for the V-1s and V-2s. It was upon this program that the United States based its first long-range guided missile technology in the post-World War II period. The past and future somehow seem compatible in his unique collection, documenting the birth of the Space Age.

On the walls, letters of commendation from generals and admirals, churchmen and popes, glint from their frames. The pictures and letters suggest the details of a life rich in experience. The stories beg to be told. Brandstetter, at the elbow, quietly fills in anecdotes. Yes, that is Jack Paar in that picture. Yes, his letter thanks me for setting up the first television interview with Fidel Castro in Havana. That, in turn, ties to another story, another anecdote, and as the visitor strolls to the outside bar to replenish his drink, the anecdotes flow on.

Brandstetter shows no compulsion to impress his visitors, but rather, in a factual and remarkably detailed way, he simply answers questions, fills in the gaps, and explains the mementos. The life of contacts and adventures, the travels to every continent, the range of experience—including information gathering over the decades for the United States government through army intelligence (G-2)—can grow fascinating and hypnotic. Scraps and pieces of a tale are here, hanging on the walls, footnotes to a narrative.

Frank M. Brandstetter, born on 26 March 1912, in Nagyszeben, a small city in the Austro-Hungarian Empire, lives on into the 1990s, charming his hundreds of friends and acquaintances, sharing memories —

Casa de la Tranquilidad, the Frank M. Brandstetter residence in Acapulco.

Jimmy Stewart visits Las Brisas in the 1960s.

some dramatic, some poignant, some instructive — all hinted at in his collection of books, papers, letters, and mementos. Here is the story of a patriot, a self-made man, a linguist, and an amusing host. His languages are English, Spanish, German, and Hungarian (Magyar), with an understanding of French and Slovak. His favorite, he says, with a glint of his piercing blue eyes, is pillow talk. That's the best way to learn a language.

What experiences yielded this personality, this man of ready wit? How did he grow into such a dedicated patriot? How and why did he so frequently cross the paths of the men and women who shaped history? What fate put him in New York City during the Wall Street Crash of 1929, in Normandy in June 1944, and in the Ruhr as Germany collapsed in 1945? Why was he present at the formation of the United Nations in New York in 1946 and in Havana when Castro took the city in 1959? What brought him to the Aegean Sea when Greece and Turkey went to war in 1974, to Argentina in April 1982 at the start of the Falklands War, and at a dozen other hinge points in the turbulent history of the world through the twentieth century? How did those events shape the character we meet in the 1990s?

Brandstetter's social and political ideas defy any effort to put them in simple categories; he seems at first meeting to be a cluster of contradictions. He fought against Nazism in World War II, shuddered with horror at the pitiful remnants of the Holocaust, and shared in the liberation of a concentration camp. Yet his view of the German enemy reflected no simple stereotype; those officers and men on both sides who fought with dedication and intelligence earned his respect. For decades he enlisted in the Cold War, one of the quiet warriors who aided Washington in its long contest against Moscow, as an unpaid volunteer. Friend to some of the wealthiest businessmen of the United States, Mexico, and Western Europe, and an active member of the American Legion, he has remained sensitive to the plight of the poor. As hotel manager, he put in place in Mexico unique programs of gratuity sharing and worker training that helped those willing to help themselves. Unless Latin America can build its middle class, he always warned, democracy would remain fragile.

In details, he demands that things be done correctly. Some would see his domestic habits as a mark of perfectionism, yet he graciously forgives small errors by his staff. As a man who once waited on tables, he recognizes the nuances of service, at once expecting excellent performance and knowing, with some sympathy, how the table appears from the waiter's perspective.

That ability to see beneath the surface, to observe in detail, to recall, to note, to catch the moment's glance, to engage another's point of view and to build a strategy upon those observations, marks a kind of genius. It makes him an excellent hand at gin rummy and a master-level player at backgammon; perhaps it also helped make him a talented "eyes and ears" for the American government that he served for nearly fifty years.

He catches the shades and flavors of words, and will quickly stop a guest from jumping to conclusions he does not approve. He dislikes the implications of such terms as espionage and intelligence. Rather, the work he did for G-2 while on active duty and while a colonel in the U.S. Army Reserve was, he insists, the gathering and reporting of *information*. His techniques had little in common with the tradecraft well known to readers of the novels of John le Carré or the memoirs of Allen Dulles.

He used no electronic bugs, signal intercepts, or bribed informants; engaged in no burglary or blackmail. His methods were more straight-forward, the simple process of traveling to the correct spot, then read-ing, observing, talking, questioning, listening, and catching the details. The experts would call his work traditional "human intelligence," not so different from the methods employed openly by military and naval attachés around the world. In short, he was a set of "eyes and ears" for those who needed and could appreciate the information. His ability to place himself where events transpired, to observe, and then to report without embellishment the facts as he saw them, made him an asset.

He always felt ambivalent towards publicity. On the one hand, too much of it, particularly about his contacts and achievements, could tend to work against his ability to quietly gather more information for the United States. On the other hand, the awards and letters of recognition are personally important to him, as evidenced by how carefully they have been collected, preserved, and housed. Furthermore, when he worked as general manager of the Las Brisas Hotel in Acapulco, he had to publicize the hotel and its attractions to a "jet-set" audience through travel magazines, newspaper columns, and an occasional news release. As a prominent member of the expatriate community in Acapulco, his name and picture would surface from time to time in the social col-umns, and in local and international news items. In fact, the more his genuine role as a hotel manager was publicized, the easier it made his other, but more quiet role, as "eyes and ears" to the Pentagon.

The life story of Frank M. Brandstetter follows and parallels much of the history of war and peace, social turbulence, and technical tri-umphs that the world has seen in the twentieth century. His life weaves in and out of those events, like a marker pen through a student's history textbook, underscoring here, adding a note in the margin there, check-ing off a fact here, providing a correction or a question there. He kept his counsel, he saved his documents, he gathered his letters and notes, and provided his reports. From time to time, his name would appear in print, giving some small reflection of his activities. And finally, at the turn of the century, he agrees to let us tell his whole story.

Child of a Turbulent Era

The empire stretched across central Europe, an uneasy balance of nationalities and nations, only loosely united under the family of Habsburgs who ruled jointly as emperors of Austria from Vienna and kings of Hungary from Budapest. In Austria and its crown lands, German-speaking Austrians governed. In Hungary, the dominant groups spoke Magyar.

Aspirations for national independence or alignment with nations outside the empire stirred in the late nineteenth and early twentieth centuries among its various peoples, sowing the seeds of later struggles. There were many such groups: Poles in the north; Czechs and Slovaks in the center; Romanians in Transylvania; Italians in the Tyrol; South Slavs in Croatia, Slovenia, and Bosnia-Herzegovina to the south.

The ruling gentry in Hungary rarely intermarried with the officer-diplomatic corps classes of Austria, but from time to time such unions brought together the German and Magyar sides of the empire. Frank M. Brandstetter's family was just such a union, the Hungarian officer class on his father's side and the Polish-Austrian titled gentry on his mother's side. The intricacy of Frank's heritage was reflected in his full name: "Maryan, Franciscus, Otto Josephus, Ladislaw, Stanislaw, Brandstetter, Drag-Sas Hubicki."

Frank's mother, Maria Luisa, belonged to the Drag-Sas Hubicki, a Polish family which had been members of the extensive aristocratic bureaucracy of the empire, and officers in the "K and K Army" — the Kaiserlichte und Koeniglichte Army of Franz Josef, emperor of Austria and king of Hungary. As an established family with the Polish baronial rank, the Drag-Sas Hubicki had been crusader-knights and later officers in the Polish kingdom of the empire.

Frank's father, Ferenc Brandstetter, was from the Hungarian side of the empire. The Brandstetters had long lived in German-speaking, Catholic Austria, close to the Swiss border. Frank's father, in common with ancestors on both sides, served as a general staff officer in the K & K army.

In the year 1912, Frank's father happened to be on maneuvers in the provincial town of Nagyszeben, Transylvania, when his pregnant wife of one year visited him in the last months of her confinement. It is for this reason that Frank was not born in the family home in the city of Bratislava, then known as Pozsony. The residence was a large villa in a nice section, with a view over the city. Bratislava lies on the Slovakian side of the border between Austria and Slovakia, the eastern republic of the former Czechoslovakia.

Two years after Frank's birth, Europe plunged into the maelstrom of war, when the heir to the throne of the empire, Archduke Franz Ferdinand, was assassinated in June 1914 by a Serbian nationalist while visiting Sarajevo, the capital city of the Austro-Hungarian province of Bosnia. Austria-Hungary presented Serbia with an ultimatum, Serbia did not comply, and Russia came to the aid of Serbia. France, an ally of Russia, joined the war. Germany fought alongside Austria-Hungary to form the Central Powers, and lunged at France through Belgium. Britain, honoring a commitment to Belgium, sided with France and Russia, becoming one of the Triple Entente or the Allies. Later, Italy would join the Allies, and the Ottoman Empire would join the Central Powers. The United States would not enter the war until 1917, fighting with the Allies. The "Great War," as it came to be called, would last more than four years, and result in the slaughter of millions of young men: Russians, Germans, French, British, Hungarians, Austrians, Italians, Americans, and the wounding of millions more.

Maria Luisa Brandstetter and
Frank, 1914.

Ferenc Brandstetter, 1911.

When Ferenc was shipped off to fight on the Russian front, young Frank was at first raised by a French nanny at home, thus learning French as his first language. His mother soon joined the voluntary nursing service and was unable to keep Frank at home. Maria's duties took her to the town of Sassnitz on the Baltic Sea, on the island of Rügen, Germany, where she worked on Red Cross trains that ran to Stockholm, Sweden, via ferryboat.

When Frank was four, his parents arranged to send him to a temporary boarding school set up and run by the Sisters of Charity for a small group of officers' children. He "fell in love," young as he was, with one of the sisters who took particular care of him. When her wedding engagement was broken, she had taken the vows. For Frank, her faith and commitment was a gentle introduction to the religious life. Even so, his memories of the cloister would not be entirely fond. The schedule was tough, with wake-up at 4:00 A.M., mass at 4:30, then breakfast and classes beginning at 6:00 A.M. The sisters were strict, even with their most youthful charges.

Frank (top center) at Sassnitz with mother and father (bottom left), 1917.

Ferenc was wounded on the Russian front and after recuperation from his wounds, was sent to Sassnitz to take charge of the Swedish route for exchange of prisoners of war between Russia and the Central Powers. Later, he received a decoration from the king of Sweden for his work with the POWs. While on active duty he was promoted to the acting rank of general. His retired rank was that of major in the general staff.

Frank learned in later years that during the war his father had been nominated for the Maria Theresa Medal for refusing to retreat as ordered. Instead, he sent a message through to his corps and linked up with another unit. Ferenc would have been promoted to general if he had received the award. His willingness to take responsibility when given an obviously incorrect order, to fight and, if necessary, die for the flag was a code with profound appeal. It burned itself deep into the child. Frank remembered one summer trip to Sassnitz during the Great War, where his father arranged a visit aboard one of the German navy's famous U-boats, the *U-9*, which had won fame for sinking three British warships. He kept and cherished the photos of those visits, preserving them among his albums and papers for decades.

On these trips to Sassnitz in the last years of the war, Frank's nickname was "Muky Pasha," apparently a diminutive of "Maryan." The "pasha" derived from a little fez he wore, a gift from visiting Turkish general staff officers. Captain Curt Meisner, a German air ace originally stationed with his squadron in Sassnitz before he was shot down over the Russian front and repatriated through Sweden, remembered little "Muky Pasha" clearly. Meisner was to meet Frank again in later years.

In 1918, when Frank was six years old, the Austro-Hungarian Empire began a turbulent transformation. In October, the Czech provinces declared their independence, and later that month, Austria and Hungary split. The Slovaks joined with the Czechs to form Czechoslovakia. The Armistice ended the Great War on 11 November. Within a week, Hungary was declared a republic, but early in 1919, its government collapsed as the Allies transferred Transylvania to Romania. Under Bela Kun, a short-lived Communist regime, the Hungarian Soviet Republic, was established in Budapest. Cruelties committed by uncontrolled Communist mobs and soldiers, including the torture of nuns and the hanging of priests, remained a vivid memory in Frank's mind.

In 1919, when he was seven, Frank's parents divorced, and the judge gave him the difficult choice of which parent he would live with. He chose his father, who then arranged schooling and residential summer camps for him over the next years. From time to time, Frank visited his father in the apartments he maintained on a fairly modest military pension. In 1920, Frank's mother married Emil Prat, a former K & K artillery officer who had joined the Czechoslovakian army in that year. The turbulence in Frank's family was perhaps a reflection of the turbulent times.

During those chaotic years, Frank returned home to Pozsony (now Bratislava) and, from a former Hungarian officer, received private tutoring that emphasized Hungarian history and military tradition. Afterwards, he was sent for a year to the Maria Theresianum school in Vienna, a school established in 1759 to train youngsters of the aristocracy, diplomats, generals, and the nephews of priests to carry forward the values of the empire. The triangular, three-legged base of the society—army, diplomacy, and the church—was to be embodied and enforced at the school. Frank attended for one year, becoming steeped in the traditions of the collapsing empire. According to legends, children from the school had fought during the revolutions of 1848. The teachers made much of the tradition of *pro patria*—"for the fatherland."

One painful situation from that period occurred during the holidays, when all of the students returned home to visit their parents. Frank, along with two young scions from Albania, children of King Zog, were left behind. Spending Christmas alone at the school was painful, despite the efforts of the teachers and parents of students living in Vienna to make the few "orphaned" students feel welcome.

Another painful occurrence at the Maria Theresianum school involved an encounter with the military chaplain, a priest who also taught music. The priest beat Frank's fingertips to a pulp for flunking his music lesson. For the first time, Frank's opinion of the clergy turned negative. It was the start of his long-lasting ambivalence towards the Catholic Church, into which he had been baptized as an infant.

Pain was also his companion during horseback training on the world-famous Lippizaner white horses. Training went beyond learning a good seat at trot, canter, gallop, and jump. As the boys rode through thorny thickets, if they bent in the saddle, they were ordered to sit upright. They had to ride with a coin under the saddle. If it slipped out, the boy was lashed with a riding crop as he bent over to retrieve it, and lashed again if he dropped it. Discipline was tough, enforced with the crop, in front of others.

In 1920 Frank went back to Bratislava, on the Czechoslovak side of the border with Austria, this time not to school, but to live with a humble family in the mountains south of Prague. In later years, Frank assumed that this disruption of his life was partly a move to destroy the influence of the old Hungarian aristocracy and officer class. He believed an order had been given by President Thomas Masaryk of Czechoslovakia (father of Jan Masaryk, the post-World War II president of the same republic) to relocate children of K & K officers to live in the homes of local, working class families. As he grew interested in the history of the period in later years, he could uncover no record of the order, and thus this episode of his life remained something of a mystery.

Young Frank was sent to the town of Brezové-Hory, near Príbram in western Czechoslavakia, less than fifty miles south of Prague. For a few months, in one of the only childhood homes he could remember, he struggled to learn Czech. The head of the household was a good family man, a miner, who returned from work each day covered with coal dust. He took a hot bath in a wooden tub and smoked his pipe. After prayers with the family, which included a young boy slightly older than Frank, they ate a simple meal.

Frank was teased at school for not speaking the Czech language. The other boys taught him some phrases by rote, which he then tried out on the teacher. The teacher flew into a rage, beat Frank, and sent him home, expelled. The boys had taught him to say, "You are a stinking Czech pig," a typically cruel schoolboy prank. His foster father, on hearing the whole story from Frank's "brother," visited the school to argue that his charge should not be punished for falling into the trap. He was reinstated. This touched the boy deeply. A father who would speak out against an injustice—it held meaning.

At last, for a few months, Frank had a home life with a sense of parental love, and a brother who shared the cramped loft attic space and helped protect him from being beaten up. He acclimated and adjusted, daily growing more fluent in Czech and earning the local school red cap and badge. He did not have the comforts of his own room or the formality of the discipline of a residential school setting, but the trade-off was not altogether bad. Then suddenly, one afternoon at the Czech home, his father appeared. He had arranged for Frank's return with him to Bratislava.

The episode in the Czech home had several long-lasting effects. Frank had learned the rudiments of Czech speaking and writing, adding it to the French, German, and Hungarian he had already acquired. He had been separated once again from his parents. He had seen and lived a simple home life and felt, however briefly, the warmth of a close-knit family with its rewards of trust, affection, and routine. He had also tasted freedom from the discipline, duty, and structure that the round of private schools imposed. The life of the simple working class, although less elegant than that of the gentry, appealed to him. He did not articulate such thoughts at the time, but the impressions were there, to surface later.

His next stay at home in Bratislava was brief, for he soon went to an *Untergymnasium*, a middle school, in Freistadt in Austria. At the end of the school session a year later, the headmaster provided Frank with tickets and instructions to take the train to Linz and then change to one for Vienna. Next he was to take a *fiaker*, a sort of horse-drawn taxi, to a ship anchored at a pier on the Danube for the overnight trip to Budapest, where his father would meet him. All the instructions, pocket money for tips, and tickets were in an envelope, and Frank, at age ten, was pleased to be able to enjoy the freedom of traveling alone. At dinner on the boat, however, he was surprised to find that his father sat opposite him.

Ferenc explained that he was next to go to an *Obergymnasium*, a military prep school, in Cegléd, Hungary, which would be a prelude to enrolling in the military school, Hunyadi Matyas Magyar Kiralyi Realiskola, and to following in his father's footsteps as an officer in the Hungarian army. During the summer, he was to attend a camp on Lake Balaton, with a private tutor to help him prepare for the *Obergymnasium*.

That fall, when he set off for the train to Cegléd, his father revealed a secret to him. When he had traveled from Linz to Vienna and got aboard the ship, he was not alone. His father had followed him every step of the way to make sure Frank could handle traveling alone, only joining him for dinner on the riverboat. Ferenc was proud of his son's abilities, and let him know it.

Although not far apart in sheer miles by modern standards, Frank's schools and homes were scattered across three countries: Czechoslovakia, Austria, and Hungary. His early education had alternated between the Austrian and the Hungarian sides of the dual monarchy's territories. Frank's cosmopolitan experiences had started early, as had his taste for international travel.

For the next few years, ethnic politics throughout central Europe generated many tensions and crises between World War I and World War II. These issues haunted the schools and the teachers that Frank observed over the next few years.

In 1924, Frank moved to the military academy at Köszeg in Hungary, near the border with Austria. The purpose of the school was to graduate a student, after seven years, with the rank of "Fähnrich," literally flag-bearer or holder of a unit's flag, a cadet rank. In warfare, the "Fähnrich" rank was an honor, since the casualty rate for flag-bearers in traditional musket warfare had been extremely high. In peacetime, young cadets passed through this rank on their way to full officer status. Although Hungary was to avoid military training under the Trianon treaty, the school operated quite openly as a military academy.

Clearly, Frank's father was preparing him to follow in his footsteps and in those of his ancestors on both sides of the family. Köszeg, like the Theresianium in Vienna, and the schools at Freistadt in Austria and at Cegléd in Hungary, represented the best traditions of education for the future officer and governing classes of both Austria and Hungary. Teachers of the Köszeg school were both Hungarian-speaking staff officers and former German officers who spoke Hungarian fluently and had fought in the Great War.

The teachers were determined to toughen up their charges, to make men of these boys in short order. Again, Frank encountered a severe chaplain, this time a lieutenant colonel in the Hungarian Army who served as language and religion teacher as well as chaplain. Functioning as altar boy at daily masses, Frank sometimes missed his Latin answers with the result that the instructor flunked him in both Religion and Language. This failure excluded him from some sports activities and his resentment became focused. Military discipline he could accept, but he found the discipline of the priest vindictive.

Frank's photographs of this time show the boys, clad in uniform gym-clothes, drilling their calisthenics in unison in an open field under the watchful eye of the instructor. Frank appears in the pictures as a blue-eyed, slim boy, with a piercing, intelligent, and eager look. Training at the school was strenuous. Obedience, studiousness, physical fitness, and endurance were all part of the preparation for the next war.

One drill sergeant, a former cavalryman, was notorious for his brutality. One day he kicked a cadet in the stomach, requiring the youngster to visit the infirmary. The senior cadet reported the incident to the officer in charge, but no action was taken, so the students planned revenge. The next Saturday, after the sergeant returned drunk from his

Cadet Brandstetter, 1928.

Rigorous drilling at Hunyadi Matyas, Köszeg, 1924.

Cadets at Hunyadi Matyas in 1928. Frank is located on the second row in middle.

evening out, all the cadets in the hall conspired to cut off one side of his waxed, five-inch-long cavalry mustache, a macho symbol he had nurtured over the years. The sergeant awoke, felt he had been emasculated by the prank, and began beating students indiscriminately. Everyone was mustered out, but the investigation revealed nothing. With the code of honor, no one would be a *spitzle*—a snitch. Accordingly, the whole class was punished, but the sergeant was also transferred to other duties away from the school.

In 1926, while still at school in Köszeg, Frank received a message that his mother wanted to see him. Since he had chosen to live under his father's jurisdiction, he was rarely welcomed into his mother's home, coming only when specially summoned. On this visit, she gave him a present that he would always cherish: a ring with the family ducal crest. He was immensely proud of the ring; he had seen it on his Uncle Otto's hand. Otto, said Frank's mother, was the last male heir of the line. Since he was childless, Otto had given her the ring to give to Frank. It would be Frank's duty to pass on the ring to his son, or if there was no heir, to order that the ring, as in the case of a crown, be broken upon his death. It was a powerful message of family connection and trust, compelling to a boy who had barely seen his family since infancy and desperately needed their approval.

His mother explained the family lineage, beginning when the Polish King Vladislaw in 1441 arranged the marriage of his own sister to his knight, companion, and aide-de-camp, creating the title of Baron Drag Sas-Hubicki. The king then bestowed on the baron a number of villages, baronial estates, and other landholdings, including the village of Hubic, from which the baron took the name Hubicki. She traced the generations down to her father, herself, and Uncle Otto, revealing that the family had held the estates through the end of the Great War. The remaining lands had been confiscated, but the baronial title remained and would pass down as it always had. In later years, as an American citizen, Frank never claimed or used the aristocratic title, thinking of the ancestry only as a source of his instinct for military service. His family had been part of the ruling elite of the Austro-Hungarian Empire, but could not identify readily with any of the new national entities. In one sense, Frank was part Austro-Polish and part Magyar; linguistically he was part French and part Czech. One line of his ancestors could be traced to fifteenth-century Polish nobility. During his first fifteen years, Frank had lived in places that now flew the flags of Romania, Hungary, Austria, Czechoslovakia, and Germany. His parents had separated and divorced. Duty, honor, service, loyalty—but to what? The entity that had represented his heritage, like his family, had rapidly disintegrated.

In June 1928, Frank again received a message to return and see his mother, who had further news for him. His father had moved to the United States. Ferenc had been given a diplomatic passport and shipped to America in connection with his work with the Hungarian Smallholders' Party, a "peasant party" of the land-owning rural population.

For Frank, the news that his father had gone to the United States was something of a shock. Ferenc had left the country without ever saying goodbye to his son, and months had passed before Frank was even told about it. His mother explained that Ferenc had sent a round-trip ticket for Frank to come to visit him in New York for the remainder of the summer holiday. A small family going-away party had already been arranged. Uncle Otto appeared, presenting the sixteen-year-old boy with thirty dollars in American cash, and mentioning he could use it perhaps to buy a bicycle. Frank was to travel by rail to France, stop off in Paris for a little sightseeing, then go on to Le Havre and cross the Atlantic by steamer. After his visit with his father, he was to return in the fall for the next term at Köszeg.

After a train ride through Vienna to Paris and a visit to Napoleon's tomb, Frank sailed, as planned, aboard the luxury steamship *Majestic* from Le Havre in late July 1928. He had a cabin all to himself on the second class deck. Wearing his striped pants, cravat, and morning coat, he felt like quite the dandy striding around the sunny decks, admiring the young ladies and being admired by them. Second class passage was an elegant way to travel for a schoolboy. The holiday had an auspicious beginning, a taste of the freedoms of the adult tourist. Frank always remembered looking down from the railing of the second class deck to the steerage passengers below, reflecting on the status of the poor immigrants huddled there, hoping for a better life in the United States.

When Frank arrived in New York City on 28 July 1928, his father met him at the ship and led him to his hotel, impressively called the Victoria, on 46th Street. With some trepidation, he walked uptown through the hot, taxi-crowded streets of New York to a hotel slightly more modest than he had visualized—even a bit shabby by contrast to the thriving first-class hotels nearby. For years he had known his father only as an occasional benefactor, a wounded and respected army officer. The memory of the reality blended with a remembered photograph of a handsome uniform and a chest of medals. He had hungered for every word of support and recognition, cherishing the moments when his father had given him approval for his ability to travel on his own.

Now, as a young man, he looked forward to a summer with his father. Many of the values he had been taught to cherish were embodied in the impressive figure of the far-away father: the military tradition, the family he yearned for, and duty, service, honor, country. Finally, he received a personal gesture, an invitation to spend some time with his father. What would the forthcoming summer hold?

As he entered the hotel room with his father, he was astounded to see a young woman there, perhaps a year or two older than he was. She was pretty and buxom. But a seventeen-year-old girl was hardly someone he expected to see in his father's hotel room.

"Frank," said his father, smiling, "this is your new mother."

Frank simply stared at his father, flabbergasted, then at the girl, who gave him a knowing look.

Furious, Frank said, "I don't know what she is to you, father—this girl. But she is not my mother and she is not going to be my mother."

His father slapped him.

"If that's how you feel about it—you know what you can do," his father said.

Frank picked up his bag and, without looking at either of them, strode out.

It was close to a final break. He saw his father only twice in later years, briefly—once in the early 1930s and again in 1940.

In shock, Frank wandered into the hotel coffee shop. Settling down with a cup of coffee, he felt absolutely alone, and absolutely devastated. The summer holiday in the United States was not going to happen. The reunion and companionship with his father was over before it had a chance to begin. He thought he would get aboard ship and sail back to Europe on the *Majestic* the next day.

As he controlled his mixture of fury, despair, and hurt, he noticed a boy his own age sitting near him at the counter, interrupting his lunch to stare at Frank's European clothes and off-the-boat look. The lad, assuming Frank was a young immigrant, said, in Czech: "Welcome to America."

The two struck up a conversation. The other boy, continuing in Czech, explained that in America he was free to do anything he wanted to do. Frank listened, not explaining that he had a return ticket, but letting the other young man give his "advice to the immigrant" talk. It was interesting.

First things first, the other continued. First you have to find a place to live. Then you find a job. If you don't pay the rent, the landlady takes your bag and kicks you out. But first, find a place to live, then the job. He recommended a stretch of inexpensive rooming and boarding houses uptown where central European newcomers stayed, where they could find people who spoke their languages, and make friends. Family does not count here; connections do not matter. You make your own way. It is free, it is equal. You get rewarded for your work and your brains, unlike the old country that is run by the aristocracy who hold everybody down. Here it is everybody for himself, all with the same chance. You'll make it, kid. Cheer up.

To Frank, this talk of democracy was a "strange song." He had been taught to do everything he was ordered without blinking his eyes. In a daze, sixteen-year-old Frank walked out into the noisy street. After all, perhaps he did not have to go back to the *Majestic*. He was blissfully ignorant of the immigration laws of the United States; his Hungarian passport indicated a visitor status only.

In 1928, Frank Brandstetter faced New York City with thirty dollars. Shocked by his father's behavior, having neither work experience nor English language skills nor friends, he nevertheless had a burning need to cut away from his entire past life. The chance to find freedom from discipline, from the teachers and priests with their impulsive punishments, suddenly seemed appealing.

Manhattan:
Down But Not Out

F rank stayed that night at a boarding house, run by a Slovak-speaking widow, on West 96th Street and Columbia Avenue. A boarding house was ideal, for it not only provided breakfast and supper, but a sort of substitute family life. The landlady charged ten dollars a week, taking the money in advance, beginning that Saturday, 28 July 1928. From his small store of cash, Frank paid a week in advance and started job-hunting the next week. By Tuesday, he had spotted a lead in the Slovak-language newspaper: a fur-cleaning job at Jackman and Sons Furriers on 35th Street.

His landlady and fellow lodgers may have been a little surprised at breakfast on the morning of Wednesday, 1 August, to see Frank dressed for his job interview. He put on his snappy jacket, cravat, and shined shoes—the best outfit he had brought with him. At the furriers, a salesman greeted Frank, invited him to sit, and after exploring his language problem, sent for Mr. Jackman. What price range was the young gentleman interested in? Something in a mink, a sable, perhaps? Frank shook his head and took out the folded newspaper ad from his pocket. When Frank finally made it clear that he was not there to buy a fur coat for his girlfriend, but to interview for the fourteen-dollar a week job as a fur-cleaner, Jackman rolled his eyes. Then all the staff who had been listening burst out laughing. Frank began to suspect he was overdressed when he was thrown out of the front showroom and hustled to a door in the rear which led to the elevator and the upper floors, where the workshops were located.

As he entered the workshop area, the employees looked up from their tasks and peered around the ranks of hanging furs, a little startled to see a young customer in their midst. A portly gentleman asked him if he was there to pick up a coat. Miserable, Frank said he had come to apply for the job in the paper.

The foreman had some of the workers come over to view the scene. Frank, more and more miserable as the butt of jokes, moved to leave, crumpling the paper into his pocket. The foreman, however, either deciding to call his bluff or taking pity on him, led him to a large flat table with bamboo sticks protruding out the back. A cart of furs for storage stood nearby. A metal hood hung from above. The job was simple enough, but tiring, tedious, and dirty. Frank had to beat the furs gently, loosening them, then throw the switch to lower the hood over the fur. Fans would suck the dust into a container, at least in theory. In fact, the loose fur and dust swirled into the muggy air, sticking to everything. The air was heavy with musty smells of fox, mink, sable, ocelot, and rabbit. Frank worked diligently, with his coat and tie on, and began to perspire. In August, the unair-conditioned sweatshops of the New York garment district earned their name. By the noon break, he looked as if he had rolled out of a chicken coop, with bits of fur adhering to his damp clothing. He had brought no lunch, not thinking he would start right away. During the break, his fellow workers explained that it was all right to take off his coat and tie to be a little more comfortable. One man loaned him an apron, and thus fortified—though still hungry—he went back to work for the afternoon. By sheer will, he made it through the long hours.

By the end of the day he had learned a lot. He bought a pair of cheap pants and an apron. He soon fell into a routine. He got up at 5:00 A.M., had a quick breakfast, took the IRT from its 96th Street stop to the 33rd Street station, and walked to the shop on 35th Street, punching the time clock by 5:45. He remembered always to take a little lunch from the boarding house, usually a banana and a sandwich. On Saturday, he received his first pay, which he dutifully turned over to the land-lady. As he began to work full six-day weeks, she always took out her ten dollars and advised him on how to budget the remaining amount.

In August, his English and knowledge of American ways still rudi-mentary, Frank walked into the neighborhood Catholic church for Mass. The usher passed around a basket, which Frank simply passed on. He noticed, however, that he got a dirty look from the person next to him. The next Sunday, the same thing occurred. Frank asked his landlady about it and she explained that the custom here was to col-lect donations for the upkeep of the church. Of course, in chapel at school, he had never encountered collection baskets before. Frank felt humiliated.

As the fall of 1928 wore on, the young man gradually increased his skill at cleaning the furs and began learning the methods of interior stitching to repair them. He worked side by side with a fur stretcher who worked overtime. Frank asked him if he could stay on after his stint was finished, to learn without getting paid overtime himself. He grew more and more knowledgeable about the furs, their stitching, and their qual-ity. By December, he was making thirty-five dollars a week, about fifty-three cents an hour—well above the twenty-one cents an hour that represented the bottom of the heap. The Jackmans, he learned, had fled Jewish persecution in St. Petersburg under the czar. He believed they had forgotten how it felt to be victims because they took out some of their hostilities on their workers, many of them Slavs. Most of the workers in the loft were also immigrant men and women: Poles, Hun-garians, Slovaks, mostly older than he. Some seemed beaten, almost derelicts, and they shared their outlook with Frank, who continued to remember the kindness of the foreman who hired him and the worker who loaned him an apron. They provided a human side to his first real job, which was on the whole a rugged experience.

The hours of work were long and uninterrupted, but the few min-utes at lunch, when he got a breath of air on the curbstone on 35th Street, or a brief coffee after work, gave him a chance to chat in Ger-man, Slav, or Hungarian. Sweatshop conditions were brutal. If you fell sick, you were out. Another immigrant was waiting for the job. Frank realized he had been lucky to get the work, for there were few opportunities unless you could speak English. Some of the older men and women seemed resigned to sweatshop jobs for life, but Frank decided to enroll in night school to learn English. There, he met others like himself, young students mastering a new language. Two brothers befriended him and took him to meet their father, Reverend Geza Takaro, a Doctor of Divinity and pastor of the First Magyar Reformed Church at 344 East 69th Street. Gradually, Frank learned English and became acquainted with a small circle of friends in the Hungarian community. On Saturday afternoons and Sundays, he spent time with the Takaro boys. Through this family, he met Mr. Louis Toth, president of the Board of Trustees of the church and one of the founders of Horwath and Horwath, a CPA firm which specialized in hotel work and issued a newsletter regarding the hotel business. In 1928, Toth and Horwath published a textbook in hotel accounting and management, which remained a standard text through several editions over the next decades and was adopted later by the U.S. Internal Revenue Service.

Frank knew his job at Jackman's was a dead-end job, so in December of 1928, he quit. The next month he began working as a soda jerk at Bleicher's Pharmacy. His English was improving, and he enjoyed practicing it with the customers. He would likely have kept this job for some time, except for an extraordinarily lucky coincidence. One cold evening that winter, while heading for the subway, he heard a voice call out, "Muky!" He had not heard the nickname for ten years.

He turned to see a well-dressed gentleman speaking German, asking whether Frank was the son of the former general staff officer who had been in charge of the prisoner of war exchange program from Sassnitz through Sweden. Frank admitted it, and then realized with whom he was talking. The gentleman turned out to be Captain Curt Meisner, the German air ace he had met at Sassnitz. Although Frank looked much the same at age sixteen as he had looked at age six—straight and lean with short-cropped blond hair and piercing blue eyes—it was remarkable that Meisner had spotted him. On finding that Frank was struggling along at a low-paying job, Meisner suggested he should look into aviation work. That is the future, he said. He should get an airplane factory job, and then study aeronautical engineering in the evenings.

Frank was interested, but remarked that he had to pay his bills and eat in the meantime. A few days later Meisner contacted Frank again, and said he had lined up an interview for him at the Sikorsky factory, where Meisner himself worked.

Frank resigned from the soda-jerk job and took the position of assistant riveter for Sikorsky in March, 1929. The Sikorsky plant, built and operated by Ukrainian-born Igor Sikorsky, was located in a former Tulip Cup factory in College Point in Flushing, on the East River across from what is now La Guardia Airport. Frank lived nearby, not far from the Takaro residence in Flushing. He continued to visit the Takaros on weekends, often having dinner with them.

Again, as at Jackman's, Frank encountered a melange of nationalities. Igor Sikorsky had hired many refugees from Communist Russia, including some former czarist officials who could not get any other type of work.

Frank's first job was to insert a rivet from below a wing, while another worker from above attached a head to the rivet. The man working below would adjust the angle at the order of the man working above. One coworker, a duke and former supreme court justice from the czarist regime, insisted that Frank address him as "Your Excellency" as he shouted down orders about the rivet angle through the wing. The incongruity of the situation stuck with Frank through the years. Titles of nobility meant nothing in the new environment, and at seventeen years of age he understood that.

Frank came to respect Sikorsky for his effort to provide jobs to his fellow Russian exiles. Photographs Frank collected at this time show him and other assembly workers posing self-consciously near the completed aircraft. Some are dressed in overalls, others in suits with white shirts and ties. Most of the polyglot group of employees were from the former czarist empire, although a few, like Meisner, had fought on the side of the Central Powers in the Great War.

Even though Frank had been earning slightly more at Jackman's when he left than he made initially at Sikorsky's, he found the aircraft work an exciting opportunity, unlike the dead-end job in the fur loft. Frank stayed on at Sikorsky as it geared up for new aircraft models.

He was later befriended by a German master toolmaker and re-

Working as a mechanic at
Sikorsky's.

ceived a transfer to work under him as an assistant. He worked on wing
fittings for the S-36 and S-37 Sikorsky single-engine amphibians, as well
as the S-38 twin-engine planes of the type purchased by Osa and Martin
Johnson for their explorations in Africa.

In July, 1929, the Sikorsky Company was purchased by United Aircraft and Transport Company and became a subsidiary of that firm. In
1930, with money from the sale of ten S-38s, the plant was moved to
Stratford, Connecticut, where a new and more efficient factory had
direct access to the Housatonic River. The work force increased from
under one hundred to over one thousand. Frank was proud of the fact
that his employee number was forty-six—one of the old numbers from
the College Point days. At the Connecticut plant, Frank began working on one of three S-40 amphibious aircraft that became the very first
used in the Pan American Clipper service in the late 1930s. One of the

four-engine S-42s from the plant in Stratford was flown by Charles
Lindbergh from Miami to Panama via Cuba, Jamaica, and Colombia.

While working at the United Aircraft plant in Connecticut, Frank
and two other young men enrolled in a night course in aeronautical
engineering at Yale in New Haven. The three chipped in on a large,
open, Graham-Paige car. For several months Frank's schedule consisted
of washing off the day's grease after work at 6:00 P.M., snatching a sandwich with the other boys, piling into the car to attend class between 8:00
P.M. and 11:00 P.M., and studying all day Saturday and Sunday. He spent
most of his earnings on the shared upkeep on the car. The oil and gas
alone kept the three boys broke. They stuck with the routine for about
four months. However, rising for work at 6:00 A.M. each morning, together with the drain of paying for the car, became too much. They
gave it all up.

Frank began taking some private flying lessons on single-engine
planes. On 9 October 1930, Frank's foreman invited him to go for a test
flight in one of the S-38 amphibians. The pilot brought the plane down
to a rough landing, and Frank fractured his arm and leg. After two weeks'
hospitalization and recuperation, Frank reported back for work and
discovered his job had been given to someone waiting on the unemployment list. The stay in the hospital with its medical costs had eaten
up his meager savings; there were no Social Security benefits or medical
insurance coverage at the time. It was not quite fair, but Frank understood he had no guarantees. Thus ended Frank's dream of becoming
an aeronautic engineer, after one year and seven months with the
Sikorsky Company. The year 1930 was not a good time to be out of
work, so Frank went back to New York City, where he had made a few
acquaintances, to see what he could find.

Frank looked up Louis Toth through the Takaros. Toth was glad to
assist. Although at the time Frank did not realize it, Toth, like Meisner,
knew Frank's father. Toth's advice about job hunting was firm and direct: "You should go into the hotel and restaurant business. There, at
least you can eat." Toth, as senior CPA for a firm that specialized in
hotels and restaurants, had contacts throughout the city and began to
steer Frank to appropriate openings.

With Toth's help, Frank soon landed a job at the Ardsley Club, a country club just north of Yonkers. He worked as a "roll boy," dressing in a chef's hat and passing hot rolls from table to table. He held this job for several months, adding reference letters from Jackman's, Bleicher's, and Sikorsky's to his growing file, which he maintained carefully among his papers into the 1990s.

Over the next eleven years Frank worked at a variety of hotels and restaurants in and around New York, gradually learning the business, collecting references, and moving from season to season to slightly better-paying and more responsible positions, all under the paternal guidance of Louis Toth. He put in seasons at the Carlyle Hotel in Manhattan; the Abraham Lincoln Hotel in Reading, Pennsylvania; the Paradise Show Boat in Troy, New York; the Laurel-in-the-Pines in Lakewood, New Jersey; and the De Witt Clinton Hotel in Albany, New York. Frank's employment at hotels and restaurants fluctuated with the seasons, some hotels specializing in holiday trade, others with summer resort traffic, still others appealing as winter vacation getaways. Toth came up with some of the leads and continued to provide advice as Frank moved from position to position. Sometimes a supervisor at one hotel or restaurant would find Frank a position one or two seasons later at another post. Louis Austerlitz, for example, supervised Frank when he served as dining room captain at the Paradise Show Boat in Troy in the fall 1933 season. Austerlitz also supervised Frank in the summer of 1936 at the De Witt Clinton Hotel in Albany. Although the Depression affected the hotel and restaurant business, Toth insisted that Frank should get a good grounding because the whole business, he believed, would bounce back when prosperity returned. By then, Frank should be ready.

At the Carlyle and other hotels, he learned of the highly organized structure of the restaurant service by serving at each level. At the lowest rank was the busboy, and just above was the "comie," the boy who would come back and forth from the kitchen with the dishes. The actual waiter was the *chef du rang* (literally, chef of rank) or the table waiter; above the *chef du rang* was the table captain, and above him was the maitre d'hotel. Each rank took orders from the rank above. The restaurant represented a structured organization table, with clear lines of responsibility. The parallel to the military, with uniforms and ranks, was often conscious, explicit, and intended.

Frank in 1933 during the period
when he worked in hotels in the
northeast.

There was not much time for recreation, although Frank kept up
with his friends, the Takaro brothers. Even though his funds were limited, he would often go to Central Park and rent a horse to go riding,
practicing the skills which he had developed in Vienna. For a while during this period, Frank roomed with another young man, William Palmer,
who worked as a "comie." They shared an apartment on West 69th Street.
Both Frank and Palmer enrolled in a home study course in the Lewis
Hotel Courses, studying Hotel Management.

After a period as busboy at the Carlyle, Frank moved up to work
under the pastry chef, learning the dessert-making business. The pastry
chef was temperamental and had worked through a host of assistants,
dismissing one after another in a rage over some minor mistake. From
time to time Frank would commit some irritating infraction, such as
passing along a cold plate when the chef had asked for a warm one or
intentionally handing over the wrong ingredient, just to watch him fly
into one of his fits. During one of these incidents the Resident Man-

ager, Harold Bock, noticed Frank being outrageously chewed out, and quietly moved him to a post as comie in the dining room.

Even though the Carlyle was a top hotel, it did not feed its staff well in those Depression days, serving them such dishes as thin soup made out of the bones removed from the thick Irish stew. Of course, the busboys and others would manage to steal a roll now and then, or take a bite off a plate of leftovers. As comie, Frank took the order from the *chef du rang*, picked up the food from the kitchen, and brought it out to the chef, or table waiter, who would serve it with a lot of flourish.

One day Frank noticed the table waiter pick up an order and hide it in the pantry, under a napkin. The waiter showed Frank how to put in an extra order for a steak or some other meal so that he would have something substantial to eat. Frank learned how to do it, and soon discovered that most of the other hungry restaurant staff also obtained extra meals in the same fashion. He vowed then that if he were ever in charge of a restaurant, the staff would be fed properly so that they would not have to steal. In later years, he followed that philosophy as manager of hotels and hotel dining rooms, and in his own home with the household help. His staff would eat the same thing that he ate, thus avoiding the degrading act of theft.

Through another lead provided by Toth, Frank landed a temporary holiday job working under a Hungarian maitre d'hotel at a famous kosher hotel in Lakewood, New Jersey, the Laurel-in-the-Pines. This hotel, which had first opened in December, 1891, was an elegant 220-room structure with an imposing twenty-five-foot copper rotunda over the front entrance, stone balustrades, and palladian-window topped French doors across its front facade. The maitre d'hotel needed an assistant captain at the door for the 1934 New Year's holiday, and Frank's facility with languages must have been attractive. A discreet sign outside of the hotel suggested a restriction on the clientele, which apparently did not apply to staff: "No Christians."

With his blond hair and blue eyes, Frank stood out clearly as a *goy* in the all-Jewish environment. However, he was pleased at the experience, since the other staff members worked to make him fit in comfortably. Frank had heard of kosher food, but knew nothing about it, so he went to Rabbi Brown and learned the logic and system behind the milk and meat separation and the other kosher rules. Frank stood unobtrusively in the kitchen, watching as the rabbi supervised kosher preparations prior to the hotel opening.

Kosher hotels were known to have fine entertainment on New Year's Day. Among the customers were several Jewish figures from the movie industry, including Georgie Jessel and Eddie Cantor. Despite the fact that the country was in the depths of the Depression in the winter of 1933–1934, the New Year's celebration that year at the Laurels-in-the-Pines was packed. As Frank stood at the door with the captain, he was stunned that the guests, as they left, slipped him large tips, some as much as fifty or one hundred dollars. By the end of the long evening his pockets bulged with over two thousand dollars in tips, a grand sum, a fortune, in the mid-1930s. It was Frank's first real exposure to a kosher hotel, to the wealthy theater clientele, and to spending on a lavish scale.

But the job at Laurel-in-the-Pines was short-lived, and Frank was back in New York in the mid-Depression winter of 1934, looking for work again.

Manhattan:
Room at the Top

Any young man searching for work in New York in the mid-thirties had a difficult task. Frank Brandstetter, however, had several assets. He was willing to take almost any kind of work that had some prospects of advancement. He had a few trusted friends, some of whom had excellent contacts. With ambition, a willingness to work hard, and multiple language skills, he began to find his opportunities. Along the way he acquired much practical knowledge.

After the Laurel-in-the-Pines job, he met again with Louis Toth, who had been watching his progress. Louis had more advice for him.

"Frank," he said, "you have enough experience now with the back of the house. Now you need to be working out front, even if it means taking a wage cut." Toth informed Frank that the St. Moritz Hotel at 59th Street and 6th Avenue, facing Central Park, which had just been taken over by new Greek partners, was advertising for a key clerk who had to speak a minimum of four languages. Frank spoke French, German, Hungarian, Czech, and English, with a smattering of Russian and an understanding of Italian because of his earlier study of Latin. He was more than qualified for the job on this count. The key clerk served as an assistant to the concierge, and the job was an excellent entrée to the front of the house. Frank took the position and received some further essentials in his schooling in the hotel business at the St. Moritz.

He worked there from January 1934 through August 1936, and again in the spring of 1939. As time passed, he progressed to assistant room clerk, room clerk, assistant manager, acting night manager, and night manager. In these positions, he continued to learn both the general theory and hundreds of specific and practical aspects of hotel management. For example, because the Depression had set back all of the first-class hotels in New York, many tried to cut utility expenses. But Gregory Taylor, a Greek, the owner and general manager who had a flair for showmanship and good public relations, kept the St. Moritz lively. He ordered the lights kept on in vacant rooms facing Central Park, so that the hotel looked occupied even when nearly empty.

Furthermore, Taylor had a plan to enhance the image of the hotel, and hiring multilingual help was part of it. Taylor began to build a truly international clientele, bringing in creative artists and musicians when they performed in New York. The Waldorf-Astoria was international, but artists and musicians did not fit its *modus operandi*—its conservative and wealthy atmosphere.

Frank observed how Taylor attracted a special clientele to the St. Moritz, getting the customers to provide both an image and a network for public relations purposes. Imitating the Café de la Paix in Paris, Taylor opened a sidewalk cafe at the hotel, one of the first of its kind in New York. It still flourishes at the corner location. Another restaurant in the hotel was created in imitation of an already famous Rumplemeyer's in Paris, and was given the same name; it also survived into the 1990s. The continental air went far beyond the decor and naming of restaurants, however. Through the judicious granting of some complimentary rooms ("comps"), Taylor attracted a potpourri of celebrities: movie moguls and their mistresses, and Ziegfield with his beautiful show girls. A few reputed mobsters even had their Ziegfield girl friends staying there. Ziegfield's theater was nearby, adding to the hotel's glamour. In addition, to give the hotel added "schmaltz," Taylor granted comps to up-and-coming artists and to influential writers and musicians, such as Eugene Ormandy and Harry Revel. Taylor also provided to Walter Winchell, the columnist, a complimentary suite that more than paid for itself in frequent mentions in the gossip columns. George Skouras, from Greece, who owned a chain of movie theaters in the Midwest, stayed there, as well as several actors and actresses. They provided a sense that this was a place where one could meet and be met by an elegant and sophisticated, yet liberal and artistic crowd.

Among the fast crowd, rather incongruously, one found the director of the FBI, J. Edgar Hoover, who maintained a suite at the hotel. Frank saw Hoover chatting with his friend Walter Winchell several times. Hoover, Clyde Tolson, and Winchell would frequent the Stork Club and other nightclubs, returning to the St. Moritz in the early hours of the morning. Again, the publicity was constant and suggested that the St. Moritz was an exciting place.

At the St. Moritz, Frank remembered greeting a member of the Rothschild family who was carrying one suitcase and a bag of diamonds that had to be placed in the hotel safe. This was probably Baron Louis Rothschild, who fled Austria in April 1939, after the Nazis looted his house and he agreed to sign over his steel mills to them. Royalty and more conservative types went to the Waldorf-Astoria, the St. Regis, or the Navarro, but the wealthy and flamboyant, without the ethnic restrictions common at other hotels, stayed at the St. Moritz.

As he worked at the St. Moritz, Frank developed a wide range of friends among other hotel and restaurant staff in the city, among the owners, among the guests and regulars at the hotel, and within the Hungarian community. His circle of friends began to widen, and many came back to assist him in one way or another later in life. One contact at a hotel and restaurant employment agency, a man by the name of M. Melvin, who later moved on to edit the *National Hotel Gazette*, kept in touch and helped Frank with job leads over the years. Melvin once landed Frank a position at the Club Jabberwocky in New Jersey, a nightclub that Frank learned later was controlled by the local head of the mob. As always, fate seemed to play a part in these contacts and friendships.

One guest of the St. Moritz, Joseph Krieger, was the owner of The Baltimore Pure Rye Whisky Distillery, located near Dundalk, Maryland. Krieger once took young Frank to a prize fight in which Max Schmeling, who briefly held the world heavyweight championship from 1930 to 1932, tried for a comeback. One evening in 1935, Krieger fell ill at the hotel, and Frank called an ambulance to rush him to the hospital. In the emergency room, the doctors said that Krieger needed an immediate transfusion. As there were no relatives present, Frank volunteered to give a pint of blood after tests showed that his blood type matched. When Joe recovered and found out about the transfusion, he was grateful and befriended Frank even more. Like Curt Meisner, Reverend Geza Takaro, and Louis Toth, the older Krieger "adopted" Frank, treating him like a family member.

Another personal contact at the St. Moritz opened an opportunity for a more responsible and better-paying post. One of the silent partners in the ownership of the St. Moritz, a Greek named Eugene (Gene) Venetos, had made a fortune in the importation of olive oil. Venetos opened another hotel, the Griswold, in New London, Connecticut, opposite the navy base. As time went on, Venetos noticed Frank's steady work at the St. Moritz, and appointed him in the summer season of 1937 as "assistant manager" of the Griswold. This, in reality, was the manager's position and the first job Frank held with the actual responsibilities of manager.

One evening while at the St. Moritz, an FBI agent that Frank had met while arranging security for J. Edgar Hoover's suite joined him for coffee and a snack at Rumplemeyer's Restaurant in the hotel. "Frank," the agent warned, "you're going to get a visit pretty soon from the Immigration Service."

Shortly thereafter, two agents from the U.S. Immigration Service tracked him down. Somehow, the government had finally figured out that Frank had overstayed his visitor's visa, granted in 1928, perhaps identifying him through the newly instituted system of Social Security numbers. The agents served him with notice. He had thirty to ninety days to get his affairs in order before he would have to return to Hungary. Suddenly, it seemed that the whole life he had developed in the United States was going to be shattered. Worse, he might face prison if he had to return to Hungary. He had not signed up for Hungarian compulsory military training, and he was already twenty-five years old. The penalty for evading service was severe. At Kőszeg, he had participated in military training to become an officer, but had simply dropped out of the program without official notice.

At the St. Moritz, Frank explained his problems to his friends. Joseph Krieger listened attentively and called his brother, Zanvyl Krieger, a former federal district attorney who was now an associate of the firm of Weinberg and Sweeten in Baltimore. Zanvyl told Joe and Frank to get on the train and come down to Baltimore immediately, which they did.

Zanvyl researched the background of the case, and found that when Ferenc Brandstetter had declared his intention to become a citizen, he had not listed Frank as his son. Zanvyl suggested that Frank work through Frances Perkins, Secretary of Labor, who was in charge of the Immigration Service, to see what she might work out. Frank traveled to Washington by train to see the Secretary of Labor.

Secretary Perkins sat silently with a stern expression while Frank explained his situation. He had arrived in the United States in 1928 as a minor. His father had established residency in the United States and Frank, assuming he would be covered by his father's status, had done nothing about it. He had been living and working in the United States for years, and it was his home now.

Secretary Perkins pointed out that Frank had received a deportation order and that he would have to obey it by leaving the United States within the time limit. She said, however, that there was space on the Hungarian immigrant quota, if Frank could apply to re-enter on a valid Hungarian passport. She explained that since 1924 Hungary had had an annual quota of 869 immigrants to the United States, based on census figures from 1920, and that in recent years space on the quota had not been filled.

Frank explained that he could hardly afford to go back to Hungary, but the Secretary pointed out that it would not be necessary to do so. He could leave the country, go to Canada, and then return on his Hungarian passport under the immigrant quota. She would touch base with the American consul in Quebec to explain Frank's situation and help assure he could enter properly. She explained that he would then be eligible for naturalization in five years.

To Frank, it was a trying time. He began to realize that he had already become an American and was living out the American dream in the midst of the Depression. He was beginning to build a life for himself, a life that was in danger of being snatched away. He felt he had earned his citizenship.

He worked quickly to obtain a new Hungarian passport, which he

soon received with a letter from the chief of police in Budapest stating
that he had no police record. Dr. Geza Takaro wrote to the Hungarian
consul general in Canada, explaining Frank's situation and noting that
Frank's father had played a role in the "renaissance" of Hungary after
the Soviet period under Bela Kun.

Armed with the documents, Frank traveled to Montreal and checked
into the Hotel Mount Royal. He verified with the authorities that indeed he was listed for the immigration quota. The load lifted from his
shoulders, he was ready to celebrate. For three weeks in September 1937,
he took a genuine vacation, going horseback riding, drinking champagne, and for once, spending money in a first-class hotel, rather than
trying to earn tips catering to guests. On returning, his passport was
stamped with an immigrant status visa dated 1 October 1937. When he
realized, with the help of a few loyal friends, that he was going to have a
place under the flag of his choice after all, another element of his character had been secured. Unlike many citizens fortunate enough to be
born under the flag, who take their privileges and rights for granted,
Frank always remembered that he had to work hard to establish his citizenship.

Frank had always lived frugally during his intermittent employment
in the hotel business, saving his earnings and occasional lavish tips during good seasons to wait out the periods between positions. By 1937, he
had enough money put aside to consider investing. In October, a few
weeks after his return from Montreal, he formed a partnership with Dr.
Eugene Hegy, a well-to-do Hungarian doctoral graduate whom he had
met through Dr. Takaro. Frank put up one thousand dollars, and later
would add similar amounts. Hegy and Frank planned to pool their cash,
make a down payment, refurbish and remodel a building, and then
make the payments and a small margin out of the rents.

Together, Dr. Hegy and Frank eventually bought five buildings in
the Upper East Side neighborhood near Reverend Takaro's Reformed
Magyar Church. Some of the buildings were originally large, comfortable homes, which now, mid-Depression, were extremely difficult to sell,
even though their prices had dropped dramatically. The homes had
rich paneling, velvet wall coverings, and other pleasant features, which
Frank hated to cover up during the remodeling. Typically, one of the

Frank's partnership with Dr. Hegy
to renovate buildings in New York
was a successful venture.

mansions could be converted into as many as three fairly comfortable apartments on each of three floors.

While Dr. Hegy handled the legal and documentary side of the business, Frank managed the maintenance and restoration of the buildings, using contacts from his hotel experience. The two partners in some cases retained the apartment houses; in others they sold them at a profit. Frank was able to obtain a decent apartment for himself on the third floor of the building at 8 East 79th Street, which he maintained as his home address over the next few years. In this neighborhood, he met Claire Booth Luce, the wife of the publisher of *Time* and *Life* magazines and later a congresswoman, as well as the heiress Doris Duke, both of whom had homes nearby.

During the summer of 1938, Frank heard that Edgewood Park School, at Briarcliff Manor in Westchester County, New York, was looking for a food manager. Frank got the job, and found himself in an enviable position as the only male employee, apart from the stable help who took care of the horses, at a girl's junior college. At Edgewood Park he was able to continue his daily practice of horseback riding, without charge, in the afternoons.

The school, which had been founded in 1936, occupied the stately hotel, Briarcliff Lodge, on a lease during the winter months. In the summer of 1938, the hotel sold out to the school, which continued to operate in the lodge facilities. At the lodge, Frank put to good use what he had learned at the St. Moritz and some of his other restaurant jobs. Life was quite pleasant as he lived on a rather princely income of some four hundred dollars per month for the season.

Checking his contacts to find a position for the next season, he received a tip from Carl Kemm, assistant manager of the Waldorf-Astoria, that Eddie Jouffret was looking for an assistant manager for his first-class hotel in Miami Beach, the Roney Plaza. At the time, the Roney Plaza had earned a reputation as one of the most exclusive and elegant hotels in the United States, and Frank regarded it as an honor when he was hired. Frank worked two winter seasons there, in 1938-39 and 1939-40, observing and learning from Jouffret, a former cavalry captain in the French army during the Great War, the qualities of military discipline as applied to hotel management.

When he first arrived in Miami by train, he was struck by a discreet sign outside the Roney Plaza that said, "No dogs, No Jews." The hotel catered to a class of wealthy, famous, and exclusively gentile customers. He noticed after working there a few months that the rule was occasionally bent. Walter Winchell, for instance, whose parentage was Jewish on both sides, received complimentary rooms. Winchell, who remembered him quite well from the St. Moritz, asked Frank to open his telegrams in the evenings while he was in the broadcasting studio and to call him if the news was important, so he could include it in his broadcast. Winchell was the preeminent radio broadcaster of the time in exposing, with help from J. Edgar Hoover, the Nazi influence in Argentina and elsewhere in South America, as well as in Europe and the United States.

In the spring of 1939, at the end of the winter season at the Roney Plaza, Frank decided on a new business venture. In May, Frank and his former roommate William Palmer set up the Champlain Corporation, with Frank as manager and Palmer as secretary-treasurer. William

Wachter, assistant general manager of the Ritz Hotel, became president. Their plan was to assume the lease of the Bluff Point Hotel on Lake Champlain and reopen it under improved management as the Hotel Champlain. The partners, all with experience in the hotel business, had carefully reviewed the operation. The hotel was well known, with over four hundred rooms, and had a good reputation. Yet in 1939 the hotel had been sold, and the former leaseholders decided not to renew their lease. Frank and his partners felt the hotel had fine prospects, having suffered simply because of bad management.

Frank and his two partners took over a lease-purchase agreement for a ten-year period, beginning in the spring of 1939. They anticipated an active summer season that first year. The hotel was successful because the lake, near Plattsburg, drew customers down from Montreal and up from New York during the summer for the cool waters. The partners plunged into the business with high hopes. Walter Winchell mentioned the hotel in his columns, and the three partners spread the word through their contacts in New York. They each had a personal reputation, and could attract customers and friends.

Governor Thomas Dewey of New York, who was running for the Republican nomination for the 1940 presidential election, held his campaign kick-off meeting on 29 August 1939 at the Hotel Champlain. The publicity from the meeting, together with the spreading word of the good accommodations, the lake front location, and the excellent food, all brought the hotel a nearly full book of reservations.

The partners were also able to arrange a dinner at the hotel for a group of foreign military attachés who were observing army maneuvers at nearby Plattsburg. The dinner was funded by Lieutenant General Hugh A. Drum, commander of the First Army, and famed for his work as chief of staff to General "Black Jack" Pershing during the Great War. With special menus printed for the event, and the display of international dress uniforms, the dinner took on a truly cosmopolitan flavor, reminiscent of the St. Moritz. The officers' brass and gold-trimmed hats stacked up on the checkroom hat rack made a photogenic picture for *Life* magazine. Frank quietly made his way around the dining room during cocktails and dinner, checking to insure that all was served correctly, in the best continental style. As he circulated, he eavesdropped on some

Frank held managerial positions while employed in Miami hotels in 1939.

Frank skiing on the cool waters of Lake Champlain in 1939.

of the conversations in French, Italian, and German among the gathered officers. He later recalled an exchange between Lieutenant General Friedrich von Boetticher, military and air attaché for Germany and Colonel Vincenzo Coppola, air and military attaché to the Italian Embassy. "When the war begins," General Boetticher said in German, "these Americans will present no threat. Imagine. They are drilling with wooden rifles and dummy tanks." Frank was irritated at the time, but within a few weeks, the words held special meaning.

War clouds had been gathering over Europe during the late 1930s. Frank followed events closely and foresaw the implications of a coming war.

When Hitler launched the invasion of Poland on 1 September 1939, setting off World War II in Europe, England and France, as protectors of the Polish borders under the Trianon and Versailles Treaties, declared war on Germany. Canada, showing its independence as a British dominion, voted a separate declaration of war on Germany.

On Lake Champlain, the impact of the outbreak of war was immediate. All of the Canadian guests left, and hundreds more wrote in to cancel their reservations. The hotel changed in a week from near-capacity rental to empty, with the rest of the season in shambles. In the New York papers a small item appeared, indicating that the Champlain Hotel was the "first American business casualty" of World War II. Frank and his partners immediately realized that the prospects of success, which depended heavily on Canadian business, had vanished.

While the season had been excellent to that point, paying off the immediate bills left a large deficit. Over thirty thousand dollars was owed to Seagrams of Canada for liquor. The three hotel partners, even though agreeing to liquidate assets and dissolve the partnership, did not want to declare bankruptcy, which would keep them out of further business ventures for years. They agreed that Frank should go to Canada and negotiate some sort of settlement with Seagrams.

Frank approached the job with trepidation. Sam Bronfman, the owner of Seagrams of Canada, had a long-standing reputation for collecting outstanding bills. Canadian whiskey had become a major import to the United States. With his background, Bronfman would not be the sort of person to forget a debt.

Frank laid his cards on the table. The outstanding debt was either thirty-six or thirty-nine thousand dollars, depending on adjustments for returns. The partners were simply unable to pay off the debt at this time, he said, but they wanted Bronfman to know that they would undertake to meet the debt, even though the hotel went out of business and the partnership dissolved. If they received enough time, they would get it paid back. They did not want to declare bankruptcy.

Bronfman listened in silence, then accepted Frank's verbal promise, shook hands, and let it go at that. Another relationship had been sealed. Over the next months, the partners worked the debt down, finally paying it off by 1941.

Frank returned to the Roney Plaza in Miami for the 1939–40 winter season and then went back to New York, continuing to work with Dr. Hegy on the apartment transactions. He followed the war news.

By the summer of 1940 the blitz of London had begun, and Americans listened to the daily radio reports of Edward R. Murrow, as he recounted the tales of Londoners taking refuge underground and fighting the fires set by German incendiary bombs. American public sympathy was shifting to the British, although officially the nation remained neutral. Gradually, defense industries in the United States geared up, and on 16 September 1940, Congress passed the Selective Service Act, establishing the military draft.

Late in August 1940, just before the Selective Service Act went into place, two navy officers showed up at the St. Moritz to see Frank, meeting him for coffee in Rumplemeyers. They suggested that he join the U.S. Navy, which badly needed mess officers. Being a hotel man, Frank could enlist as a lieutenant, junior grade, through the navy reserve, and then be activated for the navy. If war came, they argued, why should he chance serving in the army, with its high risk and discomforts? In the navy, he would have a safe berth, good quarters, good food, and as an officer, pleasant social activities.

After listening to them, Frank weighed the pros and cons and asked to think about it overnight. The next day, he saw them and discussed the same points again. Looking out of the window, he saw the army recruiting office across the street. Then and there he made up his mind. He told the navy men he was volunteering for the army, thanked them for their efforts and walked into the army's recruiting office, enlisting as a private. In his mind, he was doing the right thing. The army had been an integral part of both his upbringing and his training at Köszeg at the Hunyadi Matyas Magyar Kiralyi Realiskola. His choice was right; the army was to be his alma mater.

The training camps were not ready when he signed up, so he joined the Seventh National Guard Unit, Company C, in New York, impatiently awaiting orders to report to basic training. Those first training periods with the National Guard were somewhat disillusioning, with the socialites and sophisticates of Manhattan playing at being soldiers at the armory.

During this period, his father heard through one of their mutual friends that Frank had joined the army. One afternoon, his father accosted him. Was it true? His father asked. Had he enlisted in a "foreign" army?

When Frank admitted it, his father blew up. "Dumkopf, Idiot! Don't you know that if the Americans ever get into this war, they will be licked? Germany is bound to win."

Frank tried to explain, using all the ideals he thought his father supported—loyalty, the flag, and service to his country. But his father refused to listen. "Your bones will rot on the steppes of Russia," he said. They parted. Frank never saw his father again.

Finally, in December, 1940, Frank received his notice of induction and shipped off to basic training at Fort Dix, New Jersey. He had found his true passion. For the next five decades, in and out of uniform, Frank worked for the United States Army and his adopted country.

Enlisting for Action
as Europe Erupts

I n December 1940, Frank received orders to report for induction
on 15 January 1941 at Fort Dix to begin his term as a one-year
enlistee. The army was in chaos, with the flood of inductees and
volunteers, a shortage of supplies and equipment for training, and a
deluge of paperwork that overwhelmed the small regular army training
facilities. Through the winter and spring months of early 1941, Frank
got his first taste of army life, encountering the round of amusing and
rugged experiences that made memories bittersweet for millions of
Americans. In an ill-fitting private's uniform and a GI haircut, he was
shipped out from Fort Dix to Fort Benning, Georgia, for his basic training.

At Fort Benning, Frank was given his Military Occupational Specialty (MOS): that of typist, and was assigned to the 68th Light Tank
Regiment Headquarters Company of the newly formed 2nd Armored
Division under the command of General George S. Patton. The lieutenant in charge of personnel assumed that with Frank's hotel management experience, he could assist with the overwhelming mass of
documentation and orders. Frank tried to explain that he had joined
the newly formed army not to type, but to fight in a tank. While not
quite insubordination, this sort of back talk could not be excused, and

as punishment Frank was ordered to the task of shoveling sawdust into the ruts of a dirt road. He kept at that job for two weeks, acquiring blisters and then bleeding sores on his hands. He finally got a break in the form of an assignment as a motorcycle dispatch rider, which at least held out the promise of some action. He was excited to become a member of the "Green Hornet" motorcycle dispatch carriers. He learned how to stand up on the motorcycle and pass messages to a speeding half-track. After working there, he was boosted to sergeant of a tank platoon, skipping the rank of corporal. He served out the rest of his year's duty in Headquarters' Company of the regiment.

On 15 November 1941, one year after volunteering, he was mustered out and returned to New York. Under a War Department order, older volunteers were turned out to make room for the incoming draftees, as the nation continued its belated attempt to mobilize defenses while maintaining neutrality in the war. In New York, he returned to a position at the St. Moritz, continued managing apartment houses with Dr. Hegy, and rejoined a Manhattan unit of the Seventh National Guard on Park Avenue. Again, he found himself in the midst of a set of New York sophisticates and playboys, who regarded weekly drills as a form of entertainment.

Frank settled into civilian life and began to relax again. One Sunday afternoon, a few weeks after returning to New York, he went out for a round of golf with friends. The weather was unseasonably sunny and pleasant. As he was driving out to Westchester, he noticed a number of cars pulling off the road, but the drivers did not get out. Frank turned on his radio and discovered Pearl Harbor had been bombed. The next day, President Roosevelt requested and received a Declaration of War.

Once again Frank was back in uniform, reporting to Fort Dix on 15 January 1942, but this time he was already a three-striper, a tank platoon sergeant. Army personnel shipped Frank to his old unit, and then to the 3rd Armored Division at Camp Polk, Louisiana, in the newly-formed 703rd Tank Destroyer Battalion. He was assigned to the S-2, or intelligence section, working as an S-2 intelligence tech sergeant under a tough sergeant-major. Experienced in realistic anti-tank training, Frank and some veteran British officers supervised the soldiers under rigorous conditions with live explosives.

Instruction included methods of blowing up enemy tanks from a foxhole using magnetic mines. The British officers' training methods required the troops to crawl under barbed wire, with machine guns firing live ammunition a few feet overhead. With the troops hesitating to be first to go under, Frank, the ranking sergeant at the first such practice, was ordered to lead the way, crawling on his stomach under live fire. Later, the barbed wire and machine gun exercise became standard procedure in every basic infantry training, but the 703rd was one of the first units to receive live-fire training in the United States.

Operating under the sergeant-major in S-2, Frank worked fairly closely with Colonel Yeoman, the commanding officer of the 703rd Tank Destroyer Battalion. Yeoman noticed Frank and ordered him to apply for Officers Candidate School (OCS). Frank knew the sergeant-major for the 3rd Armored Division who handled the paperwork, and asked him to mislay the application. He preferred to stay exactly where he was, experiencing realistic military training. However, after the papers were "lost" twice, the colonel persisted and personally hand-carried

Frank on maneuvers with the 3rd Armored Division in Louisiana in the early 1940s.

Frank's third OCS application to Division Headquarters for processing. Frank was called before the OCS Admission Board.

One of the five officers on the panel questioning him did not like his accent, and thought that Frank had deserted from the German army. The officer, a West Point colonel, asked Frank: "Are you a traitor?"

"Sir, I volunteered," said Frank. "I did not ask to be an officer. Colonel Yeoman, my commanding officer, ordered me to apply to OCS. I am perfectly happy to remain where I am."

Frank was sent out of the room for a moment, and when he returned, the West Point colonel sat silently, apparently reprimanded by one or more of the others. Senior officers on the panel concluded the questioning, and Frank was ordered to attend the next class of the OCS, Class Number Eight, held at Camp Hood, Texas.

Frank graduated from OCS on 4 December 1942, as a second lieutenant in the cavalry. He assumed that his training at Köszeg and his lifelong hobby of horseback riding would be of some use. He was then assigned to the "automotive department" of the tank destroyer school as an instructor in enemy tank destruction and tactics.

Frank began to believe that he would spend his army career with no chance at action, simply rotating between courses of study, desk jobs, and training others. He volunteered for parachute training, but was rejected, at age thirty, on the basis of being too old. Although he had kept in fine physical shape before induction through horseback riding, golf, and an energetic schedule, the airborne simply did not accept men of his age as volunteers.

He made the best of his duty as an instructor. He participated in competitions with the engineers, who set up barricades and an obstacle course for his experimental tank destroyer unit to demolish or pass through. Whichever side lost hosted a beer party on the weekend. After one such late party, he fell into a deep sleep in the barracks. Someone gently shook him awake in the middle of the night, flashed an ID, and asked him outside for a talk. It was a representative of the FBI, who asked Frank to keep his eyes and ears open for saboteurs or agents. This was Frank's first experience with counterespionage.

After that discussion, word apparently drifted up to a higher level that Frank's knowledge of foreign languages was exceptional. The army

was seeking such officers and enlisted men to serve in intelligence, and
Frank received orders to report on 3 March 1943 for intelligence training at Camp Ritchie, Maryland.

At Camp Ritchie, he found himself associating with a cosmopolitan
group of trainees at the Interrogation School. Separate groups studied
German, Italian, French, Arabic, and Chinese, and received training in
prisoner of war interrogation, photo interpretation, and enemy order-
of-battle. Among the German-speaking students were some college-edu-
cated journalists, business executives, and investment bankers who had
received direct commissions on the basis of their civilian careers, foreign language ability, education, and background. Frank's unit of German-speaking enlisted men and officers, housed in tents, envied the
solid barracks of the French group across the camp lane.

Frank, with his background as an enlistee who became an officer
through OCS, was relatively unique at Ritchie. Some of his fellow students thought of military intelligence as a nice assignment to sit out the
war and avoid combat. Some of the young refugees from Europe, including the well-to-do playboy types, hoped that military intelligence

Lieutenant Brandstetter teaches German tactics at Camp Ritchie in August
1943.

would provide a soft billet through the war. Others were eager to see action and fight the Germans.

Frank submitted a second application for parachute training through Colonel Banfield, the commander of the Intelligence School at Camp Ritchie, only to be rejected again. Now the age of thirty-one, he was considered eleven or twelve years too old for such training.

Frank finished his intelligence course in October 1943 with a reassigned MOS: 9300—intelligence. He was ordered by Colonel Banfield to observe 2nd Army maneuvers in the field in Tennessee, and help evaluate how well the army division G-2s used the Military Intelligence Teams with their special training, particularly the Interrogation of Prisoners of War (IPW) teams and the Order-of-Battle teams. For two weeks in mid-October, Frank worked with the umpire teams, who officiated between a "Blue" army and a "Red" army in the maneuvers, gathering information for eventual after-action evaluation. At the major review of the action on 28 October, he was ordered to the auditorium where the officers met. With his second-lieutenant bars, he felt a little out of place in the "Milky Way" of officers' stars. Frank stood in the background as various officers conducted the briefing. Suddenly, he found himself being introduced as an observer from Camp Ritchie and instructed to comment on the use of IPW and Order-of-Battle teams by the G-2s of the divisions.

The G-2 in charge of the briefing, who had called Frank over, said, "All right, Lieutenant, what was your observation?"

"General, sir," began Frank, "our Military Interrogation teams were not used properly by our G-2 sections in all the divisions. They were used for scouting, which they were not trained for and it would be wasteful to send those men out when they are trained for a specific purpose. . ."

"That's enough!" said the general. He spoke to an aide, who approached Frank and said, in a low voice, "You report back right now to your barracks. Orders will be issued, and you'll be on the first train out tonight."

Frank reported next morning to Colonel Banfield at Camp Ritchie. He explained the whole experience to Banfield, who smiled at the brash young officer.

"Lieutenant," Banfield said, "I remember you wanted to see action. You volunteered for the parachute outfits, and you were turned down.

Now you're going to have your chance. As of this moment, you're on your way to Europe." Frank's orders to the European Theater of Operations were dated that day, 29 October 1943. Frank did not know whether to interpret the orders as punishment for being too outspoken, or as a reward for honesty. In either case, he was glad to be on his way to action.

Frank was shipped to a newly formed unit, the Field Interrogation Detachment (FID) in Broadway, England. A small town northwest of Oxford, Broadway lies in the beautiful Cotswolds country. His assignment at first seemed quite remote from the sort of military action he sought. Frank was accustomed to wearing fatigues in the tank-destroyer outfit, and he was displeased that the officers at the Broadway FID wore "pinks," the standard pastel pants that were part of the U.S. Army dress uniform from the prewar days. Adding to his annoyance, he once again found that his job seemed based on his hotel experience; he was to arrange housing and quarters for the incoming officers, including himself, in the area. He chose the Lygon Arms, an inn dating from the sixteenth century, noted for its excellent cuisine.

As the inn filled up, he continued work on the housing arrangements, laying down certain rules for the Americans he was billeting. He tried to quarter the soldiers in the homes of older people, where there were no eligible young ladies or lonely wives whose husbands were off at war. The officers and enlisted men were instructed to share their special rations, such as candy and cigarettes, and help their hosts with their gardens—Broadway was very proud of its gardens. Soon, the Americans began to integrate comfortably into the quiet town, with the more senior officers keeping a watchful eye on their younger colleagues.

The commandant at the FID in Broadway was a direct-commissioned officer by the name of Harold K. Hochschild, who had been the chairman of the board of the American Metals Corporation in New York City. Frank enjoyed working for Hochschild, who organized the training and the detachment in an efficient manner. Nevertheless, Frank personally continued to believe that an officer's leadership should be earned in the field, not conferred on the basis of political connections. Hochschild lived in a commandeered home nearby with his second in command, who happened to be his younger brother, Walter Hochschild, a direct-commissioned major. Third in command of the outfit was another commissioned officer, an attorney from New York, Major William Stremlau. The officers, although likeable, were not very "military" in their mindset, and did not seem anxious for combat.

A holding camp for German POWs was located north of Broadway. Referred to as a "cage," it was the place for officers and senior NCOs from the FID to train in interrogation methods. The training procedure did not work too well, as the same small group of two to three hundred prisoners would be questioned over and over again by new interrogation trainees. As a result of a chance meeting on Frank's part, this procedure was soon changed.

Colonel Victor Jones, a British officer who was badly wounded in the African desert fighting Rommel's Corps, was invalided home to Broadway. He observed the fine behavior of the FID contingent in the town and their relations with the civilian community, and mentioned this to a friend and visitor, Lord Ismay, who was Churchill's right arm. Lord Ismay expressed a desire to meet the billeting officer. Frank was invited to Colonel Jones's estate, along with the chief of the British constabulary in Broadway, with whom Frank had worked out the billeting problems.

Lord Ismay, over Scotch whiskey, inquired of Frank's background, which he respectfully stated. Frank further explained the lack of actual POW questioning facilities for the FID teams. They needed to train with recently captured German prisoners of war and not rely on the holding camp near Broadway, which was filled with prisoners who had been captured quite a while before.

Lord Ismay stated that he would look into the matter, which he did. Soon, Lieutenant Colonel Hochschild received orders from London Headquarters that some of the IPW team members would be allowed to train in other British controlled POW camps. Among the camps was one at Devizes, west of Stonehenge.

On Lord Ismay's next visit to Colonel Jones, Frank was again invited for drinks. When Lord Ismay asked about the progress of interrogation training, Frank replied that the FID teams were now receiving some real experience. Pleased at the progress, Ismay asked Frank if he would like to see how the British military interrogators operated. The next thing he knew, Frank received orders for detached temporary duty to

visit London to observe and learn interrogation methods employed by
the British under the command of Lieutenant Colonel A. P. Scotland of
the British Military Intelligence. Scotland had taken over three or four
buildings in a group of mews off Hyde Park. They had broken through
the common walls in the basements and left only one entrance to the
whole group of buildings. Inside was a complete complex with officers'
mess, classrooms, and interrogation rooms. In this London facility, the
most important German captives were questioned, including admirals
and generals, scientists, engineers, and Nazi party officials. Here, at the
MI complex, Frank was introduced to the British methods, including
their penchant for secrecy behind an innocent facade.

     Frank was surprised to learn that, whereas the Americans had been
warned never to touch a prisoner, British interrogation officers would
not hesitate to slap them around. This approach was justified in their
minds, Frank thought, by the fact that London civilians were being killed
daily by bombing raids. With the V-1s, or "buzz bombs," raining down
on London, Frank developed a better understanding of British feelings
about prisoner interrogation and a better appreciation for their dedication to German defeat. His understanding was to pay off many times
later during combat in Europe.

     When Frank returned to Broadway, he found out that some of the
American FID specialists who had been trained there were being sent
back from the units preparing for the invasion as unacceptable for military service. They were growing too fat and lazy, and could handle neither the rigors of disciplined training nor the combat that would soon
take place. Frank, assigned the job of improving their training, organized a strict regimen that included weapons fire, drill, and calisthenics. Although he was closer to the action in Britain than he had been in
the United States, and was now serving as a first lieutenant, he continued to fear that he might miss all the combat action himself and finish
the war as an instructor in the rear echelons. Pink pants, overweight
direct-commissioned officers, a quiet Cotswolds village, excellent dinners at the Lygon Arms, and evenings in the local pub were all very
pleasant, but were not his idea of a military career.

     One Sunday at the end of November, 1943, he took the jeep he had
been assigned and drove to a nearby camp where the 101st Airborne

Division was training. He pulled up at the gate and requested to see the commanding officer, Major General William C. Lee, commanding general of the 101st Airborne Division, the "Screaming Eagles." Frank knew that General Matthew B. Ridgway had established the 82nd, the first airborne division. Ridgway then created the 101st Division by splitting the officer cadres of the 82nd and selecting, with War Department concurrence, his old friend William Lee to take charge of developing and training the new division. Frank was brought in to General Lee, who was sitting in his large office smoking a good cigar. Frank explained that he wanted to volunteer for parachute training and that he had been turned down twice before.

General Lee asked him what his MOS was and Frank stated that it was "9300," military intelligence. Lee explained that once he had been assigned to military intelligence, his assignment could not be changed to another category. Frank replied that he thought the paratroop units should have their own field interrogation units, rather than waiting for POWs to be flown back to Britain to be interrogated, then waiting again for the information to be forwarded through channels back to the troops on the ground. He believed that FID IPW units should be assigned to the 101st Airborne Division to jump into combat with them and provide immediate intelligence from captured prisoners, maps, and documents. At that time, neither the 82nd nor the newly formed 101st had any provision for such field interrogation IPW units.

Lee heard him out. How many people served on such a FID IPW team? What equipment did they need? How did they operate? How did they report? What sort of information could they get? Frank explained the details. Usually the teams consisted of two officers and four senior noncoms, traveling in two jeeps. Prisoners were screened and interviewed by them before being sent to the rear holding areas. The IPWs reported to regimental S-2 officers, or at the division level to the G-2 officers, the specialists in intelligence. FID men interviewed prisoners, interpreted maps and photographs, gathered details of order of battle, and passed the information on. Lee immediately saw the value of Frank's suggestions.

General Lee explained that Colonel Robert F. Sink of the 506th Parachute Regiment was starting a parachute training school session in two weeks.

"Lieutenant Brandstetter, how many slots do you need?" Lee asked. "Six, sir."

"Son, you got it. Bring your volunteers here in two weeks."

Frank left, overjoyed. However, he knew he had a problem. He had acted out of channels, and this was not the army way. On Monday, he visited Lieutenant Colonel Hochschild, who seemed bemused. You did not have my permission for this, did you? No, sir. Hochschild called in his subordinates, the men Frank had thought were fairly typical of direct-commissioned officers with little imagination or commitment for action. Major Hochschild, the colonel's brother, mildly suggested that Frank should be court-martialed for acting without orders. Frank explained that he had sought out the program for the good of the service, as part of the need to stiffen the Field Interrogation Detachment training. Their reputation, he said, was zero, with the teams coming back unfit for service from the divisions under training for D-Day. The airborne program might give them a chance to uplift the reputation of the FID at one stroke; if the men could pass the tough parachute course, they would be able to handle assignments at the front. He agreed to be the first volunteer, since he had come up with the idea. Colonel Hochschild agreed immediately. The others seemed to think Frank would break his neck, but they grudgingly assented. Frank asked for a total of six volunteers, thinking that he should get an extra person in case one should wash out. He was told to pick the men.

Frank called a muster of all the officers in the unit and explained his proposal. He gave the forty or so gathered on the parade ground an energetic spiel. Many of the officers, Frank knew, were "good-time Charlies," who enjoyed the life in Britain, met young ladies, avoided military hazards at all costs, and hoped the war would end before anyone shot at them, so his pep talk appealed to their sense of patriotism, their inner courage. He offered them a chance to get into military shape, to parachute in with the airborne, to see some real action. He asked all those interested in volunteering to step forward.

Not one officer stepped forward; no one volunteered.

From Broadway
to the Bulge

Frank had promised General William Lee that he would supply a group of six volunteers for parachute training, so he decided to try the non-commissioned officers. He called all the senior NCOs at the Broadway FID together, about thirty to forty men.

This time, when he asked for volunteers, one by one, about eighteen or twenty stepped forward. He interviewed them all, eventually selecting ten. He explained that he would put them through a toughening-up program at the Broadway detachment, selecting the five best to accompany him to the 101st parachute training school. Others would be nominated to follow, if all went well. For the next two weeks, the men he selected were excused from all other duties as they worked themselves into better physical shape.

On the assigned date, he reported to Colonel Sink with his five NCO volunteers. On the day they arrived, a graduating class was completing its final jumps. One of the parachutes was a "streamer"—that is, it did not open—and the soldier fell to his death. It was an omen which Frank's group would remember when their time to jump arrived.

Colonel Robert Sink, commanding officer of the 506th Parachute Regiment of the 101st Airborne Division, ordered Frank and his men to work with the new class, and they started their three weeks of intensive parachute training. After a series of tethered jumps and active physical training on the ground, each parachute trainee had to undergo a series of five practice jumps immediately prior to the completion of the course and the awarding of airborne jump wings. Between each jump, the trainee would pack his chute for the next jump.

According to scuttlebutt, almost all of the trainees, including the IPW team members, would do well on their first jump—perhaps because the excitement and adrenaline of the first jump would carry them past any fear. However, on the second or third jump, many would freeze in fright in the plane. They would begin to question whether or not they had been crazy to volunteer for the airborne, getting such a bad case of cold feet that they would be excused from further training without prejudice.

On the night after his first two jumps, Frank had trouble sleeping. Lying in his bunk at night, he grew more and more anxious about the third jump the next day, and broke into a sweat. In the middle of the night, as he struggled with insomnia, a replacement from the States arrived, an old-timer in the service, carrying a duffel bag. As they struck up a conversation, Frank explained he was too nervous to sleep. The other soldier offered him a pill, saying that it would calm him down and give him a good night's sleep. Frank took the pill about 4:00 A.M., and was out cold until dawn when he was shaken out of his bunk to prepare for the next jumps.

He stumbled through a freezing shower, several cups of black coffee, and a visit to the chute shed. As an officer, Frank was given the slot next to the jump door on the C-47 aircraft. He hardly noticed that some of the other trainees were throwing up, shaking uncontrollably, and hanging back. When the order came, he mechanically got up, hooked his line, and jumped. In a daze, he repeated the performance on the fourth jump. Later that day, a fifth jump was squeezed into the schedule. Again Frank went through the automatic motions of re-packing his chute, climbing aboard, hooking his line, and jumping. When he returned to his barracks, which contained mostly enlisted men, the nineteen and twenty-year-old airborne trainees looked at their thirty-one-year-old companion with added respect: one cool son of a bitch, they muttered, dozing all the time prior to the jump from the plane.

Frank knew nothing of it until later that evening, when he went into the officers' mess. There, one of the officers explained that his men and instructors had been surprised at how calmly Frank took the jumps. He never found out exactly what the pill contained.

Frank wore the airborne wings and the paratrooper's boots with the same pride as the younger men in the unit. He had found his elite corps and eagerly anticipated more meaningful service.

All six members from the FID group passed with high colors, getting their parachute wings and jump boots. With his five NCOs, Frank's unit became the first U.S. Army Parachute Intelligence Team and he became the first commanding officer of the first airborne IPW team. He returned to Broadway and trained several more groups to undergo the parachute training and be integrated into the airborne units. Frank continued at Broadway through early 1944, working to assimilate the British interrogation methods he had learned in London. As the time for the invasion of Normandy neared, Frank realized that once again his role as trainer would keep him in the rear. He kept in touch with Colonel Sink of the 506th, and continued to supply parachute-trained IPW men to work with the paratroopers.

Paratroopers practice their jumps in England before the D-Day invasion.

As D-Day approached, he heard that one of his men had fallen sick, so he traveled down to the invasion assembly area to investigate. The night before the invasion, General Dwight D. Eisenhower came to address the 101st Airborne. Frank approached Colonel Sink and offered to go in the place of the sick man from his unit. Sink gave him a long look, then said, "Go ahead, Captain. After all, it was your idea, and you're the first commanding officer of the first parachute IPW team."

Thus Frank parachuted with the 506th regiment on D-Day near Sainte Mère Église on the Cotentin Peninsula, inland from the Normandy landing beaches. They were dropped into the wrong zone, that of the 82nd Airborne, because of the heavy German flak. Frank helped round up prisoners and interrogate them as the airborne troops linked up with the infantry proceeding from the beaches.

A few days later, Frank accompanied some of the captured German artillery officers back to Britain. The POWs had been manning the 88-millimeter anti-aircraft weapons, and from the locations of the weapons, Allied command could determine the whereabouts of the ammunition and fuel dumps they protected. B-25 raids and long-range artillery targeted the areas to good effect.

After returning, Frank persuaded Colonel Hochschild that a small, roving IPW unit consisting of two IPW teams, totaling twelve men, plus one MII team of six men and himself, should return to the Normandy front and assist the FID units now attached to the division's G-2s. The request was approved and he returned with his small detachment to the Cherbourg area as a roving team to provide assistance.

During one of the field interrogations, Frank questioned a captured German officer and noticed a small and unusual silver flask the officer had strapped to his belt inside his uniform. Frank asked what it was. The officer removed the flask and explained that he had served on the Russian front in the bitter winter of 1942. He carried the flask with brandy in it, dosing it out to his men when wounded to fend off shock until the medics could attend the soldiers. The officer thought for a moment, and said, "Now that I'm captured, the war is over for me. You can have it." Frank took the flask and clipped it to his belt.

During action over the next weeks, he had occasion to dose out the brandy as the German officer had advised. In the legend-hungry world of the paratroopers, he soon earned the nickname "Brandy," partly for the flask on his hip, and partly to replace his difficult last name. The new name stuck, and he became "Brandy" to his friends thereafter.

During the following months, the Allied forces broke out of the Normandy beachhead enclave and struck east towards Paris. As the Third Army moved quickly through German-held territory, they often disregarded their flanks. Brandy's small group, following them, persuaded some of the bypassed German units to surrender. He received assistance from the Third Army's G-4 executive officer, Colonel Harrison, who coordinated the utilization of empty quartermaster trucks for picking up the now-disarmed German troops and moving them to the beach area for embarkation to England.

A few days before the liberation of Paris on 25 August 1944, Brandy found himself in a jeep with his driver and two Free French (FFI) guides on the northeastern outskirts of the city. Moving through the deserted streets in the evening, Brandy realized that Paris was still in German hands. British and American troops had been held back to give Charles

Frank Brandstetter received his nickname "Brandy" soon after D-Day, 1944.

de Gaulle's Free French units time to reach the city. By the middle of the night Brandy's jeep was well inside the city, and open to possible capture by the retreating German forces.

Hurriedly, Brandy thought about his hotel contacts. He remembered Marcel Rochas, an elegant couturier from New York who had maintained his main office in Paris. Brandy had leased one of his East Side deluxe residences to be used as a branch by Rochas. Checking a phone book and a street map, he located the couturier in the middle of the night. Rochas was astounded to see Frank Brandstetter, his former landlord, now in fatigues and paratrooper boots, looking like a character from a Bill Mauldin cartoon. Rochas told the driver to bring the jeep into the courtyard and cover it with canvas. They stayed the night, and on the following night, the Resistance moved them to another "safe house." The second haven turned out to be an elegant brothel. Brandy and the driver had the "unpleasant" duty of hiding out there for three days, waiting for the formal liberation of Paris. Oddly, among those hidden in the brothel by the Resistance was a colonel in the NKVD, the forerunner of the KGB. No injuries were sustained by either the Soviet or American officers during this stay.

After D-Day, the 82nd and the 101st Airborne Divisions were united into the "XVIII Airborne Corps," actually the first U.S. Airborne Corps ever created, under the command of General Matthew B. Ridgway. At Colonel Sink's recommendation, Brandy was attached as FID's senior interrogator to the XVIII Corps on 1 September, as Assistant G-2. His boss, Colonel Whitfield Jack, was the G-2 who in turn assigned Brandy the responsibility to coordinate all the paratroop intelligence teams and other military intelligence teams attached to the Corps G-2.

Immediately after Brandy was attached to XVIII Corps G-2, the corps participated in the planning of Operation Market Garden and other airborne operations. Three airborne divisions planned to capture bridges across rivers and canals in Belgium and Holland, swinging north as far as Arnhem, with the objective of clearing the approaches to the inland port of Antwerp. Eisenhower planned for a steady flow of supplies to the front through Antwerp, to bring an early end to the war. Later, this particular operation was the basis of a book by Cornelius Ryan and a film, both titled *A Bridge Too Far.*

Between operations at XVIII Corps Headquarters, Brandy received orders regarding the kind of information sought directly from the SHAEF Headquarters G-2, Major General Kenneth W. D. Strong. Through his "Top Secret" clearance, orders arrived to be on the lookout for German engineer officers who had worked on the ack-ack defenses of Klagenfurt in Austria, of Ploesti in Romania, and of Crossbow sites in Western Europe. All of these locations had strategic significance. Klagenfurt was at the heart of a major industrial complex in southern Austria (coincidentally, the city in which Brandy's parents had been married and spent their honeymoon). Ploesti was the location of petroleum refineries and reserves for the Axis. The Crossbow sites were the launching spots for the V-1 ramjet rocket bombs raining down on London.

In November and December, Brandy was back in Britain at corps headquarters in the Midlands, planning airborne operations in his G-2 section, continuing the supervision of FID interrogators for the XVIII Airborne Corps, and visiting various British POW cages to interview prisoners. In the course of this work, he was instrumental in uncovering the

Brandy at XVIII Airborne Corps Headquarters in England.

"Devizes Plot," a planned coordinated breakout by German POWs in Britain. The plot and its details were classified "Top Secret," later downgraded to "Secret," and only declassified after V-E Day. As a consequence, there was little publicity then or later about the event, and what follows is the most complete and documented account by an American participant.

Near the town of Devizes, in Wiltshire, a large reception center for prisoners, the Le Marchant camp or POW cage, held about 7,500 German prisoners in late 1944. Some of Brandy's IPW teams worked there, interrogating prisoners. Brandy visited on 6 December 1944, on a routine trip to collect information about Crossbow sites. He learned that a few weeks previously, on 19 November 1944, ten prisoners had escaped, but had come back the next day and given themselves up.

Brandy remarked to his interrogation teams that something about the prisoners' return was suspicious, and an investigation was called for by the team's commanding officer. They had questioned the ten, but learned very little. As Brandy listened in on the interrogations, something struck him. He decided to try for himself.

The prisoners were battle-hardened troops and did not break readily under questioning, even after he grilled each one for two to three hours.

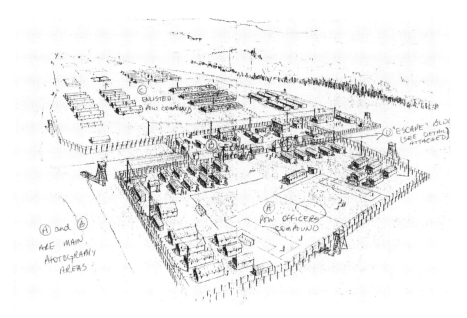

Le Marchant Camp near the town of Devizes, Wiltshire, England.

Brandy had no luck in discovering any information after interrogating the first five or six prisoners, but the next one, Staff Sergeant Hermann Storch, was different; instead of a simple refusal to answer, he displayed a kind of defiance and arrogance. Storch was a twenty-nine-year old native of Limbach, with three years of education in an agricultural college. Listening to Brandy's very accurate German, Storch assumed he was German, and therefore a traitor to the Reich. However, when Brandy explained he was Hungarian, the POW softened a little, and relaxed even more when he learned that Brandy was a Catholic, not a Jew. Over a cup of tea, Storch and Brandy discussed a range of topics, coming around to loyalty to the fatherland.

What kind of loyalty was it, Brandy asked, that would allow ten German POWs who were free to wander and conduct sabotage, to meekly return to their prison camp, like dogs with their tails between their legs? Storch looked at Brandy, steaming at the insult. He uttered one word: *Aufklarung*—Reconnaissance.

Brandy considered the implications of that one word, for it triggered a whole concept. He felt he had opened a wedge, but he pretended to ignore it and proceeded. After some more innocent discussion, Brandy returned to the word *Aufklarung*, suggesting it was simply a joke. No, it was serious, Storch said. Then, as if the momentarily suppressed trickle of information had opened a flood of self-justification, Storch proceeded to reveal the whole scheme. He claimed that he had planned a single escape for himself, and by accident had found himself joining a group planning a more extensive plot.

Storch and the others had conducted reconnaissance to learn what sort of resistance the British would have in place when a major breakout occurred and what sorts of weapons and facilities nearby would be available for seizure. The mass breakout was planned for 24 December, on Christmas Eve, to coincide with a holiday when the Allies would have their guard down. The prisoners would attack two local hospitals and obtain weapons, then storm a local tank park, commandeer the tanks and fan out, releasing prisoners from other camps. After driving onto airbases and capturing aircraft, the Germans would head for London to assassinate, if possible, leading political figures and spread havoc. These actions would tie down Allied strategic reserves, such as the airborne divisions, in Britain. The leader of the special commando troops in Germany, Otto Skorzeny, planned to coordinate with the escapees by ordering some limited parachute drops and shore landings of raiding forces, which would add to the chaos.

Brandy was shaken. The plot sounded fantastic, almost as if Storch were inventing it. Yet certain details gave it the ring of truth. The leader was an officer by the name of Herbert Wunderlich, who had been in touch with two German agents among the guards. Storch did not know the names of the two British guards of Irish origin acting as collaborators, but he described them in detail. Storch claimed that Wunderlich was actually a lieutenant of the Luftwaffe, disguising himself as an enlisted man. Some eighty rifles had been hidden within eight hundred to nine hundred yards south of the camp. Storch did not know exactly where, but one of the other prisoners had that information. During the November escape, two of the prisoners had reached an airfield and almost managed to steal a trainer aircraft, abandoning the effort when they could not start the plane. Brandy knew that the first major military objective, the tank depot, had two hundred Sherman tanks available. The men from A1 compound, who would seize the Shermans, included experienced Panzer tank drivers and SS men. Men in A3 compound included Luftwaffe troops to commandeer the nearest airfield. The other camps marked for possible prisoner release included an American camp, Morton, and a British camp, Springhill.

Brandy sent Storch back to his cage with the warning that he should keep quiet about what he had divulged, otherwise his fellow prisoners would execute him. Meanwhile, Brandy reported his findings directly to Lieutenant Colonel Scotland, with copies to Lieutenant Colonel Upton and others. As a similar plot had been uncovered earlier in Tunisia, after the German surrender there, this plan did not seem entirely impossible. Brandy reported to Colonel Jack, his G-2, who passed on the information to General Ridgway. Brandy assigned Captain Joseph L. Hoelzel to return to Devizes and assist in the questioning. Hoelzel, born in Germany, was a former ski-champion and fluent in German.

As Hoelzel continued questioning Storch, Brandy was ordered by General Ridgway and Colonel Jack to report to General Strong, G-2 to

Eisenhower. Brandy respectfully suggested to General Strong that British officers wearing German uniforms should infiltrate the camp to verify and uncover more about the plot. Several officers were moved in disguised as new German prisoners, including Captain T. H. Pancheff from British Military Intelligence. Between the questioning of Storch, the breakdown of one or two of the other conspirators, and the undercover work of the British officers, G-2 gained many more details over the next few days. The British MI officers verified and confirmed the facts that the American officers uncovered.

The moment for the start of the escape was to be announced by a speech that began: "Men of the Freedom Movement, the hour of our liberation is approaching and it is the duty of every German once more to fight with arms in hand against world Jewry." POWs would seize weapons and attack nearby hospitals across the road from the Le Marchant camp. Wiltshire Barracks, which abutted the camp to the west, also had small weapons detachments to be seized, and vehicles that would be taken from the camp's motor park. Besides Storch and Wunderlich, the names of five other ringleaders were discovered, as well as the organizational structure in the different compounds. The prisoners would be organized in *Kampfgruppen* of 150 to 180 men, about company size. They would be under strict orders to avoid looting and obey the international rules of war. The plan called for the opening of *Die Dritte Front* or the Third Front, across England. The password for the operation was to be *Hans-drei, Gustav-vier*, or "Hans-three, Gustav-four."

On 13 December 1944, as the questioning proceeded, Storch indicated that the planned breakout had been advanced to the night of 14 December. The British undercover agents, who had been placed in each compound, confirmed that the date had been moved up.

Accordingly, on the night of the 14th, with searchlights beaming down on the camp, a motorized unit of the Sixth British Airborne Division approached. Over a public address system, Colonel Upton announced to the camp that the whole plot had been uncovered. Upton and several other British officers including Captain Pancheff, moved in with British MI, Brandy, and others. The ringleaders were arrested in the presence of the officers. On 16 December, as General Gerd von Rundstedt launched the Ardennes offensive, the reason for the advanced date of the Devizes Plot became apparent. The escape was coordinated to precede the German attack in Belgium.

After the conspirators had been sent to London for questioning, a prisoner at Devizes who was suspected of being an informant, was hanged by other prisoners. It was not Storch, but Wolfgang Rosterg. In October 1945 the British tried and executed five prisoners for Rosterg's murder, including two from the group of ringleaders originally arrested at Devizes, Heinz Brueling and Joachim Golitz.

The British kept the clamp of secrecy on the entire Devizes Plot for several months, finally releasing a short version of it which was published in the *New York Times* on 11 May 1945, the day that censorship was lifted. One of the writers who prepared more complete cables on the story was John McDermott, a war correspondent for United Press International attached to the XVIIIth during the Ardennes offensive. Later a political writer for the *Miami Herald*, McDermott provided Brandy with copies of his original dispatches years afterwards. Brandy was never certain why the story was so severely censored. He assumed that either the British leaders felt it would have been destructive to public morale to reveal how close they had come to chaotic disruption, or they thought that good schemes should be kept classified in case they might prove useful in some future war. McDermott explained that his book on the episode had been suppressed on the personal instruction of Winston Churchill, who was running for re-election in the summer of 1945 against Clement Attlee. Churchill feared the incident would reflect badly on him during the election. In later years, Sheldon Leonard, a novelist and writer for both television and films, suggested to Brandy that the story would make the basis for a good thriller. Brandy maintained all of the clippings, despatches, correspondence, and copies of interrogation reports in his files.

Both Hoelzel and Brandstetter were decorated by General Ridgway for their part in foiling the uprising which, had it started, could have had a major impact on the Allies' ability to meet the German advance across Belgium. Some historians have supported this interpretation. An attack of a large number of the 75,000 prisoners in Britain might have tied down the tactical reserve troops there. At the same time von Rundstedt would have pushed back to the coast of Belgium, aiming his

wedge of forces between the British and Canadians under Montgomery, and the Americans under Bradley and Patton to the south, to cut
through to the supply port of Antwerp.

However, at the time, Brandy immediately put the events behind
him and flew over with the XVIII Airborne Corps, when it was ordered
to block von Rundstedt's Ardennes offensive.

From Belgium
to Copenhagen

As soon as the message concerning von Rundstedt's offensive was received, Ridgway ordered his whole headquarters staff from Britain to France to the advanced command post of the corps. They flew with a group of fifty-five C-47 aircraft into Rheims. Both the 82nd and the 101st Divisions were ordered to move on Bastogne, but the 82nd got there first. Ridgway ordered them to keep on rolling to the north, towards Spa. By accident, the 101st was then isolated at Bastogne, instead of the 82nd, and was surrounded by the advancing German units. Ridgway moved his headquarters up to Werbemont to be near the action with the 82nd.

Brandy moved with Ridgway's command post. The next few weeks were a blur of actions, some too painful for detailed recall. Brandy was present at the discovery of the massacre of American prisoners of war at Malmedy. The bodies were found partially buried in the snow and Brandy remembered having his G-2 men place numbered placards on them. Later, photographs of those numbered bodies became one of the most remembered of the tragic pictures of the war. In the days immediately after that discovery, he noticed a decrease in the number of German prisoners taken alive to interrogate.

On one of his searches for possible important prisoners of war, he

American prisoners massacred near Malmedy, 1944.

was proceeding with his sergeant to the S-2 of the 505th Parachute Regiment, fighting in the Trois Point front, when they were ambushed by a German patrol. In the ensuing close-quarter fight, Brandy was bayoneted. The sergeant drove him to a medical area near Spa, Belgium, for treatment. The chief nurse, Captain Irma Kovacs, happened to be an old friend from New York City. "Frank, you are going to be evacuated to the rear, and here is your Purple Heart." Brandy replied, "No soap! Patch me up, I'm going back to my unit." She relented, and Frank returned to duty without his Purple Heart, thanking her for looking the other way. She understood that paratroopers did not wish to be put into a replacement unit.

For a time, Ridgway set up improvised headquarters at Harze, Belgium. Brandy established an interrogation unit there. One prisoner, an officer in the German navy who spoke fluent English, was particularly obnoxious. Brandy for a while assumed he was one of Skorzeny's infiltrators, but when captured he was in a German uniform. The prisoner gave only minimal information, and refused to listen to any "stinking American Jews." Brandy's sergeant was Jewish and, understanding the

replies, seethed with anger, his weapon at the ready. Finally, the German soldier spat on a small American flag that Brandy had on his desk.

Infuriated, Brandy jumped up and slugged the German in the face,
knocking him senseless. He realized that he must humiliate the prisoner, so he ordered his sergeant to undress the German while he was
unconscious. When the POW revived, he was quite humbled. Standing
at attention in the brisk, cold room, without a stitch of clothing on, he
answered the questions without further resistance. In the midst of the
interrogation, two British officers accidentally stepped into the room,
took one look, then left.

Brandy thought they might report him for demeaning the prisoner,
but he concluded the investigation. Years later, by one of those strange
quirks of fate that seemed to trace his life, Brandy met the British actor
David Niven, after his filming of *Around the World in Eighty Days*. Niven
had been a Phantom during the war, and when comparing notes with
Brandy, he asked if Brandy had ever heard the story of an American FID
officer who had questioned a German prisoner in the nude! Niven, it
seems, had been one of the two officers from General Bernard
Montgomery's headquarters who had interrupted the questioning, and
he remembered the moment for years afterwards as one of the most
gratifying he had experienced in the war.

Within six weeks, the surrounded troops at Bastogne were relieved.
The Ardennes offensive had been stopped, and Ridgway was placed in
command of a special corps operation involving the 6th British Airborne
Division and the 17th U.S. Airborne brought from Britain. During this
period, Ridgway appointed Brandy as a special intelligence officer to
the commanding general, effective 21 March 1945. The United States
Army did not have an official position of military aide de camp, although
for the British it was a regular rank. Nor did the American forces have a
special group like the Phantoms, which Montgomery used as his "eyes
and ears" for both enemy and allied actions on his flanks. However,
Ridgway retained Brandy to serve as his military aide-de-camp and as his
"eyes and ears," working in a role similar to that of the Phantoms.

The corps dropped the two airborne divisions on 24 March across
the Rhine, near the city of Wesel. Brandy jumped in with the 17th Airborne Division, catching up with General Ridgway near General Will-

iam Miley's temporary command post in a foxhole, close to the Diersdorf Forest. After being briefed by Miley, he inquired if contact had been established with Brigadier Derek Mills-Roberts, 1st Commmando Brigade, fighting in the city of Wesel. The answer was negative. Ridgway turned to Brandy and ordered him to penetrate the German lines and establish contact. General Miley, in turn, suggested that a unit of the Special Air Service (SAS) Ground Force should assist to fight through the German lines. This was done and contact was established, late at night, in Wesel with the 1st Commando Brigade.

At daylight, Brandy returned to Ridgway's forward command post. As fate would have it, it was his turn to be on duty, holding down the midnight watch until 6 A.M., and preparing the G-2 reports for the morning briefings. At 4 A.M., General Ridgway walked in and Brandy read out his reports on the enemy situation. Instead of sticking with the G-2 phases, he trespassed into the operations phase, the G-3 area, which he should not have done. Brandy stated that from the information on hand, there were heavy artillery concentrations in the woods near the towns of Chermeck, Dorster, and Haltern. However, they could be overrun since they did not have experienced ground forces to protect them. He suggested a swift, aggressive attack with tanks and airborne troops, causing a breakthrough and a resulting end-run all the way to the Haltern and Dulman areas. These forces would then make contact with other American forces coming up from the south. Ridgway heard him out, and then asked him to repeat the report. The general next ordered Brandy to brief the members of the general staff, which he did. Brandy thought he would get a good chewing out by some of the general staff officers later on.

Ridgway ordered his chief of staff to set up a meeting with the commanding general of the Second British Army, General Dempsey. The briefing with the British general and other officers was well received. General Dempsey agreed to the plan with General Ridgway. Orders were issued to attach the British 6th Guards Armored Brigade to the corps, and with the 513th Parachute Infantry Regiment riding on top of the tanks, they would commence the attack plan. The meeting concluded. Ridgway turned to Brandy, and in front of all the assembled British and American officers said the following: "Captain, since this was your idea, *you* will lead the point of attack." Brandy saluted, saying "Thank you, general, will do!"

On 27 March 1945, Brandy rolled out in his jeep in front of the tank column, with the troops riding on top. Not until later did he learn that General Ridgway was behind the first tank during the attack. The operation was a complete success. Contact was made by the combined tank and paratroop forces in the Haltern-Dulman areas with the 2nd U.S. Armored Division, thereby forming the famous "Ruhr Pocket," which ultimately broke the back of the German resistance in the west.

Having completed the encirclement of the Germans, General Omar Bradley ordered Ridgway, commanding general of the XVIII Airborne, to move four infantry divisions newly assigned to his corps: the 86th, the 8th, the 78th and the 97th, and one armored division, the 13th, forward from the south. Their mission was to eliminate the Ruhr Pocket, the industrial heartland of Germany to the east of Wesel. British and American troops had already taken vast numbers of prisoners. They had cut off the retreat of German Army Group B, who were defending the Ruhr under the command of Field Marshal Walther Model, and were within a few miles of his field command post.

Brandy suggested a plan while talking to some members of the Counter Intelligence Corps, the CIC. It was known that the German industrialists wanted the balance of the factory areas preserved and clearly hoped for a surrender of troops rather than a hard fought battle through the Ruhr. The CIC units were penetrating German lines regularly by this time, and Brandy arranged with the CIC to meet with five or six German industrialists and one general, who were receptive to surrendering the Ruhr area, in the town of Siegen. Brandy met with the group as planned on 13 April and got them to agree to transmit a request for surrender to Field Marshal Model. The message to Model was never delivered, because the SS executed all the delegates prior to its delivery. The bloodstained copy of the surrender request, which was recovered later in Model's headquarters, ended up in Brandy's files.

Brandy explained what had happened to Ridgway. The general decided on a more direct approach for surrender. He gave a message to Brandy for personal hand delivery to Field Marshal Model. Brandy, Major Jack Crowley from the G-3 section of the corps, and a driver drove slowly

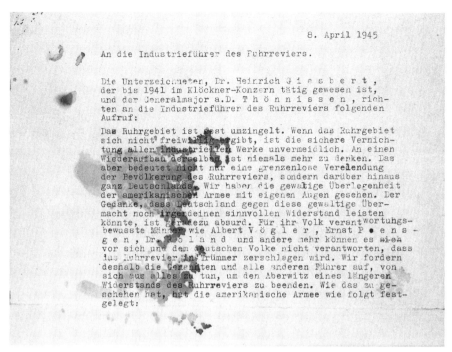

```
                                         8. April 1945

    An die Industrieführer des Fuhrreviers.

    Die Unterzeichneten, Dr. Heinrich G i e s b e r t ,
    der bis 1941 im Klöckner-Konzern tätig gewesen ist,
    und der Generalmajor a.D. T h ö n n i s s e n , rich-
    ten an die Industrieführer des Ruhrreviers folgenden
    Aufruf:

    Das Ruhrgebiet ist fast umzingelt. Wenn das Ruhrgebiet
    sich nicht freiwillig ergibt, ist die sichere Vernich-
    tung aller Industriellen Werke unvermeidlich. An einen
    Wiederaufbau derselben ist niemals mehr zu denken. Das
    aber bedeutet nicht nur eine grenzenlose Verelendung
    der Bevölkerung des Ruhrreviers, sondern darüber hinaus
    ganz Deutschlands. Wir haben die gewaltige Überlegenheit
    der amerikanischen Armee mit eigenen Augen gesehen. Der
    Gedanke, dass Deutschland gegen diese gewaltige Über-
    macht noch irgendeinen sinnvollen Widerstand leisten
    könnte, ist geradezu absurd. Für ihr Volk verantwortuhgs-
    bewusste Männer wie Albert V ö g l e r , Ernst P e n s -
    g e n , Dr. Pol a n d  und andere mehr können es sich
    vor sich und dem deutschen Volke nicht verantworten, dass
    das Ruhrrevier in Trümmer zerschlagen wird. Wir fordern
    deshalb die Genannten und alle anderen Führer auf, von
    sich aus alles zu tun, um den Aberwitz eines längeren
    Widerstands des Ruhrreviers zu beenden. Wie das zu ge-
    schehen hat, hat die amerikanische Armee wie folgt fest-
    gelegt:
```

Bloodstained copy of German industrialists' surrender request to Field Marshal Model.

across the front lines in a jeep with a white flag of truce on the fender. Brandy was unarmed and acted as a negotiator. The trio was captured by a German patrol, one of whom threatened to shoot them. A German general staff officer, *Oberst* (Colonel) Fritz Shultz-Madler, intervened. Brandy explained that he had a message to deliver to Field Marshal Model, and he would wait for a response.

The three men were blindfolded and driven by Colonel Shultz-Madler to Model's headquarters. On the way they were stopped by the SS, who immediately ordered that the captured men be shot. Only through another argument by Schultz-Madler was an execution avoided. The identical situation occurred a third time upon arrival at Model's headquarters, where the SS made ready to shoot not only Brandy and his group, but also Schultz-Madler, for bringing the negotiators to headquarters. Once again intervention, this time by one of Model's generals, saved Brandy and his patrol. Brandy then personally delivered this letter into the hands of Field Marshal Model:

                                                            APO 109 In the Field
16 April 1945

To the General Officer Commanding ARMY GROUP "B":

Sir:
1. Powerful Allied forces are today deep in the very heart of GERMANY. Its complete and rapid conquest is now beyond GERMANY's power to avert.

2. Of the encircled forces under your command, more than 180,000 have been taken prisoner. Your forces are completely surrounded by overwhelming UNITED STATES forces. Their fate is irrevocably sealed. The alternatives are death or honorable submission.

3. Neither history nor the military profession records any nobler character, any more brilliant master of warfare, any more dutiful subordinate to the State than the American General, ROBERT E. LEE. Eighty years ago this month, his loyal command, reduced in numbers, stripped of its means of effective fighting, and completely surrounded by overwhelming forces, chose an honorable capitulation.

4. This same choice is now yours. In the light of a soldier's honor, for the reputation of the German Officer Corps, for the sake of your nation's future, I ask the immediate unconditional surrender of your forces. The German lives you will save are sorely needed to restore your people to their proper place in society. The German cities you will preserve are irreplaceable necessities for your people's welfare.

5. The bearer of this communication, an Officer of my Staff, is authorized to conduct your emissary to my Headquarters.

                                                            M.B.Ridgway
                                                     Major General, US Army
                                                            Commanding

Model replied verbally to Brandy, rejecting the offer and asking him to convey it to Ridgway. The German *Generalstab* colonel who had accompanied Brandy's jeep in his own staff car escorted him back to the lines. On their return to the front, the German officer stopped and left his car to walk back to Brandy's jeep. In his hand he had his P-38 pistol, and for a moment, Brandy thought the mission, and his life, were over.

But Colonel Shultz-Madler put the gun in the palm of his hand and held it out.

"I want to surrender to you," he said. "I am your prisoner."

Brandy explained that they still had some further lines to cross, and that both American and German troops might fire on them. Nevertheless, Shultz-Madler wanted to surrender. But he had one condition. Brandy would also have to accept the surrender of his driver. If he refused, they would both attack him with their bare hands, and Brandy would have to shoot them. The convoy proceeded with Shultz-Madler continually intervening at the roadblocks, preventing Germans from shooting Brandy, Crowley, and the driver.

The jeep passed through the lines safely with the German officer and his driver. Arriving at the American lines, they were shot at and then roughly manhandled by U.S. troops, who suspected they were all infiltrators. An American officer appeared who, at Brandy's insistence, called his G-2. The G-2 then called corps headquarters to get Brandy and his escorts, now prisoners, forwarded through channels. When they all arrived at Ridgway's command post, Brandy was astonished to learn that the German driver was actually the son of the colonel. Both were happy to be prisoners.

Next, General Ridgway put Brandy in command of a large detachment that raided through the lines to capture Model, since he had refused to surrender. Unfortunately, when Brandy's armored task force arrived at Model's command post, they found that the field marshal had just fled, leaving his breakfast uneaten and still hot on the plate. Brandy later reported the facts to Ridgway.

A few weeks later, Ridgway and Brandy learned from the British that Model had escaped the encircling net at the last moment, and then during the retreat, quietly walked into the woods and shot himself. Later,

Model's son recovered the body. Over 300,000 German troops surrendered in the Ruhr Pocket.

As the Allied troops moved forward, Brandy received a variety of special assignments, sometimes arranging the surrender of isolated pockets of German troops. As he had done with his FID unit when following Patton's rapid tank advance through France, he would approach German command posts in his jeep, at times with a white flag, to convince the German major or colonel in charge to surrender. Several times he arranged for the German officer to order his own men to stack their arms, secure the perimeter, and keep order that would prevent spontaneous resistance when the American troops arrived. Once he had such a discussion under the muzzles of several Panzer tanks.

When they were south of the town of Essen, which was surrounded by the 8th Division on the east and the 13th Armored Division on the left flank of the XVIII Airborne Corps, the advance was extremely slow. The commanding general of the 13th Armored Division was relieved and temporarily replaced by XVIII Airborne Artillery Corps Commmanding General Lemuel Mathewson. Ridgway ordered Brandy to capture Just Dillgardt, the mayor of the town, in order to declare Essen an open city and thereby limit casualties by avoiding street-to-street fighting. Essen, often regarded as a model community, was one of the first planned company towns in the world, housing employees of the giant Krupp munitions works.

Brandy and his driver moved ahead of the rapidly advancing infantry patrols, even though some areas were still held by the Germans in an extremely fluid situation. Driving past a large estate, he noticed a Nazi flag still raised and assumed it might be a Nazi headquarters. As they approached the gate to the park-like compound, to their surprise, they spotted an old German civilian cleaning two guns.

The man explained that he was a *jagtmeister*, literally "master of the hunt," a high-ranking combination of private game warden and guard, and therefore perfectly entitled, he believed, to have weapons. It was clear that the elderly *jagtmeister* expected deference. Brandy explained firmly in German that to be seen with a Nazi flag and a weapon would make him a likely target, and that he should hand over the guns and take the flag down.

"But the guns are not mine," the old man replied, "and I can't allow them to be confiscated. They belong to my master."

Even with the driver's Thompson submachine gun pointed at him, the *jagtmeister* refused to yield up the hunting rifle. Instead, he ordered the two trespassers off the estate.

"So," Brandy asked, "who is your master?"

Brandy learned that the master was Baron Alfried Krupp von Bohlen und Halbach, residing in the Villa-Schloss Hügel, the castle, so he decided to drive there. The front door was unlocked. Brandy and his sergeant pushed in gently, Brandy with his service .45 and the driver with his tommy gun at the ready. There were no servants in the large front hall, and the whole mansion seemed deserted. At the end of the hall they came to a large oak door, which again was unlocked. Brandy turned the handle and walked in.

The room was a luxurious library with a highly polished floor. At the end of the room was a large table with a leather top. Seated at the table, reading some documents, was Alfried Krupp, the German industrialist and munitions manufacturer, one of the most wanted civilian war criminals of the Reich. Krupp was heir to the three-hundred-year-old Krupp arms fortune and employer of thousands of slave laborers. As managing director of the firm from 1936 on, he had supplied Hitler's armed forces with a steady stream of tanks and munitions.

Krupp did not look up at the intruders. When Brandy started to question him, he disdainfully replied that he was not about to talk to any lowly captains or sergeants. Brandy's driver, a young German-speaking Jewish refugee who had fled Germany, stiffened at Krupp's arrogance, raised his tommy gun, and aimed directly at Krupp. Instinctively, Brandy knocked down the barrel and the bullets ripped into the front of the desk and the polished floor. Krupp blanched, but did not move. None of the shots had hit him.

Quietly, Brandy took the sergeant's weapon from him and explained that their orders did not include killing one of the most wanted men in Germany. Brandy told Krupp that he was under arrest as of that moment. As they walked out, Krupp remained at his desk, immobile.

Leaving the estate, Brandy ran into a U.S. infantry combat patrol and told them to put a guard at the gate and notify the CIC to come for

Krupp. He ordered the *jagtmeister* to place the hunting guns in a canvas cover and surrender them. He lowered the Nazi flag, had his driver take a posed picture of him with the flag and Krupp's hunting guns, then confiscated the flag. Krupp was picked up a few hours later by the CIC and held for the war crime trials at Nuremberg. As it turned out, Krupp's father Gustav was released without trial due to his age and health, and Alfried was not tried until 1948. He received a twelve-year sentence, but was freed by amnesty in 1951 and returned to operating the firm.

Brandy and his sergeant pressed on to find the mayor. Just Dillgardt was at his home on another large estate nearby, at Bredeney. By contrast to Krupp, Mayor Dillgardt was almost jovial as he explained that all the records of the town were in order and available to the CIC. When Brandy told Dillgardt that he must accompany him to General Ridgway to arrange for an open city, however, the mayor was mildly annoyed. He asked for permission to tell his wife where he was going and explain to her that he would soon return when the Americans finished with him. When Brandy, remembering the estate at Hügel, asked him to turn over all of

Brandy next to Krupp's Nazi flag outside the Villa-Schloss Hügel.

the Bredeney guns, Dillgardt laughed. "Guns? Guns have no place in our affairs." Brandy thought the remark a little ironic, coming from a confirmed Nazi and mayor of a planned community at the heart of the weapons manufacturing complex of the Reich. Brandy later learned that the mayor, despite his cooperative behavior, was put on trial for war crimes and served a total of twenty-eight months, about the equivalent time eventually served by Krupp.

For the Ruhr action, Brandy received the Silver Star and was promoted to major.

After the collapse of the Ruhr Pocket and the destruction of German Army Group B, Allied troops moved forward more rapidly, crossing the Elbe and anticipating a link-up with the Russian Army moving

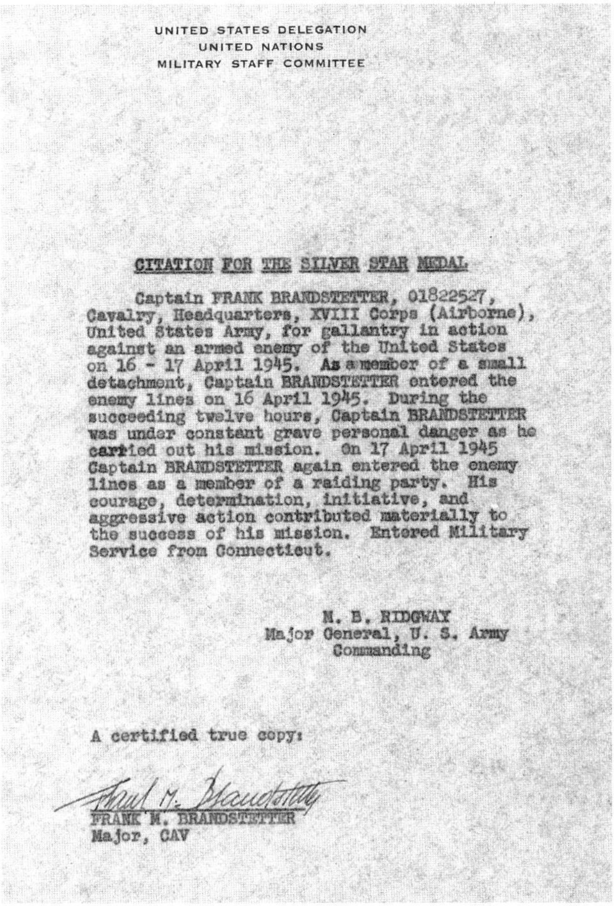

UNITED STATES DELEGATION
UNITED NATIONS
MILITARY STAFF COMMITTEE

CITATION FOR THE SILVER STAR MEDAL

Captain FRANK BRANDSTETTER, 01822527, Cavalry, Headquarters, XVIII Corps (Airborne), United States Army, for gallantry in action against an armed enemy of the United States on 16 - 17 April 1945. As a member of a small detachment, Captain BRANDSTETTER entered the enemy lines on 16 April 1945. During the succeeding twelve hours, Captain BRANDSTETTER was under constant grave personal danger as he carried out his mission. On 17 April 1945 Captain BRANDSTETTER again entered the enemy lines as a member of a raiding party. His courage, determination, initiative, and aggressive action contributed materially to the success of his mission. Entered Military Service from Connecticut.

M. B. RIDGWAY
Major General, U. S. Army
Commanding

A certified true copy:

FRANK M. BRANDSTETTER
Major, CAV

Frank Brandstetter's Silver Star Medal citation for his missions to Field Marshal Model, 1945.

steadily west. Sudden opportunities presented themselves. Ridgway used assault boats to put one battalion of the 82nd Airborne across the Elbe, then hastily put the 244th and the 552nd Engineer Combat Battalions to work building a pontoon bridge across the river on 30 April. While the bridge was being completed, the Germans began shelling it with heavy artillery. On his way to the bridge to check the progress, Ridgway did not see the engineers, who had taken cover. He ordered Brandy to find the commanding officer of the engineers, which he did and returned to the pontoon bridge. Ridgway walked out on the partially completed bridge to observe the shells falling in the water, which he later noted were very well directed. Brandy stood three feet from his commander.

Ridgway walked back and gave the engineers a pep talk, and with his example and encouragement, they completed the 1180-foot bridge in just over thirteen hours, even though it took two hits and the engineers sustained thirty-two casualties. A few days later, when it was quite safe, General Montgomery walked out with Ridgway to view the bridge and pose for some photographs, with Brandy standing behind them.

Generals Ridgway and Montgomery discuss the completed bridge over the Elbe, May 1945. Brandy can be seen at the back.

At the instruction of General Ralph "Doc" Eaton, Ridgway's chief of staff, Brandy later prepared a report of the event which Eaton used to recommend General Ridgway for his second Silver Star. Brandy's admiration for Ridgway was profound. Later, as he recorded his memories of this period, he tried to capture the nature of the example set by General Ridgway, whom the fighting paratroopers had come to call the "soldier's soldier":

> Yes, the General was tough, but fair. He never asked anyone to do anything that he could or would not do in battle. He drove his chief of staff, General Eaton, to exasperation, and all division commanders under the XVIII ABN Corps also.

> His habit was to have an advance forward Command Post in the attacking Regiment's area, from his XVIII Corps HQ close to him and the front he was inspecting. . . . This way, he shamed the Division commanding generals to spur on their respective regimental commanders and catch up with the Corps' Advance CP from where the General directed the entire front. . . . He brought down long-range artillery, personally directing it from the battalions' forward position.

> I know, I was there with him. . . .he was a man of guts, but expected the same from his officers close to him. It was always a "can-do" spirit which prevailed under his command. . . . I was there then, and later on the bridge during this entire episode. Was I scared? Damn well I was. But the example of the soldier's soldier did not give me time to think— do it. That's it. It is your duty.

During one of the forward artillery post observations with Ridgway, Brandy received a wound from the shrapnel of an 88 mm shell that exploded nearby. Brandy was knocked flat on his back, but when Ridgway turned and asked if he was all right, Brandy, not realizing he had been hit, said he was fine. A few seconds later, he realized he had been hit.

The shrapnel had penetrated his pistol pouch and opened up his left side. Unobtrusively, his sergeant patched him with a bandage. Later, Colonel Wolcott L. Etienne, the Corps surgeon, stitched the wound. The pouch had saved his life. Brandy declined a Purple Heart, but saved the pouch and the piece of shrapnel as mementos.

Events moved rapidly in late April and early May 1945. Hitler committed suicide on 30 April in his bunker in Berlin. Two days later, the Soviets subdued the last resistance in Berlin, and the remaining German troops, under Hitler's successor, Admiral Doenitz, began to arrange surrender. On 7 May, the Wehrmacht capitulated, and at midnight on 8 May 1945, the Reich unconditionally surrendered. Brandy's movements through these days kept him close to the unfolding events.

Allied troops had advanced rapidly in the northern sector, covering sixty miles in less than a week. On 2 May, American and British forces met up with the Russians at Ludwigslust near the Baltic, in what was designated to be the Russian occupation zone. The Russians continued to pound away at the last defenses of Berlin on that day. The British and American drive to Wismar on the Baltic successfully cut off the Soviets from any advance into Schleswig-Holstein and Denmark. The German troops there thus would surrender to the Americans and British, not to the Russians, assuring that there would be no penetration of Soviet forces into the Atlantic coast of Europe.

Briefly, the Allies celebrated the linkup with the Russians at Ludwigslust with a round of toasts, but Brandy found the Russian officers quite arrogant. Their attitude, it seemed, was that the Americans and British were merely observers and latecomers, and that Stalin's forces had accomplished the bulk of the fighting. After a few days, Ridgway pulled his command post back to Hagenow, a few miles inside the American lines.

At Hagenow, Brandy was present as Ridgway's troops liberated Wöbbelin, one of the many concentration camps full of slave laborers from all over the territories conquered by the Reich. The nearby camp, although small, was appalling even to the battle-hardened paratroopers, who had to sort the living from the dead and administer help to the survivors. Brandy, with General Ridgway's approval, ordered arrangements to be made for the burial of 144 emaciated corpses right in the town square, next to the bandstand, to serve as a permanent reminder. Others were to be buried at the nearby communities of Schwerin and Ludwigslust.

At the orders of the American troops, able-bodied civilians dug the individual graves in Hagenow. The local townspeople protested that they had no idea what had transpired at the camp, causing the men of the liberating army to be appalled at their bland indifference.

Ridgway's troops rounded up the townspeople to attend the burial ceremony, held on 8 May 1945. Colonel Harry Cain delivered a speech, which Brandy wrote in German and translated into English for the American troops. He had it printed overnight in both languages in the form of a small pamphlet.

> In these open graves lie the emaciated, brutalized bodies of some 144 citizens of many lands. Before they were dragged away from their homes and their livelihoods to satisfy the insatiable greed and malice, ambition and savagery of the German nation, they were happy and healthy and contented human beings.

> They were brought to this German soil from Poland, Russia, Czechoslovakia, Holland, Belgium and France. They were driven and starved and beaten to slake that unholy thirst of the German war machine. When possessed no longer of the will or ability to work or fight back or live, they were either tortured to death or permitted to slowly die.

> What you witness and are a part of in Hagenow today is but a single small example of what can be seen throughout the length and depth of your German Fatherland.

> Untold numbers of other Allied Soldiers and German citizens shudder before similar burial services, as you shudder now. The Allies shudder because they never dreamed that human leadership, supported by the masses, could so debase itself as to be responsible for results like those in these open graves.

You Germans shudder for reasons of your own. Some of you, having been a party to this degradation of mankind, shudder in fear that your guilt will be determined—as in fact, it will. Others among you shudder because you let depravity of this character develop while you stood still. The civilized world shudders on finding that a part of its society has fallen so low. That world isn't content to believe that what we are horrified about was the work of any small group of German gangsters, maniacs and fanatics. That world must, as it does, hold the German people responsible for what has taken place within the confines of this nation.

Time will prove to what extent the German people recognize the enormity of their crimes and to what extent they will shoulder a full national responsibility for making amends. That any future conduct can eradicate the knowledge and memories of something like this—this is a matter of high dispute. If there be a soul within the German nation, it will rise now to make impossible the doing of such future wrongs. If there be not a soul in this German nation, its future is forlorn and totally lacking in hope.

The bodies in these graves came yesterday from Wöbbelin. They were buried in a common grave, or lying piled high on the open earth. Bodies from Wöbbelin will be buried in Ludwigslust and Schwerin as they are being buried here— under the sight of God, and true words consecrated by the Protestant, Catholic and Jewish faiths are being spoken over them. In death these bodies are receiving from Allied, Christian hands, the decent, humanitarian and spiritual treatment they didn't receive in life from German hands. As we listen, Allies and Germans alike, let us ask an understanding which Germany must find if there is to be a future life for her.

In a service last Sunday held in the German cathedral in Wismar, 2,000 Allied soldiers —the same who had helped beat down and crush your military machine— spoke a prayer aloud that drifted into your German skies—God's skies—"Pray," they said, "for the German people, that they may one day take their place again among honorable peoples."

This was the first time that U.S. troops made an example by revealing the atrocities committed by the Germans through the honorable burial of victims in the middle of a German city. Later, in the XVII Airborne Corps areas, other divisions followed this example.

With the first full day of peace, 9 May 1945, and after the strain of the burial service, Brandy thought of flying up to Denmark, which had been relatively unscathed in the fighting, and getting a good meal. Copenhagen was about 160 air miles from Hagenow. Denmark was to be in the British occupation sphere, but Brandy assumed that no one would object if Ridgway unofficially visited for a day's relaxation. According to information Brandy received from 6th British Airborne Divi-

STATEMENT

delivered at Hagenow, Germany,

on 8 May 1945 at Public Burial Service

for 144 dead uncovered at Wöbbelin

Concentration Camp

ANSPRACHE

die am 8. Mai 1945 in Hagenow

zur Begräbnisfeier der im Konzentrations-

lager in Wöbbelin gefundenen 144 Toten

gehalten wurde

Cover page of the statement made at Hagenow, Germany, May 8, 1945.

sion intelligence, the city was in British hands. Ridgway assented, and as special intelligence officer, it was Brandy's job to plan the excursion.

As the staff flew into Copenhagen in a C-47, the pilot, John Day, pointed out to Brandy that a turret of German 88's guarding the airport were tracking them. Brandy and Day looked through binoculars, but could see no British. Brandy said quietly to the pilot that he should circle gently, without taking evasive action that would draw ack-ack fire, and on landing, make sure that Brandy was the first out the door.

When he stepped out on the tarmac, a German staff car pulled up and a Luftwaffe officer got out. It was clear the British had not yet arrived and Copenhagen airport was still in German hands, although the war had officially ended twelve hours before. In his best High German, with a peremptory tone of command, Brandy informed the German officer that they were there to take over the surrender of the German forces. Then Brandy ordered two additional Mercedes cars for transport, and made clear that their first business would be lunch. The German commanding officer, who had been expecting the British, was perplexed but cooperated.

A small motorcade, with German motorcycles as escort, proceeded into the city. The word must have spread, for the convoy had to stop several times, blocked by rejoicing civilians who showered the cars with flowers and by girls rushing up to kiss the U.S Army officers. Patiently, the German drivers wended their way through the throngs.

On arrival at the center of Copenhagen with the German escort, Brandy contacted the acting mayor, pulling him out of earshot from the Germans, and asked, "Where the hell are the British?" The mayor answered that they were on the outskirts of the city. Brandy told him to get a message to them through the Copenhagen underground and inform them that a strong unit should be sent immediately to the city. He told the mayor to tell the British that the entire XVIII Airborne Division's general staff, including General Ridgway, were now in Copenhagen.

The small group then drove across the square to D'Angleterre Hotel, well known for its excellent cuisine. Inside all was in readiness, and a full-course meal was served up for them with table linen, fine china, and silverware. Brandy was astounded at the service and food, reminiscent of the finest in New York's pre-war days. However, he had trouble enjoying the fine meal because his stomach was in knots. He was not sure what orders the Germans had received, what was holding up the British occupation, or how they would react to finding the United States Army there ahead of them, with no clearance through channels. He sat by the window, anxiously watching the mayor's office and hoping the British units would arrive, his eyes on the Luftwaffe vehicles and motor- cycles parked in front. At the end of the meal, he kept ordering various desserts, coffees, liqueurs, fruits, cheeses, and nuts, hoping to stall for time. Finally, after two hours, a small unit appeared. A British Landrover came slowly poking around a corner into the square in front of the hotel, as if expecting armed resistance.

Brandy quickly walked out of the dining room and up to the ar- mored car. One of the Brits, a little suspicious of a Yank in paratrooper boots coming out of a hotel guarded by Luftwaffe vehicles in a city that was supposed to be in British territory, aimed his weapon at Brandy's chest, demanding an explanation.

Brandy smiled and turned the tables. Where were the British troops? Well, reconnaissance was necessary. What was the delay? German forces still had their arms.

Brandy continued, telling him in no uncertain terms to radio for a larger force. The British soldier snapped off a salute and drove off. Brandy could feel the dampness in his shirt as he returned to the hotel and gathered the general and staff together for the trip back to the airport. Thus ended the American "occupation" of Copenhagen.

Years later, Brandy told this story to the Danish Ambassador to Mexico, who had invited him to visit Copenhagen. He stayed at the D'Angleterre, had a relaxed meal at the same table, and insisted on paying his own bill.

The victory established in Europe on V-E Day, 8 May 1945, however, only meant that the war was half over; the United States still faced Japan in the Far East. Ridgway's staff prepared to return to the United States before heading to the Pacific.

A Troubled Peace

Perhaps because he had been rejected by his own father, young Frank Brandstetter always sought a mentor, a man on whom he could model his life and whose approval would be worth earning. In New York, Kurt Meisner, Louis Toth, Geza Takaro, and Joe and Zanvyl Krieger had served as role models. In the Army, he found that figure in General Matthew Ridgway, whose personal courage and pure commitment to serving his nation earned Brandy's respect. Ridgway, for his part, found an excellent military aide in Brandy. Toward the end of the war in Europe, he promoted Brandy to major for his action in the Ruhr. He also secured his transfer from the reserves to the regular establishment based on a glowing rating, the "highest I have ever given any officer, 6.8 out of 7.0," according to Ridgway. Brandy sometimes found it hard, but he always tried to live up to those words in both his personal and business life.

Brandy openly admitted then and later that Ridgway was like a father to him. The feeling was clear and explicit, and over the next four and a half decades Brandy kept in close contact with Ridgway by mail, phone, and frequent visits to his home, as his house guest, in Pittsburgh.

Brandy's experiences in the year following V-E Day firmly sealed the close, personal relationship to Ridgway. When the war in Europe ended,

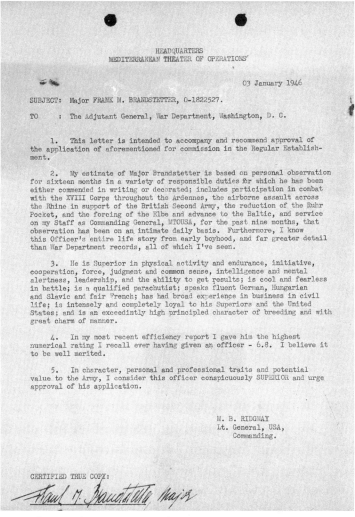

HEADQUARTERS
MEDITERRANEAN THEATER OF OPERATIONS

03 January 1946

SUBJECT: Major FRANK M. BRANDSTETTER, O-1822527.

TO   : The Adjutant General, War Department, Washington, D. C.

1. This letter is intended to accompany and recommend approval of
the application of aforementioned for commission in the Regular Establishment.

2. My estimate of Major Brandstetter is based on personal observation
for sixteen months in a variety of responsible duties for which he has been
either commended in writing or decorated; includes participation in combat
with the XVIII Corps throughout the Ardennes, the airborne assault across
the Rhine in support of the British Second Army, the reduction of the Ruhr
Pocket, and the forcing of the Elbe and advance to the Baltic, and service
on my Staff as Commanding General, MTOUSA, for the past nine months, that
observation has been on an intimate daily basis. Furthermore, I know
this Officer's entire life story from early boyhood, and far greater detail
than War Department records, all of which I've seen.

3. He is superior in physical activity and endurance, initiative,
cooperation, force, judgment and common sense, intelligence and mental
alertness, leadership, and the ability to get results; is cool and fearless
in battle; is a qualified parachutist; speaks fluent German, Hungarian
and Slavic and fair French; has had broad experience in business in civil
life; is intensely and completely loyal to his Superiors and the United
States; and is an exceedingly high principled character of breeding and with
great charm of manner.

4. In my most recent efficiency report I gave him the highest
numerical rating I recall ever having given an officer - 6.8. I believe it
to be well merited.

5. In character, personal and professional traits and potential
value to the Army, I consider this officer conspicuously SUPERIOR and urge
approval of his application.

M. B. RIDGWAY
Lt. General, USA,
Commanding.

CERTIFIED TRUE COPY:

Frank Brandstetter received the highest efficiency report
rating given by General Ridgway, a 6.8 in January 1946.

Ridgway was called back to the United States and given the task of re-
constituting the Airborne Corps for action in the Pacific Theater. Many
of the enlisted veterans who had survived the European Theater of
Operations were mustered out, and new recruits were to be trained to
replace them. In the summer of 1945, Ridgway recalled his staff from
Europe to the United States. Brandy, together with the other staff officers, began the rebuilding of the Airborne with fresh recruits.

Early in August, Ridgway flew to San Francisco, and then on to Mindanao in the Philippines, to take up his post. In Mindanao, he began to assemble the Airborne Corps for the final assault on Japan.

While flying in and out of San Francisco, Brandy enjoyed some well-earned relaxation in the better restaurants of a city famous for its hotels and dining. With his rank as major, his dress uniform, parachute boots, blond hair, neat mustache, erect bearing and European manners, he was noticed everywhere. One day at lunch in the Palace Hotel, he spotted an attractive and sophisticated young lady at a nearby table looking at him intently. He mentioned it to Baron Rieder, his friend, who was the vice president and the general manager of the Palace. Baron Rieder recognized her as one of the young members of the San Francisco social register, Barbara Peart.

Baron Rieder explained more about her family. She was having lunch with her aunt, Mrs. Genevieve Harriman O'Brien, a widow highly-placed in social circles in San Francisco. Barbara's father, Hartley Fiske Peart, was one of the most prominent attorneys in the city and chairman of a group called the Cabinet Table, which met to discuss matters of national and international importance, often determining who would be nominated or selected to represent California at the Republican presidential conventions. The Table had been established by Peart's father-in-law, Jim O'Brien. Hartley Peart, also a director of the Santa Fe Railroad Corporation, was legal counsel to Bechtel Corporation and other banking and insurance firms and a leader of the Republican Party in California.

Frank made a bet with Baron Rieder and the Swiss Consul at lunch that, snobbish or not, he would have dinner with the charming young Miss Peart that evening. Frank was introduced to Barbara, and with a courteous bow, he kissed her hand. He was impressed with her, not only for her beauty, manners and elegant outfit (à lá Marcel Rochas), but also for her awareness of world conditions. She, in turn, was struck by his charm, looks, and sophistication. The result was a whirlwind romance, conducted mostly by long distance telephone between Washington, Fort Campbell, and San Francisco, while Brandy awaited final orders to ship to the Philippines with the balance of the XVIII Airborne Corps.

After the official signing of the surrender by the Japanese in September, 1945, Ridgway asked to return to the United States on leave. He flew to Washington, where he was offered the post of Ambassador to Argentina, replacing Spruille Braden. Brandy was to accompany him to this post, which would have been ideal for him because he could use his fluent German in an Argentina with a large German colony and a military trained by the Germans. Ridgway declined the offer, however, and later General George C. Marshall nominated him to the post of commanding general of the Mediterranean Theater of Operations of the United States Army (MTOUSA), taking over the transition from combat troop units to military governance of Italy during the stage of "occupation."

Meanwhile, in San Francisco, Brandy proposed marriage to Barbara Peart, and sought advice from Ridgway about fitting the marriage into his commitment to the army. Ridgway advised him to ask his fiancée to set a date, and go with it. Accordingly, Brandy, Barbara, and her parents arranged a small Catholic wedding ceremony at the military chapel at the San Francisco Presidio, on 13 October 1945. On the morning of the wedding, Brandy waited at Hamilton Air Force Base for the arrival of Ridgway, who was to serve as his witness at the wedding. While he waited for the overdue plane, the army air force general in command of the base summoned Brandy into his office and handed him an "eyes only" note for Ridgway. Brandy told the officer that, as Ridgway's aide, he was authorized to read the "eyes-only" mail. He opened the envelope, finding it contained orders for both Ridgway and himself to report to Italy immediately. His heart sank. It would certainly require a change of wedding plans. After Ridgway arrived, Brandy handed him the orders in the car as they headed for the wedding. Ridgway offered to get Brandy a transfer to the Military Attaché branch so he could serve in an embassy. In such a post, Brandy could have his bride with him. Another option Ridgway offered was a two-week vacation for his honeymoon, after which Brandy could join him in Italy. Brandy preferred to go directly to Italy and Ridgway agreed, pointing out that his would not be the only honeymoon interrupted by military orders. His future father-in-law and his bride also agreed.

The wedding was a small ceremony, attended by Ridgway and his wife as witnesses, the Pearts, Barbara's aunt, Mrs. Earl Harriman O'Brien, and Barbara's sister and her fiancé. Brandy was particularly moved as the priest, Chaplain and Lieutenant Colonel Thomas L. McKenna, in-

toned the words, "in sickness and in health." He accepted the commitment as profound and binding.

Hartley Peart arranged a private compartment on the Santa Fe Chief
bound for Washington, and Brandy ordered a case of champagne and
one hundred roses for the honeymoon aboard the railroad. Meanwhile,
Ridgway delayed his departure for Italy by a few days to allow Brandy to
rejoin him on the East Coast.

On 17 October, Ridgway and Brandy flew to Italy in a converted B-
17, which was assigned to General Joseph T. McNarney. Ridgway was
flown over to replace McNarney, who in turn was replacing General
Eisenhower as Commander, ETO. The plane had a galley and bedroom
compartments. Both Ridgway and Brandy were impressed that they could
sleep in a bed while airborne, a far cry from the rough arrangements
they had experienced during the war, when they often slept on the
ground. The plane went by way of the Azores, where it was listed and
presumed lost due to faulty radio communications. The plane, however, continued on to Casablanca and to Naples.

Ridgway's headquarters in MTOUSA was located in Caserta, Italy,
just north of Naples. The general and Brandy moved into a "cottage"

Frank Brandstetter, Barbara Peart, General Matthew Ridgway, and Margaret
Ridgway pose at the wedding ceremony in October 1945.

there, a comfortable two-bedroom converted Nisson Hut with its own kitchen, set in a mixed grove of evergreens and palm trees. Here Brandy worked with Ridgway from October through December 1945, receiving a number of orders from him with a special status: "VOCG," that is, Verbal Orders of the Commanding General. These would sometimes later be committed to writing in order to maintain an official record. Some of the assignments required Brandy to put his language skills and information-gathering abilities to work directly for Ridgway.

One of his first duties was a difficult chore, fraught with the perils of diplomatic protocol. Ridgway had decided to arrange a large luncheon in the Hassler Hotel in Rome, to which he invited high-ranking military Allied personnel from Italy, including the British and Russian diplomatic missions. Ridgway added as guest of honor the King of Italy, Victor Emmanuel III, who was due to be restored to his throne shortly after the reception. The morning of the luncheon, Ridgway received notice that General Mark Clark, stationed in Vienna, would be in Italy and expected to attend the luncheon. Since General Clark was the "Liberator" of Rome, it would be necessary that he be the guest of honor, not the king, especially since a state of war still officially existed between the

Secretary of State James F. Byrnes visits General Ridgway at MTOUSA headquarters in Caserta, Italy. Frank Brandstetter can be seen on the right.

United States and Italy. Yet Victor Immanuel, who had already received his invitation designating him as guest of honor, could not very well be told he was now relegated to the "number two" guest at the luncheon. Clark and Ridgway had a history of ill will, going back to the invasion of Italy. At that time Ridgway felt that Clark had intended to sacrifice airborne troops, and had argued him out of the tactic in front of British officers, much to General Clark's annoyance. Both Ridgway and Brandy assumed that Clark was putting Ridgway in the diplomatic hot spot on purpose. Ridgway was disgusted. He turned to Brandy: "Handle it!"

Brandy immediately flew to Rome, where he received a motorcycle escort to the Quirinale, the residence of Victor Emmanuel III. The king's pompous aide-de-camp, a major-general in the Italian Army, made Brandy cool his heels in the reception room. The time was 11:45 A.M., and the luncheon was set for noon. After five minutes, Brandy insisted on explaining to the aide that the king could not attend the luncheon. The aide fumed that this was unacceptable, an insult, a humiliation. Brandy replied sternly, explaining that Italy was still an occupied country and the king had not yet been recognized. A solution was required that would be satisfactory to all. While they were discussing the situation, King Emmanuel entered. Despite the protests of the aide, Brandy made the situation clear, politely suggesting to the king that a short note be written for General Ridgway, conveying regrets due to a sudden illness. The king calmly ordered that the note be prepared apologizing to every representative for his inability to attend.

Brandy rushed out with the note and, accompanied by military police motorcycles, dashed to the Hassler Hotel. He then unobtrusively passed the note to Ridgway, who was in a receiving line greeting the guests. Ridgway read the note, nodded, took a deep breath, and continued with meeting the notables. Later, at the luncheon, Ridgway read aloud to the group the king's apology for not being able to attend. The reception was a great success. Brandy remembered later that the exercise was a lesson in "how to tell a king to go to hell, in a nice way."

In northeast Italy in 1944, the British and American troops had driven the Italians back and established the "Morgan Line," which placed the province of Venezia Giulia in Allied hands. The area surrounding Trieste to the north was on the Allied side of the Morgan Line. The British and Americans hoped that the region and at least part of the Istrian peninsula could be established with an international jurisdiction, to keep it from falling within the Communist sphere of influence. However, the Yugoslavs expected that Trieste and the surrounding countryside would be turned over to them. The United Nations eventually scheduled a plebiscite to determine the status of the Trieste region, but during Ridgway's appointment in Italy, the exact boundaries of the region subject to the plebiscite had not yet been fixed.

This troubled area attracted Ridgway's attention, and he gave Brandy "Verbal Orders from the Commanding General" to investigate. Brandy made trips to inspect the areas controlled by two regiments of the 88th Infantry Division. The 351st Regiment was charged with responsibility for an area near the Austrian border to the north of Udine, while the 349th Regiment was responsible for an area facing the Yugoslav side of the Morgan Line.

On his tour, Brandy stopped and interviewed the small outposts of American troops. He found that the troops had only a vague idea of the location of the Morgan Line, that there was practically no liaison between British and American troops guarding different sectors of the frontier, and that the American guards did not inspect most vehicles crossing their lines. At the northern border with Austria, he heard that trains regularly crossed into Italy without border control, carrying thousands of displaced persons. The local troops along the border were also uninformed concerning their responsibilities, making the international line seem perfectly open to both legitimate and illegitimate crossings.

Brandy closely investigated one report by a CIC agent suggesting that ten to twelve thousand persons without documentation were crossing the Austrian-Italian border. Along with a CIC lieutenant, he commandeered a locomotive and estimated that no more than fifty people a day could make such a trip, rendering the earlier CIC report a great exaggeration. Nevertheless, he agreed that the border was very loosely patrolled at that point and that clear orders needed to be issued, along with guards posted at the crossing points.

Working under separate VOCG orders, Brandy examined the lines around Gorizia to assess the operation of the 349th Regiment and the

degree of Yugoslav penetration through the Morgan Line. He found
the conditions there "unbelievable." The officers had neglected the
troops, not maintaining supplies or detailing instructions for the guarding of the borders. Some of the American troops had begun supplying
their meals by shooting pigs and goats, roasting the cuts on their bayo-
nets. His report shocked Ridgway, who assigned Major General Bryant
E. Moore to take over command of the 88th Division and replace the
officers at the regimental level. Ridgway's shakeup soon brought some
order to the area.

Before the Americans could propose a detailed boundary for the
plebiscite zone, more detailed information concerning the topography
and the defenses of the area was required. Again on VOCG orders,
Brandy conducted a clandestine trip into the territory south of Trieste
to determine the degree to which that area would be militarily defensible in the case of a Yugoslav, or possibly a Russian-Yugoslav, incursion.
Reports of Soviet motorized artillery and military trainers in Yugoslavia
added to the concerns of the British and Americans. The difficulty, however, was that Tito's forces already patrolled sections of the proposed
zone.

Brandy left Gorizia, where the 88th Division maintained a command
post, and then proceeded south on the British-American side of the
Morgan Line towards the port of Trieste, which was in British hands.
South of Trieste, the Yugoslavs held the town of Pola on the Istrian peninsula. With a sergeant, under the cover of darkness, Brandy took a jeep
on dirt trails to the little town of Gimino, over fifty miles into the Istrian
peninsula. Outside the town, they ran into a Yugoslav patrol that fired
on them. They took cover, and as another patrol approached to sur-
round them, they hurriedly drove out of the area back to the British
outposts at Trieste. When Brandy reported to Ridgway about his midnight adventure the general smiled, perhaps because Brandy's cool "invasion" offset a bit the painful report concerning the condition of the
349th Regiment.

Brandy's research revealed that during the First World War at Gorizia,
the Austrian forces had fought the Italians at the Battle of Caporetto.
The Italians had held the Austrians at the Isonzo River, which flowed
alongside a road leading into Gorizia. Brandy suggested that the same

military frontier might be defensible if the western allies had to with-
stand a military advance by the Yugoslavs.

General Ridgway decided to inspect conditions in the Trieste area
personally, staying at the headquarters of the British commander, Sir
John Harding, who had led the British 7th Armored Division—the Desert
Rats—at El Alamein. Harding situated his headquarters on the outskirts
of Trieste in an old castle, "Miramar," which had once housed Emperor
Maximilian and Empress Carlotta. After spending the night, Ridgway
and Brandy set off for a tour of the harbor in a small launch. As they
boarded, Brandy noticed that the general's eyes seemed glassy. They
were pulling out into the harbor when suddenly Ridgway collapsed in
the launch. Brandy felt for a pulse, but could not find one. He ordered
the launch back to the dock and told the boat captain to radio for an
ambulance. Brandy began artificial respiration. In the ambulance on
the way to the hospital, the young and inexperienced intern blankly
told Brandy that the general had stopped breathing. Brandy urged him
to do something, anything. Finally, in desperation, he screamed, "Do
you have any adrenalin?" The doctor gave Ridgway a shot, and the
general's heart rate improved slightly. He began to breathe, with a little
color gradually coming back to his cheeks.

At the hospital more experienced doctors took over. Brandy called
Caserta for assistance from General Lyman Lemnitzer, Ridgway's Chief
of Staff. Lemnitzer reached an American army doctor stationed in
Naples, a heart specialist, Major Homer Dupuy, who called Brandy and
then conferred with the British doctors. Dupuy flew to Trieste and took
personal charge of the general's case. Both Brandy and Dupuy were
assigned an adjoining room in the hospital next to the general's, so
they could be close to him for the next few days.

Dr. Dupuy told Ridgway he would have to be relieved of duty.
Ridgway refused to even consider reassignment to the United States.
The doctor objected, but Ridgway was able to fly back to Naples and
return to his headquarters at Caserta. Dupuy kept close watch on him
there. Ridgway recuperated quietly at the Caserta cottage, later noting in his memoirs that he wanted no word of his collapse getting back
to Washington. Brandy and Dupuy cooperated in keeping the details
quiet. As Ridgway noted in his memoirs, had word of the incident be-

come known to headquarters, his career would probably have ended at that point.

While at Caserta with the general, Brandy was reading some CIC reports on resistance to the Nazis in central Europe when he noticed the name of his younger sister, Marie, on a list of participants in the German resistance in Austria. Brandy's sister, born in 1916, had been a young member of the German resistance during the war years in Vienna. According to the CIC report, she had been caught and tortured by the Nazis while broadcasting in both French and German for the French intelligence services. Brandy mentioned this to Ridgway, adding that he had not seen his sister since 1928. Ridgway's response gave Brandy reason to appreciate the warm-hearted side of his commander even more.

"Frank," said the general, "you are going to Bratislava. You will see your sister, help her out. Take my car and driver. I'll send along Major Dupuy, so if she needs medical attention, he'll be available. Load up the car with C-rations and medicines and get them to your sister. She can probably use them."

Orders were cut, indicating that the three men were traveling on a personal mission for the general, in his personal limousine, with the three-star general's flags flying from the fenders.

The trip to Bratislava took them through Communist-controlled territory. In contrast to Brandy's brief clandestine penetration behind Yugoslav lines, he and Doctor Dupuy traveled openly to Bratislava. At that time, the eastern section of Austria was under Soviet occupation, with Vienna jointly administered by the British, Americans, French, and Soviets. Czechoslovakia was also under Soviet occupation. Since Czechoslovakia was regarded by the Allies as a victim nation, not an Axis aggressor, the Czechs expected the occupation to be of short duration until a local civilian administration could be elected. In the meantime, however, a trip from Naples to Bratislava took Brandy through Soviet-occupied eastern Austria and into Soviet-occupied Czechoslovakia.

Brandy later filed a full intelligence report on the trip, keeping a copy among his papers. He, Doctor Dupuy, and a driver departed on 15 November 1945 at 2:00 P.M. in the afternoon. They drove the length of Italy from Naples to the Austrian border. Brandy took a snapshot of Doctor Dupuy at the Brenner Pass, with snow surrounding the simple gate that barred the road. Arriving in Austria, they contacted the G-2 section in Linz and received instructions about crossing into the Soviet sector, which they did at Enns on the evening of the 17th. They received a pass from a nonchalant American guard, who interrupted his conversation with a German girlfriend to say that he gave a pass to anyone who asked for one. On the other side, the group received a big smile from the Russian guard, who glanced at their papers and waved them on.

In the dark, they overtook and passed a regimental-strength unit of troops with horse-drawn anti-tank guns, infantry howitzers, and wagons full of fodder, moving towards St. Polten. Russian officers waved them past. Whenever they encountered a roadblock or convoy, Brandy would shout out "Americanski Officia," which seemed to work like a magic password.

The group proceeded towards Bratislava from Vienna, after receiving permission from the Czechoslovakian consul general. East of Vienna, Brandy and Dupuy noticed the heavy traffic of refugees moving into Austria, under the watchful eye of Russian guards, while trucks laden with furniture and cattle moved east. At a pontoon bridge across the Danube into Bratislava, a steady flow of refugee traffic coming out of Czechoslovakia forced them to halt. Finally a Russian air force officer who wanted to cross into Bratislava drove up. All of the traffic was stopped, and Brandy's sedan followed the Russian across the bridge, arriving in Bratislava at 8:45 P.M. on Sunday, 18 November.

In a method which would later characterize all of Brandy's reports, he spelled out exactly the sort of people he used as sources for his detailed information, documenting his "eyes-and-ears" approach with an evaluation of the reliability of those interviewed. He spoke to a Czechoslovakian full colonel, a businessman, the wife of a Czechoslovakian political leader and professor, a Slav major and his wife, and three other "reliable" civilians. They all explained the lengths to which local men had been driven to hide their wives and daughters during the first Russian occupation, due to the constant raping of all women from age eight to eighty.

Some of the sources for his official report were the members of his own family. Brandy learned that his mother had remarried and that she was now with her daughter. He had not seen her since 1928. He learned

Surrendered German military columns and locals on the move, in 1945.

a good deal about the life of the family since he had broken contact. In his typed report to General Ridgway, Brandy gave full details on the life of his mother's husband, Emil Pratt, who was a colonel of artillery and who had worked with the Czechoslovakian government-in-exile in military resistance to the Germans. All of the family, and most of their friends, were concerned that Soviet influence was growing, particularly among the Slovak population. All of the contacts looked to the United States for support against the threat of a Russian takeover, and were concerned about the upcoming elections.

In Bratislava, Brandy found not only his sister, but his mother as well. It was true that in January 1945 his sister, captured by the SS, was incarcerated and tortured. She had been broadcasting in French to the underground fighters throughout the region. After the liberation of Vienna, French forces hospitalized her. Dr. Dupuy examined her and later contacted an American hospital in Vienna to provide further care.

Brandy and Dr. Dupuy were approached by a Slav couple while they waited at the bridge to leave Bratislava. The couple tried to engage them in a discussion about the evils of the Soviet occupation, but Brandy assumed they were provocateurs attempting to get the Americans in trouble by inducing them to make anti-Soviet statements. He suggested that future American visitors be warned of such clumsy attempts to provoke incidents. As they drove through the Soviet zone of Austria on the return trip, a Russian guard stopped and delayed them for about two hours. The guard laboriously examined their papers, filling out forms in longhand. As they were finally released, Brandy learned from the translator that a Russian officer was looking for a new car to confiscate, and had all the papers of suitable vehicles inspected, looking for some irregularity that could justify the seizure.

On their way back through Vienna, Brandy and the doctor talked to several people and heard complaints about the Soviet occupation, the molestation of women, and the ineffective methods used by the Communist party to campaign in elections. Brandy also noted the movement of weapons towards the zonal boundary with the American sector while whole trainloads of furniture, livestock, and machinery were being removed from Austria for shipment to Russia. A two-day drive to Caserta was completed when Brandy and Dr. Dupuy arrived on the morning of 23 November 1945.

The information Brandy collected on the trip was personal, political, and of strategic military importance. His personal reasons for going meshed easily with his need to gather important information for the army. Neither motive, personal or informational, was a false "cover" for the other; rather, both motives were legitimate.

One of the more painful orders of business for Ridgway during his stay at Caserta was to arrange for the execution of General Anton Dostler, a German officer who had been tried and convicted of war crimes well before the extensive and more famous Nuremberg trials. Dostler had ordered the torture and execution of U.S. Army prisoners of war, in violation of the international conventions on the treatment of prisoners. General Ridgway's predecessor, General McNarney, had left the execution of sentence in Ridgway's hands. The date was set for the morning of 1 December 1945, but Ridgway did not address the issue until 24 November. He had never before had the responsibility for the execution of a fellow general. He arranged for an execution by firing squad, as befitted a military officer, rather than by hanging.

Still, on the night before the execution, Ridgway asked Brandy to assist him in reviewing the files to search for any mitigating circumstances that would allow for an act of clemency or a commutation of the sentence. Both Brandy and Ridgway worked all night reviewing the files, and in the morning both concluded that the military tribunal had been fair, and that no grounds for amnesty could be found. At 5:00 A.M., Brandy answered a phone call from the Vatican. Ridgway signaled Brandy to stay on the extension as he took the call.

Pope Pius XII was put on the line, and in a calm and reasoned way explained that he had been asked by General Dostler's wife to intercede for him, and that he was doing so. Ridgway listened respectfully, then replied. He had been through the file carefully, hoping to find some reason to grant mercy to the accused, but had been unable to justify any such action. Pope Pius said calmly that he understood, and that he would appreciate General Dostler being informed, before his execution, that on the request of his wife, the Pope had asked for clemency and that it had been refused.

"Your Holiness," Ridgway said, "your wishes will be carried out."

The Pope thanked the general and hung up. Ridgway turned to Brandy.

"OK, do it."

Brandy called the provost marshal and asked him to prepare for the execution, which was to take place in Naples. With an escort of MPs, Brandy drove to Naples, arriving at 6:55 A.M. Anton Dostler was in civilian clothing, already tied to the execution post.

With Father Gruber, a German ex-army chaplain, Brandy proceeded into the execution courtyard, where the firing squad was drawn up. Standing a few meters from Dostler, close enough for the condemned man to hear, Brandy read out the memorandum he had prepared, in German, to Father Gruber:

> The communication of Anton Dostler to His Holiness was received. His Holiness addressed a plea for clemency to the competent authorities, saying that should it be found possible to exercise a measure of clemency in this case and to commute the sentence of capital punishment, His Holiness

would be grateful since the mitigation of a death sentence
is always a source of satisfaction and comfort to him.

Brandy stepped back to join the witness group behind the firing
squad while the priest comforted Mrs. Dostler. The execution—the first
military war crimes execution of a German staff officer after the war—
was carried out.

The stress of the Dostler execution, the conditions of the frontier
with the Yugoslavs, Brandy's news of his family, Ridgway's medical problems, and the daily life in the Caserta "cottage" all contributed to bringing the general and his aide closer. That December, Brandy arranged a
holiday for the general's staff at the Isle of Capri. He broke the news
with some trepidation to General Ridgway. To his surprise, Ridgway
thought it was a good idea and accompanied the staff for an outing
there over Christmas. All of the men, Ridgway and Brandy included,
needed the break.

Matthew Ridgway, with
Frank Brandstetter on the
left, prior to the general's
courtesy call to the Pope in
the Vatican, October 1945.

On 1 January 1946, Ridgway reported to the U.S. delegation in London to be present at United Nations discussions headed by President Harry S. Truman's former Secretary of State, Edward R. Stettinius. On arrival, Ridgway wrote a glowing recommendation of Brandy for his commission in the regular establishment, moving him from the status of a reserve officer. Ridgway noted that he formed his opinion of Brandstetter based on observation "on an intimate daily basis" over the past years and particularly during the past months in the Mediterranean Theater.

Brandy reported with Ridgway to London. At their headquarters at the Dorchester Hotel, he met the rest of the American delegation to this initial meeting of the United Nations General Assembly. The civilian delegation included Senators Arthur Vandenberg and Tom Connally, Eleanor Roosevelt, Adlai Stevenson, John Foster Dulles, and Ralph Bunche.

The military group in the American delegation included nine officers, three from each service. General George Kenney of the air force and Admiral Kelly Turner of the navy were among the delegates. In addition to Ridgway, Major General William F. Dean and Major Frank Brandstetter represented the army. Truman had personally approved the nine, selecting for this delegation only officers who had seen action in the war— who had "smelled gunpowder," in Brandy's words. Brandy was impressed with Ralph Bunche, the distinguished black diplomat, whose experiences as a lone representative of his people moving in white social and governmental circles intrigued Brandy. He remembered the concept when later the tables turned and he found himself in a minority position.

The group had a few weeks until the formal sessions were to begin in February, giving Brandy and the others in the military delegation an opportunity to meet with their Soviet counterparts on a daily basis. After several meetings with the Russian officers, Brandy was incensed. The American delegation had presented a position outlining mutual inspection of military facilities, but the Russians refused to cooperate. Brandy reported to Ridgway that the Russians were behaving impossibly, distastefully, and crudely.

Brandy's report irritated Ridgway, and for the first time Brandy was "royally chewed out" by the general, who was known as a master of the art. "Our mission is to make peace, not to enlarge difficulties with the Russians," Ridgway pointed out. The officers had been hand-picked to carry out President Truman's direct orders. With a sinking feeling, Brandy feared he had lost the general's confidence. After that, Brandy simply kept his nose to the grindstone and performed his duties as ordered.

During this period, Brandy received disturbing news from his in-laws. His bride, Barbara, had a breakdown that was diagnosed as symptomatic of schizophrenia. Her parents committed her, with Brandy's consent, to a sanatorium in San Francisco. Brandy paid for her care out of his army salary, but worried that his absence was contributing to her condition. Soon, Brandy received orders to return to the States, to transport some two dozen metal boxes of top secret documents of the U.S. Military Staff Committee to the office of the Joint Chiefs of Staff at the Pentagon. Ridgway knew of Barbara's situation, and the orders to escort the documents to the States appeared to be a thoughtful way of getting Brandy back home sooner.

Accordingly, Brandy sailed to the United States aboard the *Queen Mary* on 6 February 1946, with two armed guards to help protect the documents. Aside from the crew, his guards, and a few army doctors, Brandy and Congressman Sol Bloom from New York were the only males aboard the ship. All the rest of the nearly ten thousand passengers were war brides, many of whom were pregnant. Brandy stayed in his cabin during the trip, sleeping directly on the metal boxes containing the documents, and occasionally taking the air on deck with the congressman. Once, as the two men looked down on a lower deck where hundreds of young European women strolled around, Bloom remarked that the ship probably held the all-time record for transporting pregnant women.

At the dock in New York, a small convoy of MPs met the ship. Brandy signed over the boxes of documents to the MP officer-in-charge. His two armed guards traveled to Washington as passengers in the truck, with MPs in a jeep in front and another in the rear. Brandy, planning to follow later by train for final delivery of the documents, had a few hours to kill. Suddenly, he felt a load was lifted from his shoulders. He called his business partner, Dr. Eugene Hegy, to meet him for lunch at Longchamps Restaurant on Fifth Avenue and 33rd Street.

Brandy was in a mood to celebrate, in spite of his worry over Barbara and the still-stinging rebuke from Ridgway. For him, it seemed the war was finally over. As he traded memories with Hegy, Brandy ordered one or two double martinis. Then he had a round of oysters, followed by a large steak, smothered in onions. He finished off with a large dish of ice cream. It was the sort of meal that GIs had dreamed about in trenches and in chow lines for years. But it was too much. He felt dizzy and got up, hoping to get to the men's room.

Suddenly he passed out.

Nine days later, he woke up in a hospital ward.

9

Waiting for the Bubble to Break

Like thousands of other GIs, Brandy was suffering from battle fatigue. He was unconscious for nine days at the Staten Island Military Hospital in February 1946 and then woke up in Walter Reed Medical Center in Washington, where he was held for observation for another two months. As an officer, he received excellent treatment, but the rounds of tests dragged on. General Ridgway visited from New York City, and Brandy discussed his deep concerns about his wife and his ability to support her now that he looked forward to a lifelong Regular Army career. When he was finally released from the hospital, the doctors provided a rather cryptic diagnosis: "exhaustion, acute; anxiety state, mild." As with Ridgway, the moderate diagnosis allowed him to continue on active duty in the Regular Army. He reported to General Ridgway in New York for continuing duty with the United States military mission to the United Nations. The problems with Barbara continued to mount, however, and finally on 4 September 1946, he reluctantly submitted a letter requesting relief from active duty. The general understood, and Brandy's separation order, dated 24 September 1946, was signed by Army Chief of Staff Dwight D. Eisenhower.

Brandy drove to Camp Beale in California for his final release, which was dated 22 April 1947. He left with the rank of lieutenant colonel, which he retained in the mobilization reserves, ready for recall to duty on a moment's notice. Over the next few years, Brandy developed two careers simultaneously, bringing to each a similar degree of intensity. On the one hand, he resumed his civilian career as a manager in the hotel and restaurant business, advancing from post to post as he had in the 1930s. On the other hand, he kept his military career alive in the Reserves.

He brought to the civilian jobs not only the rich background of his New York and Miami experiences and the clues he had picked up from his tutelage under Louis Toth, but also several ideas about commitment, training, and service which reflected his military experience. His accumulated records and mementos from these positions often reflected some aspect of his military style. His management on one job seemed to echo the army's method of breaking complex tasks down into specific parts for which there was detailed training. For another company, his organization charts reflected the army's explicit designation of chains of command and responsibility assignments. He collected logos and badges, and by giving attention to the design of insignias, he provided symbols of the esprit de corps he hoped to instill among his employees.

As Brandy continued his civilian work, he maintained his connection as an active reservist with the army's intelligence service. While the nation went through the stages of peacetime status, then brief mobilization for the Korean War and demobilization again, Brandy found it difficult to find assignments that put him at the center of the action. Yet he kept trying, taking whatever duties came his way. In the first years of his retirement in the Reserves, his activities involved the preparation of reports and engagement in training. He never viewed the assignments as make-work or routine, but plunged into them wholeheartedly. He treated his short active duty assignments as if he had been fully mobilized to a war footing, even when the nation was at peace. He thought of each study or training assignment, no matter how specific or local, as a matter of national security.

Brandy had the ability to perform successfully in two separate careers simultaneously, giving to each the sort of drive which had pushed him through the Depression in New York, the combat in Europe, and the demands of serving as Ridgway's aide. He had balanced personal and military motives during his 1945 trip to Bratislava when he located his family and conducted reconnaissance for Ridgway. This balance between personal and official "eyes-and-ears" motives that had mixed so well in Bratislava continued, appearing from time to time through the late 1940s. As a hotel and restaurant manager he brought the same kind of loyalty and leadership that made him excel as an officer; in turn, his promising civilian career, with its contacts and travel, began to enhance his value to army intelligence over the next decades. The blend evolved in the post-war years, setting personal patterns that would continue.

His father-in-law, Hartley Peart, provided several contacts to assist him with information for possible civilian positions. One of these was the Bechtel Corporation, which obtained the contract to build facilities for the consortium of Standard Oil of California and Texas Oil Company operating in Saudi Arabia. Brandy called on Mr. O'Brien, Hartley's cousin and a vice president of the CalTex firm, who offered him a position managing all of the residential facilities for the corporation in Saudi Arabia, including a 150-room hotel for visiting VIPS and others to be constructed. Brandy turned him down politely by indicating he did not want to be separated from his ailing wife.

He sought a position on his own and landed a job, starting in November 1947, as Assistant Manager of the "front of the house" at the Santa Barbara Biltmore Hotel, working for Robert S. Odell. That evening he mentioned to his father-in-law his good luck in landing the position. Peart was worried, however, because only the week before, as President of the San Francisco Bar Association, he and a group of attorneys had recommended that Odell be brought to court on charges of fraud. Nevertheless, Brandy served at the Biltmore through the next season, trying to work up business for the elegant, but aging, hotel. Brandy participated in the planning of the Christmas and New Year's holidays, with the entertainment of a choir on Christmas Eve and deluxe dinners. Planning also included the use of an advertising campaign, managed by a San Francisco merchandising firm, and direct mail invitations to members of the "Coral Casino" Club, which met in the hotel. He filed reports and suggestions to improve management and promotion and at the same time, he sought to discover personnel who had tried to make the hotel a failure in the hopes of an eventual sale.

On his resignation in September 1946 from active duty in the army, Brandy and Ridgway had agreed that if an international crisis developed, Brandy would step forward for active duty and Ridgway would help to get him activated immediately. Brandy kept his eyes on the news, believing the time to volunteer was near. The international situation between the Western Allies and the Soviet Union came to a head in December 1947, when the Soviets walked out of the London Conference, demanding a share of the industrialized Ruhr region. In February 1948, the British, French, and Americans announced the unification of their occupation zones in Germany, without Soviet participation. The long-range split of East and West Germany was developing.

That February, Brandy visited the Presidio and received only vague answers about the state of affairs. He wrote to Colonel Carter Clarke, former Assistant G-2 to the Army Chief of Staff on 5 February 1948, inquiring what plans had been made for mobilization:

> As the present world situation deteriorates from day to day, I sincerely hope that some plans are laid in your department where some of us will be recalled prior to D Day, to receive some indoctrination due to the fact that we are not getting any here in our branch from the 6th Army. I had a long [talk] personally with the Assistant G-2 of the 6th Army, volunteering my services and time, but so far have not heard from him or the department. I feel very strongly about the European and Asiatic situations. I can't see how we can avoid it. Again, may I mention that I would like to have it on record that if the Department feels that my services can be of use, they are available at any time.

With the crisis over the Soviet blockade of West Berlin on 1 April 1948, Brandy felt the time had come. He called General Ridgway as prearranged in 1946, inquiring "Yes" or "No." General Ridgway's answer was "Yes," so Brandy resigned his post in Santa Barbara, and on the same day, appeared at the Presidio in San Francisco for activation.

The G-2 of the Sixth Army at the Presidio knew of no order by which a reserve officer could simply appear for duty when the international situation seemed to call for service. Brandy had no orders, nor did the

G-2 have an immediate active duty assignment in mind. Brandy insisted that he call the Chief of Personnel in the Army Chief of Staff's office, the G-1, to confirm that he should be activated. Brandy knew that Ridgway held that post at the time. Brandy overheard only one side of the conversation, as the G-2 presented the question, and then stiffened, replying on the phone, "Yes, Sir....Yes, *Sir*!" After the call was completed, the officer put Brandy immediately to work.

From April to August 1948, Brandy served with Headquarters Sixth Army, G-2 Section, in the planning division in San Francisco. His official duties, as later listed in his military record, were "Strategic Intelligence Staff Studies" and "Active Duty Training" at the G-2 Section, Headquarters, Sixth Army, Presidio, San Francisco. Brandy was assigned to Lieutenant Colonel Andrew Kirby. Working with Kirby and two majors, Brandy compiled information for a proposed "City Handbook." He was assigned the task of contacting local sources of information that included transportation and utility executives, state and local police, the FBI, health departments, fire departments, radio stations, and hospital administrators. The purpose of the guide was to provide a list of crucial facilities that should be protected by civil defense guards and army detachments in case of sabotage or attack. A copy of it would be provided by G-2 to "City Fathers," the FBI, the telephone company, railroads, police, hospitals, and utility firms.

Because information compiled a few years earlier by California state disaster authorities and military personnel was out of date, Brandy had to start from scratch. He worked hard to obtain current information, collecting details on industry, labor, agriculture, port and harbor facilities, water reservoirs, oil and gas fields, truck terminals, emergency facilities, and police departments from 1946 and 1947. The data covered not only San Francisco, but also the surrounding counties of Alameda, Contra Costa, Marin, and San Mateo. Some of the information ranged throughout the Sixth Army area of jurisdiction, from the nuclear facility at Hanford, Washington, down to the Mexican border.

Brandy learned a great deal at this time about the local business community and leadership, and also about the structure of the G-2 office in the Sixth Army. He carefully collected the organization charts and task descriptions of the G-2 units, detailing the role of various units, including Training and Combat Intelligence, Collection, Counter Intelligence, Reserve Components, and the group in which he served: the Planning Intelligence Division (PID). On the list of the PID duties was the heading: "Provides intelligence required for planning pertaining to the Army mission," which Brandy circled and underlined as his particular mission. He grew familiar with the duties of the Training and Combat Intelligence group, which the year before had conducted a school for intelligence officers in Kansas. Brandy collected the syllabus and lecture notes for another such course that would prove helpful later on.

By the end of the summer of 1948, the Berlin Crisis had settled into a routine, with the air force providing an airlift of food and fuel into land-locked and blockaded West Berlin. At the end of his four-month period of active duty with the Sixth Army, Brandy accepted assignment to a Reserve Composite Group, G-2 Section of the Sixth Army, and returned to civilian life. In his request for release, dated 4 August 1948 and forwarded through Colonel Pape, Brandy noted:

> The present G-2 assignment and cities study will be completed prior to departure. If any additional information will be required to enlarge the present Bay Area Cities Study, they will be collected and furnished to the G-2 Section Sixth Army at the writer's own time and with no expense to the Department of the Army.

Brandy made the point that he was willing to serve without pay, and later highlighted the phrase. He would return to that pattern many times, volunteering his services at his own expense. Later that fall Brandy wrote to Ridgway, noting that General Mark Clark, Commanding General of the Sixth Army, was to head an experimental unification program to examine how utilities could be organized in time of war in the western states. Apparently Clark would make use of some of the information which Brandy's team had filed through Colonel Pape's G-2 office. Brandy explained in his letter to General Ridgway that he was going to continue the project for Colonel Pape on his own time and at his own expense.

While working in Santa Barbara, Brandy and Barbara had lived in nearby Montecito. When he was assigned to the Presidio, he moved there, since he believed it was dangerous for him to live outside the base with that much information in his head. Barbara had lived with her parents on Hyde Street in San Francisco, in the Russian Hill neighborhood. With great surprise and some amusement, he found his name listed in the *San Francisco Social Register*, where it remained until 1978.

In August 1948, when he finished his tour at the Presidio, Brandy took over the management of the Orinda (California) Country Club, and settled into a routine life for a few years. The club provided an apartment for Brandy and Barbara and she lived with him there, with intermittent stays in sanitoriums. At Orinda, Brandy organized the golf club's food and liquor services along efficient lines. He also worked to improve the staff, hiring a French chef, Jean Joaquin, who had won a prize at the 1936 Paris Food Exposition. He obtained a training film from the Wine Advisory Board to show to his mostly Filipino staff and enrolled all of the waiters in a free correspondence course developed by the Wine Institute for the Wine Advisory Board.

Noting the conventional high mark-up on wine, Brandy began tracking its sales at Orinda, and then engaged in a plan to increase them by offering a ten percent commission on each bottle of wine served by waiters. Every day, the waiters met with the chef and the hostess to choose wines for each dish on the menu. In the dining room, he created a special wine display, consisting of grapes, a sugar-icing model of grapes, a champagne glass made by the chef, and special menus of the day. After five months he had increased wine sales from about twenty bottles a month to over three hundred a month. To cap the effort, much like a report on his duties for the military, he wrote an article about the entire wine program and published it in a magazine for club managers. Brandy's organized methods of training, incentives, and elegant catering to the guests began to pay off, and the club's officers were impressed with the rapid improvement in revenues and quality of service.

Brandy communicated with Ridgway regularly by phone and mail during this period. Ridgway, having assumed the Caribbean command of the U.S. Army, was stationed in Panama. He offered to provide Brandy an introduction to the United States Ambassador in Venezuela, if he sought work there. It appeared that Ridgway was building a network of former officers who would be able to act as his "eyes and ears" in this

Brandy's marketing innovations at Orinda Country Club produced a significant increase in the sale of wine.

region. Brandy suggested in a letter that "should the bubble break in
the next year or so, no need to say that it would be an honor to serve
under you again." The increasing tensions of the Cold War suggested to
both Ridgway and Brandy that a shooting war might break out at any
time.

Meanwhile Bill Palmer, an old friend and partner in the Champlain
Hotel, drove through California and stopped in Orinda for a visit. Palmer
told Brandy he was on his way east to sell his holdings in order to invest
in a Jamaican hotel.

Later that winter, on 19 December 1949, Brandy was reassigned without activation, from the Reserve Composite Group to the command of
the 418th Strategic Intelligence Team. The "command" seemed to be a
title only on paper, for Brandy was not in charge of any troops, but of
205 officers. Over the next few years, Brandy put in short tours of active
duty, including three weeks in May 1950 at the Presidio.

In the summer of 1950 the bubble did indeed break, with the invasion of South Korea by Communist forces and the beginning of the
Korean War. At the time, Ridgway was stationed at the Pentagon. A few

days before Christmas, Ridgway was ordered to Korea to take charge of the Eighth Army, replacing General Walton Harris Walker who had been killed in action. Brandy was visiting General Ridgway when he received the order from General Joseph Collins, Army Chief of Staff, and he volunteered to accompany Ridgway to Korea immediately.

Ridgway told Brandy as he was leaving his quarters at Fort Myers in Washington, "Frank, this is Christmas. You stay with Barbara, and then after I get to Korea, I'll let you know." While waiting for the call, Brandy continued his routine of civilian work and reservist activities.

In February 1951, Brandy put together a resumé reflecting both his hotel and military experience. His list of references was impressive. It included General Ridgway and former Secretary of State Edward R. Stettinius, Louis Toth of Howarth and Howarth, Joseph Krieger in Baltimore, and M. Melvin of the *Hotel Gazette*, as well as a number of corporate executives and managers he had met in and around San Francisco and the officers of the Orinda Country Club. The resumé and his contacts landed him an excellent position with the Santa Fe Railroad Company, with the help of its chairman Fred Gurley. In March 1951, Brandy took over the management of the restaurant chain for Continental Trailways, a newly formed subsidiary of Santa Fe. Continental was to be headquartered in Dallas, Texas. Over the period 1948 to 1953, Continental, under the leadership of Maurice E. Moore, consolidated and took over dozens of small bus lines to move from obscurity to the number two position behind Greyhound Corporation. By 1953, Transcontinental Bus Systems Incorporated had 1,475 buses (compared with Greyhound's 5,000) and a solid second place in the motor transportation business. Brandy and Barbara moved from Orinda to Dallas, where Moore appointed Brandy as president of the restaurant subsidiary, Continental Restaurants Corporation. Brandy created a series of improvements by setting up standards, developing training, and writing handbooks and instruction sheets for hundreds of small bus stop restaurants around the nation. He planned the construction of new bus depots, incorporating the restaurants within the stations. He worked on a system that would supply pre-cooked frozen meals from a central kitchen in Dallas to all the smaller kitchens within a four hundred-mile radius, probably the first widespread use of frozen food for fast-food purposes. From his corporate headquarters, Brandy set prices, health regulations, sanitation checklists, management rules, systems of shift organization, and job descriptions for the various ranks within the organization. He designed a logo for the restaurant: a stylized figure with pointed moustache, monocle, and chef's hat. Employee identification tags were made with the logo. He retained Tag Number One in his collection as a souvenir, and noted that the menus, roadside billboards, and electric signs all used the logo he had developed. To keep all restaurant areas up to standards of cleanliness, Brandy insisted on tile flooring, stainless steel and Formica tables, and stainless steel kitchen equipment.

Using systems of cost controls, Brandy aimed at reducing the cost of the food served to 33 percent of the price, and the cost of the items sold in curio shops down to 75 percent of the price. He more than achieved both goals by 1953, increasing sales through lower prices and mass volume. He increased total sales for his company from $215,000 in 1951 to $1,228,000 in 1953, and at the same time, increased the profit margin percentage as well.

Brandy's move from San Francisco to Dallas resulted in his transfer from the Officers Reserve Control Group with the Sixth Army in San Francisco to one with the Fourth Army in San Antonio in the G-2 section. Brandy sought to maintain his security clearance and raise his

Brandy's logo for the Continental Restaurant chain is seen at right.

The logo appeared on the exterior sign of the Continental Bus and Restaurant building in Corsicana, Texas. Photo by Taylor Studio, Corsicana, Texas.

Stainless steel kitchen equipment, tile flooring, and formica tables were standard components of the Continental Restaurants. Photo by Ed Hayman's studio, Monroe, Louisiana.

mobilization availability level from "C-1" to "A-1." This change in designation would mean that during an emergency, instead of being called up 91 to 180 days after a general mobilization, he would be available immediately from "day one." He specifically requested the change, "with the purpose," he said, "that the undersigned will be available for active duty orders." Although the change in status was put in effect in early November 1951, Brandy received no call. Continuing to work with the army bureaucracy, in December 1951 he was assigned to reserve duty training in Dallas. In March 1952, his file was submitted for a security background check. That work was finally completed on 30 June 1953, and he was once again cleared for material up to and including Top Secret. The next month, however, brought a truce in Korea and he was not called to duty, thus missing his chance to work with Ridgway again.

Brandy soon began teaching and participating in a few courses in specialized intelligence studies. In September 1953, he gave a lecture for Naval Reserve medical officers in Dallas on "Prisoner of War Interrogation on Subjects Pertaining to Pre-Invasion Areas." That October, while on his annual fifteen-day active duty assignment, he completed a study with the subject: "Assume that the Eastern Mediterranean Area becomes a Theatre of War in 1955. What contributions to the Allied effort might be expected from Israel?" The topic was prescient. In October 1956, Israel, England, and France launched a short war against Egypt, during which Israel took the Sinai Peninsula.

Despite his commitment to the reserve assignments, it was clear that Brandy sought more significant participation. He wrote to Colonel J. P. Kaylor of the Fourth Army's G-2 section, headquartered in San Antonio, recommending more intensive training for "mobilization designees" like himself. Brandy praised the two-week training, but urged that they include additional activities. He suggested monthly or semi-monthly briefings in a private area "where classified material could be read and secured," meetings with Civilian Defense Authorities for liaison in case of emergencies, and correspondence courses. He also proposed two- and three-day active duty tours for training or organizational work, and an exchange of phone numbers among the mobilization designees for more rapid call-up "at an instant's notice."

His requests for more activity received some recognition, for in December 1953, he and several other officers were attached to different units for the first three months of 1954 as "Inspector/Advisors." Their sole mission was the voluntary inspection of different units on their assembly dates. Brandy's unit was a hospital group, meeting in Dallas. That September, he reported for his regular two weeks of duty. On completion of that session, he requested permission to attend a two-day planned exercise at Fort Hood, named "Cloverleaf I." He once again did not insist on compensation.

While at the Presidio, Brandy had prepared a draft of a Domestic Emergency Plan, which he revised and submitted in 1954 as part of the Cloverleaf I exercise, to G-2 of the Fourth Army Command in Dallas, Colonel M. H. Truly. The plan referenced standing orders, laws, memoranda, and duty officers' books to create a set of instructions for staff response and intelligence estimates in times of domestic emergency. It was devised to be a general plan, to respond to an enemy attack, a natural disaster, or a domestic disturbance in which social dissidents of the far left or far right in the United States attempted to foment disorder. The plan defined the structure of spot intelligence reports, intelligence summaries, periodic intelligence reports, counterintelligence summaries and reports, and the proposed structure and responsibilities of an expanded G-2 office in coordination with the FBI. Colonel Truly sent him a letter of appreciation for his work.

Through this period, Brandy was very serious about his reserve activities, even after the truce of July 1953 ended the war in Korea and the country returned to a demobilized and peaceful interlude. His attitude and commitment to the service was not typical of the national mood of apathy pervading in the "Peace and Prosperity" atmosphere that characterized the years of the Eisenhower Administration. His performance continued to attract the attention of superiors, with at least one attempting to get him promoted to full colonel.

In 1955, he put Trailways behind him and searched for a new opportunity.

10

Jamaican Ventures, Dallas Doldrums

Over the years since 1940, Brandy had kept in contact with William Palmer, his old friend from the hotel days in New York. Together they had served at the lowest rank of the hotel business; they had roomed together, stretching a meager budget with a diet of eggs and bananas; they had worked through Lewis Hotel School home study courses together. Later, William Palmer had been one of Brandy's partners in the venture to reinvigorate the Hotel Champlain on the eve of World War II. Palmer had visited Brandy when he was managing the Orinda Country Club to explain about a possible resort hotel venture in Jamaica. Finally, Palmer got back in touch with Brandy early in 1955, having decided to sell his home in New Jersey and invest the proceeds in a partially constructed resort hotel on the north shore of the island of Jamaica at Ocho Rios. The hotel, Sans Souci, meaning "without care," was named after a palace built by Frederick the Great in the eighteenth century. Unfortunately, the venture would live to contradict its name.

Palmer sold his Pound Ridge, New Jersey, home on 11 February 1955 and took over the British-owned Sans Souci Hotel in March. The owners had filed for bankruptcy, and Palmer believed that, like the venture on Lake Champlain, with good management and good public relations he could make the Sans Souci show a profit. BOAC, Pan Am, and

Delta Airlines were flying into Montego Bay on the north shore of Jamaica, but there were few first class resort hotels in that area of the island. The partially completed hotel had potential, but needed to attract American tourists.

Palmer explained his proposition to Brandy. With Brandy's extensive experience in New York and his experience in restaurant management at the Orinda Country Club and Continental Trailways, he could run the front of the house, while Palmer took care of the back of the house, particularly the financing.

Brandy liked the idea. Barbara needed constant care, and doctors advised that a change of climate to the tropics might do her some good. In Jamaica, household help and a good nurse could be obtained reasonably. Brandy could construct a beach cottage for her on the hotel grounds, where she could benefit from the relaxing Jamaican life style. Meanwhile, Brandy could participate in a new opportunity. Flights back to Texas for army reserve duty would be easy enough. Brandy agreed, invested as a financial partner, and went to work improving Sans Souci in July 1955.

The business went quite well at first. Using stone construction, a pool area was separated from the ocean by a retaining wall. Most of the early guests at the hotel were British, but with promotions, Brandy worked to bring in more American tourists. The site was attractive because a reef protected the beach from the direct surf, providing an area for safe swimming. The white sandy beach was lined with palms above a stone seawall. Although traveling down from the steep hills behind the hotel required either a tough drive down a precipitous driveway or a ride down a special hillside elevator, the isolation and protection of the setting was part of its charm.

Palmer, who had always been somewhat the playboy bachelor, decided to settle down and marry, and he brought his new Swedish bride to live at Sans Souci. With Brandy and Barbara settled in as well, the hotel was beginning to resemble something of a family operation. However, as the business grew through 1955 and into 1956, the cash reserves put together by Palmer began to dwindle. He flew to New York to attempt to arrange a bank loan. Negotiations went so well that he returned early, arriving unexpectedly at the hotel. As he entered his apartment,

Palmer discovered his wife in bed with a Jamaican lover. Palmer was devastated, and so distraught that he began to lose his grip on management. Palmer left again in late 1956, forcing Brandy to handle the winter season alone. Through the period November 1956 through January 1957, Brandy knew that the hotel could not survive. He struggled to keep a clear record of the increasing expenses, while Palmer searched for a buyer.

With debts mounting, Brandy began to pay bills from his own pocket. Eventually, in February 1957, Brandy left Sans Souci after paying off all the debts and moved to Kingston, Jamaica, to deal with auditors and to wrap up the affairs of the resort. A small clipping in the *Kingston Gleaner* noted the closing of the hotel. Palmer succeeded in selling Sans Souci to a group that eventually converted the facility into a set of condominium apartments. Palmer informed Brandy that the proceeds would be some $170,000. Brandy and Barbara moved back to Dallas and waited for Palmer to make his payment of their share.

Unfortunately, Palmer refused to pay, even denying the funds Brandy had paid out to cover the debts. Brandy then filed suit in Dallas, and in

Sans Souci, an attractive resort on the Jamaican coast, was not a successful venture for Brandy due to the failings of his partner, William Palmer.

a long, drawn out civil case, fought to recover his outlay, lost wages, and share of the proceeds. Palmer's company was incorporated in Texas, so the court had jurisdiction. Brandy's side prevailed, handled ably by attorneys Bill Brice and Joseph Geary, with the court finding for him and awarding a total of $64,700 plus attorneys' fees in several amounts against Palmer individually and against the William Palmer Company. Unfortunately, by that time, Palmer had disappeared. Over the next few years, both Brandy and Brice made a number of efforts to track him down, following up rumors that he had surfaced in Chicago, or that he had been seen in Turkey or Paraguay, countries without extradition treaties with the United States.

Although Brandy never recovered any money and his memories of the betrayal by an old friend cut deeply, he did gain one positive result from the Jamaican venture. He and Bill Brice became lifelong friends and later became neighbors in Acapulco, where Brice maintained a home to entertain and visit on vacations from his Dallas law practice. Brice became famous as the attorney who handled the landmark Carter Phone case that challenged the AT&T monopoly on long distance lines.

In Dallas, Brandy began to search for new opportunities. General Carl L. Phinney, an attorney for Continental Trailways and commanding general of the Texas National Guard, knew that Brandy was looking for new ventures. Clint Murchison, Sr., one of the most prominent millionaires in Texas during the 1950s, was also a member of the board of directors of Continental Trailways. Phinney, who served as his attorney, helped arrange an interview for Brandy with Murchison. Brandy and Murchison hit it off immediately.

"I have an idea," Murchison said, "to build various big real estate developments throughout the United States. To support them, we need in each development a swimming club, together with a full range of country club facilities. I want you to make a feasibility survey, and if we do it, to manage the real estate development with the club idea."

Brandy began by placing all the proposed developments against a map of the United States. The sites were in Louisiana, California, Kansas, Minnesota, and Texas. A question immediately came to Brandy's mind: what would be the season for outdoor swimming pools in Kansas and Minnesota? How would you operate considering northern winters?

Brandy obtained meteorological reports for the whole country and began to work on the calculations, including year-to-year and month-to-month average temperatures.

He planned locker rooms, pools, a bar, and children's playrooms, as well as the grounds for each club along a standard design. Brandy spent nearly two months making the basic layout, working up figures to show the length of a club's profitable season in each location, and detailing the average expected seasons of 60, 90, or 120 days, depending on the meteorological records. Annual cash returns would be far worse in the North because of the shorter seasons. Putting together figures for all the locations, he produced a bottom line that showed a negative figure—a loss for the whole club operation.

Brandy knew that Murchison wanted to have the whole club system pay its own way as a self-sufficient operation, with dues paid by each resident. If the clubs from all the sites were to be regarded as one single enterprise, run from a central office, the fees would have to be so high as to make the clubs in the warmer climate zones noncompetitive with others in the same area. On the other hand, if the fees were set at a competitive rate for the warmer areas, the bottom line would be a loss. Murchison did not want to subsidize the clubs or pay for them out of other revenues. The plan could not work as a single, large-scale operation.

At the end of several weeks of study, Brandy took his full report, together with the maps and supporting documentation, and laid it out on a conference table for Murchison.

"I don't want to see all that," Murchison said. "Just tell me—what's the net result?"

Brandy gave him a little briefing, then said: "The point is, Mr. Murchison, I think the idea is great. Some of the locations would be negative, some would be positive. But because of the locations, the end result—the bottom line is—you will lose money on it."

Murchison looked at Brandy.

"Would you repeat that?"

Brandy did so.

"Frank," said Murchison, "do you realize you are talking yourself out of a big job—a big position?"

"Mr. Murchison," said Frank. "The facts are facts. That's all. I can't tell you any different. That's it."

"You're quite a guy," said Murchison.

And indeed, that was it. Murchison paid Brandy for his consulting work, but the project was over.

Through the whole period of 1955 to 1958, Brandy remained active in the Army Reserves. In November 1955, for example, he undertook a short tour of active duty as a "Mobilization Designee," still attached to the Staff G-2 at the Headquarters of the Fourth Army in Fort Sam Houston, Texas. Among his responsibilities on the November tour of duty was a fifteen-minute briefing for the commanding general and staff of the Fourth Army on the "present situation in Israel," with particular emphasis on the strategic positions of the Arab states and Israel. He spoke to the question of Soviet arms support for Israel's neighbor states.

He also revised a briefing on French North Africa, detailing recent changes in the military and political outlook there. He had several other duties during this short tour, including revising the classification procedures for aerial photography and making suggestions for a revised format for a portion of the Fourth Army newsletter. He reviewed daily intelligence briefings and studied the emerging integrated intelligence system. As in the past, Brandy took these duties very seriously and wrote detailed reports on his work.

He verified that a rapid call back for duty was possible from Jamaica in time of mobilization and gave his mailing address in Dallas as that of a friend, Gordon McLendon, the "Old Scotchman" of radio fame, who could call him by phone if anything urgent came through from the Reserves.

In September 1956, Brandy reported back from Jamaica to Fort Sam Houston for another fifteen days of active duty. After leaving Jamaica in early 1957, Brandy served as assistant troop commander and provost marshal of the Fourth U.S. Army Area Intelligence School for two weeks in August 1957.

These intelligence school sessions reviewed procedures and studies in a wide variety of areas for reserve intelligence officers, including a review of a Central Index of Investigative Intelligence and Domestic Subversive Files. Also reviewed were procedures for handling foreign visitors and students, control of classified funds, control of Q (nuclear) clearances, and procedures regarding record checks for the Counter Intelligence Corps, the Atomic Energy Commission, the Office of Naval Intelligence, and other agencies. Plans and documents reviewed included mobilization plans, foreign intelligence reports, strategic intelligence briefs, and plans for the coordination of information collection with tactical level organizations.

As was common for Brandy, he received a fine commendation for his work from his commanding officer, at this time Colonel George Lumpkin.

> In fulfilling a position of considerable responsibility, you demonstrated a receptive, agile, and well-disciplined mind and a high degree of facility in applying the techniques of military leadership and command. Your exemplary personal conduct together with your generous application of time, interest and energy to your duties served as an inspiration to others of the command and reflects most favorably upon you and the service.

Brandy kept in contact with Colonel Lumpkin over the years. In his civilian life, George Lumpkin was deputy chief of police in the city of Dallas, a post that he held through the dramatic events of November 1963, when President John F. Kennedy was assassinated there.

Brandy was invited back for the August 1958 Fourth U.S. Army Area Intelligence School to play a role similar to one he had performed in the 1957 exercises. Meanwhile, he received some bad news. After the 1958 summer exercises, the army decided to cut back. Those officers who could not find alternative Active Reserve roles would be transferred to a "U.S. Army Reserve Control Group (Reinforcement)" in 1959. In effect, Brandy's participation would be reduced. The Table of Distribution eliminated altogether his position as a member of a Corps G-2 section. Colonel F. C. Cook was almost apologetic as he explained to Brandy that the elimination of his position in no way reflected on his efficiency as a mobilization designee. Brandy kept in touch with officers both at the Fourth Army and others who came through on inspection tours from the Pentagon, in hopes of hearing of an active assignment to which he could be attached. In particular, he met Lieutenant Colonel William B. Rose, chief of the Army Intelligence Reserve Branch of the Office of the Assistant Chief of Staff, Intelligence (ACSI) at the Pentagon. The contact would later prove momentous, changing the course of Brandy's military career.

Despite Brandy's career changes in his private life, he meant to continue his service to army intelligence. He vowed he would not disappear into a reserve control group without duties.

Over the next year Brandy, at age forty-six, began a series of adventures which allowed him to pursue both his personal career in the resort hotel business and his military career as an intelligence officer which he had kept alive through the doldrums of the 1950s. Interestingly, he accumulated more U.S. Army Reserve credit points than any other officer in the Reserve.

11

Cuba Si!

W hen Brandy was pursuing legal action in Dallas to recover his share of the proceeds from Sans Souci, he had obtained a copy of Conrad Hilton's life story, *Be My Guest*. He thought about the new concepts in Hilton's hotel work, especially the idea of an international chain of hotels. Brandy considered that there might be a match between his own background in languages, his rich experiences, and the needs of the expanding chain. He checked business directories and discovered that the president of Hilton International was John Hauser. Hilton International had set up a hotel in Puerto Rico as their first, semi-overseas operation, and then had plans to expand in Latin America, Europe, and the Near East. Accordingly, Brandy wrote a letter to Conrad Hilton, who answered that he had passed it on to Hauser. The letter detailed Brandy's background in the hotel business with a file of references, some from before the war. His letter of inquiry received a quick response by return mail.

In late 1957, Brandy went to New York to meet Hauser. The two men immediately liked one another. Hauser, a marine combat officer in the war, suggested that Brandy might appreciate an appointment as manager for a planned hotel in West Berlin, and after a lunch at the Waldorf-Astoria in New York, they shook hands on the offer. Brandy was aboard with the Hilton organization.

He began a training course in Hilton methods in New York. Although he was an experienced hotel man, with his background from the early thirties and his employment with the Santa Barbara Biltmore, Orinda Country Club, Continental Trailways, and most recently the resort in Jamaica, Brandy was not insulted by the concept of being "trained." Hilton had its own procedures, and furthermore, he always liked to observe exactly how a training course was organized, remembering all his activities in the army both as trainer and trainee, and his own training programs at Orinda and Continental. Unlike some of his fellow experienced executives in the course, Brandy took the work seriously. He finished his exposure to Hilton standard operating procedures by January 1958.

Suddenly, Hauser called him in. The hotel in Germany was still under construction. Hauser told Brandy to take a plane to Havana that night. There were some problems getting the hotel there into operation and they needed a trouble-shooter. Brandy was not fluent in Spanish, but with his French, his smattering of Italian, and grounding in Latin, he felt he could move quickly into the new language.

Brandy turned to Hauser and asked, "To whom do I report?"

"To me!" Hauser said. OK, Brandy thought, the channels are set. Next question.

"What is my mission?"

"Finish and open the Havana Hilton, no matter what," said Hauser.

"OK," Brandy said. "Will do!"

Brandy flew to Havana that evening, 13 February 1958, to undertake the position. Barbara, who was under medical care at Timberlawn in Dallas, could visit him periodically with a nurse in attendance.

The hotel, like many in the Hilton chain, was owned locally. Hilton International had a contract to operate the hotel on the basis of a seven percent fee against gross receipts.

Local ownership was in the hands of the Cuban Culinary Workers' Union. The union's leader, Sr. Aguille, had required that the union's own man, José Menéndez, be appointed as general manager. Menéndez, a Cuban, had worked for Hilton International as an auditor, but had no managerial background. As Brandy investigated both the delayed delivery of materials and work, he discovered that a system of bribes reach-

Frank Brandstetter was sent by Hilton International to complete the Havana Hilton in 1958.

ing ten or fifteen percent over cost had been required for every detail of construction. Many bribes had already been paid out to the Cuban union leader, Aguille. Menéndez was complaisant about the delays, expecting that eventually the work would be completed. Brandy advised him of the situation, but no corrections were made.

The hotel was a mess. Carpets and furniture had not been delivered, and the painting of the rooms had not been finished. In particular, "Conrad Hilton Suite," a set of rooms on the top floor, was simply an empty construction site that required painting, finishing out, and furnishing. Conrad Hilton himself always attended the opening of new hotels in his chain, and he would be occupying that suite when the occasion arrived later in the year.

Hilton had sent a project manager, Peter DeTulio, to oversee the completion of the work, but DeTulio was finding one frustration after another in his attempt to finish the hotel. Brandy visited several of the back-of-the-house departments, such as the kitchen and laundry, helping and overseeing the work. Then he checked in with DeTulio with a list of ideas about what needed to be done. DeTulio asked him what he was doing there.

Brandy replied he was there on a temporary basis, to get the hotel open on schedule, per the orders of Mr. Hauser. DeTulio, in a stressed and nervous state, shouted at Brandy to leave. When Brandy did not move, DeTulio took a swing at him, which he ducked. After a moment, DeTulio swung again, and again Brandy dodged the blow.

Brandy stared at him and said calmly, "If you try that again, you are dead. I'm a karate expert."

DeTulio calmed down, and the two men were able to work together after that. Even so, due to DeTulio's state of nervous exhaustion, many of the project management duties fell to Brandy.

Brandy had less success with José Menéndez, the thin and gregarious local bookkeeper. Menéndez simply ignored him, while Brandy took on the actual tasks of finishing out the hotel and disregarding the unpleasant situation.

Although the hotel was still being completed, a casino had already opened. It could be entered through the lobby of the hotel, but was a separate operation with a series of problems of its own. Hilton's only concern and interest in the casino was that it be operated in a clean fashion, so as not to cheat the guests and ruin the Hilton name.

Conrad Hilton had recruited the noted gambling expert and author, John Scarne, to serve as the corporation's representative for inspecting casinos associated with the various hotels in the chain. Brandy was impressed with Scarne, who could walk through the casino and spot the dishonest dealers who were allowing their friends to win, were cheating customers, or otherwise "plucking the pigeons." In effect, Scarne's job was to identify staff members who were stealing, either from the house or from the customers. Brandy himself knew nothing of the gambling business, and he grew to trust Scarne and his decisions. Scarne had served during World War II in the navy, spotting card sharks and cheaters at navy bases, and his military background appealed to Brandy. Scarne quietly pointed out that the gambling operation, like most of the major casinos in Havana, was conducted through contract by a group with mob connections. He identified one or two famous members of the American underworld who would stop by the casino occasionally, including Meyer Lansky.

Brandy was irritated to see the casino flourishing, with its mob connections, while he struggled to get the main hotel into operation. Brandy began holding daily morning meetings with heads of departments, stressing the need to hire competent people and concentrate on work that was needed to open the hotel on time. He planned to delay for the time being the less visible work on the back of the shop. Menéndez was notable by his absence from such meetings, but progress was made as the planned date for the grand opening drew near.

There were numerous other problems at the Havana Hilton. For one thing, after examining the books, Brandy found that the hotel was overstaffed. A month before opening, he reviewed the personnel records and was surprised to discover that the total staff numbered 1,500. He froze it at that figure for the time being. A large staff in the opening phases in itself was not unusual. As guests arrived and problems were identified, extra help could be pared down gradually.

The morning before the day of the planned opening, a distraught employee ran into Brandy's office. There was a disaster: the Conrad Hilton Suite literally stank. The fresh paint had not dried and the odor permeated everything. When Brandy raced up to the room, he found Arthur Elminger, vice president of Hilton International from Mexico City, who had flown in a day early. He was standing in the suite, shaking his head. They conferred and at Elminger's suggestion, dozens of carnations and roses were ordered to fill the room, in hopes of covering the paint smell. Whether the effect was psychological or real, Elminger was happy to have been of help. The next morning, as the two assessed the smell, Elminger was further horrified to discover that the inside of the door to the suite had been left unpainted.

The painters were gone, so Brandy took off his shirt and went to work painting the door, sweating profusely despite the blast of the air-conditioner. He was finishing up when an assistant manager stuck his head in with the word that Conrad Hilton had arrived with his entourage at the airport, a day early, and they were on their way to the hotel. Brandy took a few more swipes to finish the door, when the assistant manager quickly checked back: the party was in the hotel already, inspecting things. In fact, he said, they were on the floor and were about to look over the Conrad Hilton Suite itself.

The shirtless Brandy, sweat and paint on his face and chest, a jar of paint in one hand and a brush in the other, had no place to hide. He stepped behind the door just before the party looked in, glancing at the vases of flowers and the fresh room. Elminger stepped in, and without batting an eye, spotted Brandy behind the door. The entourage did not enter the room, however, and passed down the hall, commenting on how nice everything appeared.

Brandy dashed out, hurried to his quarters and cleaned up, placed a carnation in his buttonhole, and appeared back at the suite with a calm countenance. He went in to meet Conrad Hilton and apologized for the odor of fresh paint. Hilton brushed it off—all new hotels smelled like that, he said. The opening was off to a good start.

Yet the extra staff, coupled with the finishing costs and expenses associated with the opening day, ran the books of the hotel deeply into the red. The party of Hilton executives, including Conrad Hilton himself; John Hauser; Charles Bell, who was in charge of food and beverage for Hilton International; and Arthur Elminger, along with assistants and some of their girlfriends, all were provided rooms that were charged to opening costs. In addition, travel writers from newspapers and magazines, who were invited to the opening, also received rooms, food, and beverages on a complimentary basis. Even long distance international phone calls were charged to the hotel's own tab. With these heavy charges, it was nearly impossible to show a profit in the first weeks, even with a full house of tourists. Yet all of the complimentary rooms and good service made sense. Managers and personnel from other parts of the chain, if impressed, would refer guests to the hotel. Happy travel writers and tourists also would bring new business.

As soon as the opening party left, Brandy began to concentrate on cost control, to move the hotel into a profit-making mode. Unfortunately, the publicity extravaganza had yielded low results and guests stayed away. He called his daily morning meetings and explained the facts to the staff. They had a brand-new 630-room hotel, overstaffed with 1,500 employees, and only 150 guests. The ten-to-one ratio of workers to guests was simply unworkable. The rumors of Fidel Castro's forces raiding against the repressive regime of Cuban dictator Fulgencio Batista, had apparently scared off the tourists, even though the attacks were concentrated several hundred miles away on the eastern end of the island in Camaguey and Oriente provinces. Despite publicity and the apparent safety of the capital, the revenue was simply not forthcoming. He asked his department heads for advice.

One by one, they all warned against cutting the payroll. The Batista regime would never accept the concept that a foreign company would conduct layoffs because of distant troubles to the east. Any increase in unemployment would in fact feed the local support for the revolution and would not be allowed.

Day after day, as the hotel payroll expenses climbed and cash reserves dwindled, the Cuban department heads refused to accept the concept of a payroll cut. Finally Brandy decided there was no choice. Unilaterally, he ordered a cut of fifty percent. Each department was to lay off half its workers, bringing the staff down to 750. All of the department heads were horrified. Manuel Ray, the chief engineer, who had struck Brandy as a thoughtful type with little to say, warned that there would be some serious consequences as a result of the layoffs. Brandy stated that any department head who did not agree with the layoffs could resign. No one got up to leave, and the cuts went into effect.

The next morning, 9 April 1958, as Brandy was receiving reports concerning the progress of the cuts and their effect on the various departments, he was suddenly interrupted. Four Cuban security policemen strode into the room: two enlisted men and two officers. The officers had pistols on their belts, the enlisted men held machine guns at the ready. Calmly, they looked around the room. "Which one is Brandstetter?" they asked. Brandy stood up. "Did you cut the payroll?" they asked. "Yes," he said, and the men marched him out. As he left the room, he noticed that Manuel Ray modestly looked down and covered his eyes with one hand.

Outside the Hilton, Brandy was appalled to see a large blue Buick to which the security policemen marched him. The security force's "Blue Buick" had grown famous under the tough regime of Batista; those arrested for questioning and taken away in it usually never came back.

Inside the car, he received a once-over. A burly security police type on each side squeezed him in with his arms and legs locked back; each delivered tight blows to his stomach, kidneys, and face. Saying nothing, they continued to beat him as the big car drove slowly through the busy streets of Havana to the headquarters of Police District Nine.

Like the "Blue Buick," District Nine headquarters had an ominous reputation. As Brandy was dragged into the building, the beating continued. He could hear screams and moans from doors as he was led down the hall, pummelled with fists and sometimes smashed with a rifle butt by the other guards standing in the hallway. Finally, he discovered himself at the end of the hall, in front of a door to a private office. He was hustled in.

Brandy did not at first recognize the imperious major, a Himmler-type, leaning back with a contemptuous posture in his leather chair behind the desk. Clearing his head, Brandy read the nameplate: Major Ventura. This man was notorious, the so-called "Butcher of Havana."

With a languid wave of his hand, Esteban Ventura motioned Brandy forward. As the guards released him, Brandy stepped up and snapped to attention, as if reporting to an officer in the military. Ventura at least responded by sitting up straight. He glared at Brandy, then pointed his finger at him.

What reason could Brandstetter offer for firing hundreds of Cuban workers? Quickly, Brandy thought it over. Someone inside the Hilton was feeding information to the security people.

Brandy gave a straight answer.

"I have cut the payroll because I am under orders to make the hotel profitable. I simply do not have the money to continue to meet the payroll. If we keep on the full staff, the hotel will collapse financially, and then everyone will be laid off. The closing of the hotel, the layoff of 1,500 people, could lead to an even bigger crisis. Maybe riots. I'm sure you do not want that."

Ventura slammed his hand down on the desk.

"If this is a Hilton Hotel," he said, "why don't you just ask Hilton for the money to pay the workers?"

Brandy explained that Hilton did not own the hotel, the Culinary

Workers' Union did. Hilton had only a management contract based on a fixed percentage of the receipts.

"Nevertheless," Ventura said, "Hilton has an interest. He wants to see the hotel succeed. Why haven't you tried to get the funds from the company?"

Brandy explained that he had indeed already tried, three times. The answer was no. Hilton headquarters in New York were sympathetic, and they were sorry to hear there were startup problems. But providing funds was not company policy. Things would work out. They were polite, but they refused to help.

Ventura was disgusted.

"Get this man out my sight," he ordered the guards.

Brandy, assuming the interview was over, was momentarily relieved. But the interrogation had only begun. He was slammed into a chair to the side, where he was ordered to sit without moving. From that spot he watched Ventura for hours. The major read reports and signed them; then he quickly interrogated other individuals brought before him, frequently dismissing them with initials on a form. They would leave as they came, escorted by tough guards. Brandy imagined that each document was a decision: execution, torture, release, disappearance. From time to time a soldier would carry off a document to implement the sentence, Brandy assumed. He knew the stories: a shot in the back of the head in the basement of District Nine headquarters, and then the body driven to a remote beach and dumped.

As the hours passed, Ventura would rise, walk over, stand in front of Brandy, and repeat his question: "What are you going to do to preserve the jobs at the Hilton?" Brandy would repeat his original answer that dismissals were the only way to save the hotel.

Finally, he thought of another response. The next time Ventura strode up and demanded an answer, Brandy struggled to his feet and stood at attention. "Colonel," he said—knowingly promoting the major considerably—"Colonel, you are a military man. You are used to taking orders. I, too, am taking orders. My orders are to have the hotel make money. The Havana Hilton has great potential; it is a good setup. Like all hotels, it is going to be cash-poor during the startup period. So if we want to carry the full payroll during these times, we need a loan. You could loan us the money personally, or the government, or the Culinary Workers' Union. I would personally honor the repayment schedule and guarantee that a loan be repaid, with interest." Ventura stared at him as if he had completely lost his mind, shook his head, and returned to his desk. One of the guards slugged Brandy for his insolence.

During the next questioning, Brandy repeated his insistence that there simply was no way to pay the workers. Ventura stared at him.

"Brandstetter," he said, "you are one tough son of a bitch."

"You, as well, colonel," said Brandy, as if returning a compliment.

A few minutes later, Major Ventura briefly changed his tone, whether from the implied promotion or out of respect for Brandy's resistance. He treated Brandy to a tray of sandwiches and a cup of coffee that Brandy remembered as one of the most delicious in his life. After the break, the same routine began again: long interludes of sitting in his chair, enduring intimidating questions, replying that nothing could be done or that Ventura should loan him the funds, and feeling an occasional smash of a fist in his face. From time to time he was led out to a bathroom, then back to the chair for more questioning, beating, and intimidation.

Finally in disgust, Ventura whispered something to the guards, who then pulled Brandy from his chair and out of the office. They dragged him down the hall, past the open doors from which moans and cries emerged. At the front door, they simply threw him into the street, bleeding all over. He pulled himself together. Luckily, he still had his watch. It was nearing 3:00 A.M. He had been in the office since the previous morning, over fifteen hours earlier. He still had his wallet, so he flagged a taxi and returned to the hotel.

In his room, he poured himself a glass of good stiff brandy, ordered a glass of warm milk from room service, then stripped and examined himself in the mirror. One eye was swollen shut, and his torso was covered entirely with bruises, and his face was bleeding. Sipping the drinks, he examined the hotel's books for the day. Occupancy had not gone up. He put in a call for the regular staff meeting the next day, took a hot shower, and went to bed.

At the next morning's meeting, Brandy appeared, neatly dressed, but with the marks of his beating clearly showing on his patched face.

The staff was shocked, but with the exception of Manuel Ray, said nothing. Ray muttered that the police could be brutal.

The payroll was still too high, Brandy said. There would have to be another cut to pare down further, another 250 people, down to 500. There was no choice. The department heads agreed, but silently filed out of the room. Manuel Ray murmured to Brandy: I hate to think what the government will do when they hear this; you won't live through it. "Pase lo que pase," Brandy replied—what happens, happens—so be it.

The next day, Brandy was again hauled off in the "Blue Buick" and found himself again in Ventura's office.

"I let you go once, and you did it again!" screamed the major.

"You didn't get me the money," said Brandy. "I had no choice."

Ventura claimed that Brandy had promised that there would be no further cuts. Brandy denied it. He repeated his assertion that if the hotel went under and payrolls were not met, there would be a riot. Brandy explained that if Ventura had him killed it would only make the situation worse. The hotels were having trouble because tourists were afraid to come; they had heard about Castro and the troubles in the east. If word got out that the police killed an American businessman, the remaining tourist business would dry up altogether. You have already frightened off most of the tourists. Do you want to frighten off the rest?

Ventura asked if Brandstetter was a Castro supporter. Brandy replied that he was completely in the dark about politics. He had come to open a hotel, and then to stay on for a while as manager, and he knew nothing about Castro. He could not run the hotel without tourists and with a huge staff. The troubles had kept tourists away, and it was bad for business. That was all he knew about Castro.

Ventura took another tone, explaining the logic of the situation patiently. The government did not want to encourage Castro supporters in the city. Layoffs and labor unrest would only feed the Castro cause. The army would deal with Castro in the countryside, but to prevent labor problems in the city, they had brought Brandstetter to headquarters to try to reason with him. Yet he insisted on provocative actions.

Ventura warned Brandy: "Very rarely does anyone ever come in here twice. No one ever comes and goes a third time. There are to be no more staff layoffs at the Havana Hilton. If you have to come back again, you will not be going home." After more beatings, he was again thrown into the street, early in the morning.

As Brandy left Police District Nine the second time, he knew that Ventura was correct. The hotel could barely operate at the new levels of reduced staff. If business did not pick up, there would not have to be further reductions in force; rather, the whole hotel would just be closed down and the workers paid off.

With its reduced staff, the hotel began to show a small profit. Brandy continued to make friends with journalists, and their favorable mentions of the hotel in a few stories in the *New York Times*, the *Chicago Tribune*, and *Time*, caused guests to trickle into the hotel during the late summer of 1958. Other assistance was provided by the New York headquarters of Hilton in the person of Fred Lederer, an excellent food and beverage manager, and a first class crew of Swiss chefs, who soon established a fine reputation for the restaurant.

The Hilton organization, however, could not spare Brandy for a three-week reserve duty. After some difficulty, Brandy was later able to put in two weeks at the Summer Fourth Army Area Intelligence School in Texas. When he returned to Havana, he wrote to Colonel William Rose at the Pentagon, in the Office of Assistant Chief of Staff-Intelligence (ACSI). Brandy reminded him that he would need a new billet in 1959, and sent along a collection of documents amplifying his military background. Rose remembered Brandy very well and responded within a week that he was glad to hear Brandy was "back in Havana, where [he could] take good care of our interests." Rose suggested that Brandy contact Colonel Sam Kail, the U.S. Army military attaché at the American Embassy in Havana. Brandy followed up, conferring with Kail regularly about the situation in Cuba.

Brandy began to learn more about the political situation by listening to discussions and gathering information from ordinary people, from journalists like Jules DuBois, and from guests and hotel staff. At one staff meeting, when someone pointed out that "the Communists" were in the hills, Manuel Ray corrected him. A few of the Castro men, some who were close to him, were in fact Communists, but many were not. The peasant soldiers wore crucifixes and many were devout Catholics, not Communists at all. In the summer, Brandy sent a confidential report via Colonel Kail to Army G-2, suggesting that an overthrow of the Batista regime by Castro's forces would soon take place. If Castro were not neutralized, he warned, the Communists in his group could take over. Through channels he heard back the response to his report. State Department, CIA, and the military services were well aware of the situation, and the CIA and State were not unsympathetic to Castro. Brandy felt, however, that they missed the point. Raul Castro, Fidel's brother, and Che Guevara, an Argentine revolutionary and known Communist who had joined Castro's cause, were stressing that the Batista regime was a puppet of the United States. Unless care was taken, the Communist element could easily dominate the new regime when it took power. As an army man, Brandy found the all-knowing tone from State and CIA frustrating, even wrong-headed, but at least he had reported the news and the tenor of the conversations in Havana. What Washington did with the information was out of his hands.

He settled into the routine of managing the hotel, making the rounds with John Scarne, supervising the kitchen crew, and trying to meet expenses as the hotel occupancy fluctuated with every news item from the growing revolution in the east.

12

Yankee No!

During the fall of 1958, Brandy encountered several difficulties in the hotel. For a time, the elevators unaccountably lost power, and it would take hours to get them running again. One noon, Brandy had lunch with Colonel Sam Kail, the military attaché from the U.S. Embassy. Kail and Brandy worked out tentative plans for an evacuation of American tourists if the revolution reached Havana. After lunch, they were irritated to find themselves stuck in the elevator between floors. They clambered up through the trap door to the elevator roof, reached up to the doors on the floor above, and pried them open, giving Brandy insight into why the hotel guests who became trapped from time to time in the elevators during power failures sometimes panicked at the shutdowns and the other daily crises.

A spate of stink bombs, with an odor exactly like that of a skunk, were set off in the hotel's air conditioning system. Somehow the self-contained water system of the hotel became contaminated and gave everyone diarrhea. The Hilton name, Brandy feared, was attracting more and more anti-American attention. Manuel Ray explained that he thought the perpetrators could either be Castro agents trying to harass the American tourists or Batista agents trying to discomfort the news reporters staying at the hotel in order to generate anti-Castro feelings among them. A convoluted plan, but possible, thought Brandy.

Every evening at 7:00 P.M., like clockwork, bombs would explode around Havana. Brandy noted that he could sit on the veranda and set his watch by the explosions. The bombs rarely did much damage, but psychologically, they could be nerve-wracking, especially to civilians who had never seen action in wartime. At one level, he admired the precision of the bombs' timing; at another level, he knew the sabotage and nightly explosions were destroying all prospects that the Hilton would show a profit for the year.

Brandy noticed with satisfaction that after his cruel beatings by the police, the disturbances and sabotage at the hotel appeared to decline. Perhaps his willingness to stand up to Ventura had, among Castro's sympathizers, offset the impact of layoffs on the Hilton reputation. He could only guess. Soon, however, he picked up a rumor from his grapevine that Manuel Ray was a Castro supporter. It seemed to fit, the more he thought about it. Ray's muttered support when Brandy was arrested, his passing comments that not all Castroites were Communists, his complex explanations regarding the sabotage, and the decline in hotel problems after his own beating—Brandy had a feeling in his gut.

One evening, when Brandy was out walking near the hotel, he confronted the young engineer. "Listen," Brandy said, "I know where your politics are. But keep your hands off the Havana Hilton. I won't say anything, but for heaven's sake, stop any damage to the hotel." Ray did not answer directly, but from his eyes, Brandy knew he had struck a nerve. He had no idea how correct he was, or how deeply involved Ray had become. A few days after the revolution was completed, Manuel Ray, former chief engineer of the Havana Hilton, received a cabinet appointment in the new Castro-led government as minister of public works. Ray had apparently been in charge of all the sabotage in Havana in the summer of 1958.

Listening to reporters and his other sources on the grapevine, Brandy heard another, even more frightening rumor. The word was circulating that when the Castro people took over Havana, they would burn the Havana Hilton to the ground. He decided to establish a liaison with the Castro forces, and planned to carry a letter through the lines to Castro inviting him to make the Hilton his headquarters, when and if his troops arrived in Havana. Young Fred Lederer found Brandy in his office, preparing the letter, and asked him why he seemed so distressed. Brandy was staring at the small sign on his desk that read "Illigitimatum non Carborundum"—Don't let the bastards wear you down.

"Look," said Brandy, "I'm going to take this letter through the Batista lines and get it to Castro—I've got to save the hotel." Lederer and Brandy discussed the logistics of having Castro and his battalions at the hotel. They had only 630 rooms, but thousands of troops. Where would the food come from? Where would the men sleep? Brandy had it all charted out. The ballroom itself could accommodate over eight hundred, bunked down. Food would be requisitioned by the troops. The troops could enter, one "battalion" at a time, get cleaned up, get their uniforms dry-cleaned, receive a round of meals and a good night's sleep, and then move on. The Conrad Hilton Suite could be the CP—the Command Post—for Castro himself. Brandy visualized the communications lines, internal security, and defense perimeter. He had experience setting up and staffing CPs in World War II, so it would be natural.

If Castro came to the city, the invitation would save the hotel. If he never made it to Havana, Castro would not be telling anyone he had received an invitation, and the threat to the hotel would be moot. It was worth the risk to carry the message through the lines. Brandy may have been thinking of his earlier crossings: urging surrender on General Model; testing the Morgan line; visiting his sister in Bratislava. But Brandy was forty-seven years old and no longer an eager young paratrooper.

"Are you nuts?" asked Lederer. "You don't speak fluent Spanish like I do. And I know the back alleys. Let me do it." At first, Brandy resisted. Lederer explained that Brandy was already well known to the Batista forces because of his earlier arrest. He would never make it. The Batista troops would either arrest or shoot him; the Castro people would suspect a trick. Lederer insisted on delivering the letter.

Brandy felt guilty letting him assume the mission, but Lederer came from a Prussian military family, was bright, and had guts. Furthermore, if he was caught, Lederer held a German passport, and neither side would care to create bad feelings with a European country.

Brandy took the letter out of the typewriter, signed it, and gave it to the young man. So Lederer left, and Brandy chewed his nails. When Lederer returned, hours later in the early morning, he gulped down a stiff shot of brandy and then reported. He had trouble getting across the Batista lines, and spent several hours in detention. Then he had to backtrack and find another route to the Castro lines. There, the Castro forces held him for further questioning. He had not been allowed to deliver the letter personally, but it was taken from him by a *barbudo*, a bearded Castro soldier he assumed was a staff officer. Then he was released to go back.

Was the mission a success? Had the word gotten through? How would Castro react? Nothing was clear, but at least the effort had been made. Brandy remembered the Lederer mission years later as he followed the younger man's career in the Hilton and the Hyatt chains, and finally, in the 1990s, as he successfully built hotels on the Baltic in the former East Germany.

Lederer's attempt to get through to Castro occurred on Christmas Eve, 1958. Not knowing when, or if, the Castro forces would succeed, Brandy continued with his plans for a gala New Year's Eve party at the hotel, a last chance to fill some of the hotel rooms with Americans flown in for a Caribbean New Year's fiesta.

The party began for several hundred guests attending that evening. As Brandy was preparing in his room, dressing in his tux for the party, he took a phone call. His face was still lathered with shaving cream. The call was from Jules DuBois, the *Chicago Tribune* reporter who had written favorably of Castro, and had contacts in the revolutionary camp. DuBois had left Cuba and was calling from Chicago. "Tonight's the night," he said. The razor slipped, and Brandy cut himself shaving. He knew exactly what DuBois meant. Brandy called his doctor in, on the pretext of looking at the cut.

Later that night, confirming word came through Brandy's own informal sources that Castro forces were on the edge of the city, and that Batista had fled for the Dominican Republic. Brandy later calculated that, through DuBois, he might have been the first American in Havana to know that the revolution had succeeded. Years later, after reading CIA officer David Atlee Phillips's account of the same evening in *The Night Watch*, Brandy noted that Phillips claimed to have been the first to hear of the evacuation of Batista at 4:00 A.M. The next time Brandy saw his friend Phillips, he told him he had the jump on him!

He knew the end was coming at 8:00 P.M. the night before, beating the CIA by eight hours. Phillips and Brandy had a good laugh over the issue.

During the New Year's celebration, small arms fire could be heard, putting the dwindling group of guests at the party on edge and punctuating their celebration. Quietly, Brandy told the doctor that his sources indicated the city would fall that night and Batista would be leaving. He asked him to bring his medical gear to the hotel, call other doctors and nurses to join the New Year's festivities as his guests, and be ready to set up a clinic and help in an evacuation if needed. The doctor was curious about Brandy's information, but as the sound of sporadic firing neared through the night, he complied. Inside, the revelers toasted the New Year. In the distance, the tempo of the guns increased.

As the party wound down, the early morning hours became increasingly chaotic. Brandy issued an order that guests should not check out—he had in mind the evacuation plans developed earlier with Colonel Kail at the American Embassy, as well as the plans for Castro forces to stay in the hotel. It would be difficult to juggle the two confidential plans, and as Havana fell to the Castro forces on the morning of 1 January 1959, the two well-laid arrangements began to collide.

A few guests began nervously to call the front desk staff asking if they could check out and get a taxi to the airport. The staff replied negatively, recommending that everyone stay in their rooms until further notice. Before dawn, one of the newsmen rushed in and breathlessly collared Brandy. A mob of Castro revolutionaries had formed in the street and was headed towards the hotel. They were shouting anti-American slogans and planned to burn down the Hilton.

Briefly, Brandy had an exchange with Manuel Ray, who confirmed that the mob intended to burn the hotel. Brandy handed him his jacket and went down to the lobby. From the mezzanine, a few guests observed what happened next. Among them was Philippe de Vosjoli, head of French intelligence—the SDECE (Service de Documentation Exterieure et de Contre-espionnage)—in Cuba, Canada, the United States, the Caribbean, and Mexico. Unknown to Brandy, de Vosjoli was staying in the hotel with his wife. He later recorded the events in his autobiography, *Lamia*, dedicated to Brandy, wherein he recorded seeing "a physically-fit man in a white shirt with short sleeves . . . calmly blocking the path of an armed, angry mob."

Brandy met the mob and stood his ground at the entrance to the hotel lobby, explaining that the hotel was *not* American property. It belonged to the Cuban people—to the Cuban Culinary Workers' Union. Hilton managed it, but if the mob burned down the hotel they would be destroying the Cuban workers' savings, not American property.

The crowd waved machetes, pistols, and rifles; some gestured as if to club Brandy with their rifle butts. Brandy's shirt was drenched with perspiration. He explained that American tourism would be needed to keep Cuba strong. He pointed out the cornerstone of the building, indicating the hotel was property of the Culinary Workers' Union.

Gradually, the crowd began to quiet, then broke into groups and argued. The standoff lasted only about fifteen minutes, then the rioters moved on. Two of the bearded officers in charge of the Castro troops drew Brandy aside. They quietly asked him if arrangements could be made to feed the troops. Brandy explained that he already had made that offer directly to Castro in his letter of Christmas Eve, and that he fully expected not only to feed the troops, but also to provide facilities for the Castro command post and lodging. He would need help, he explained, in gathering enough food.

That morning, the officers brought up several of their large army trucks and accompanied Brandy to the other hotels, confiscating food supplies from their storerooms. The whole process distressed Brandy because he thought that, when everything settled down, he might be charged with looting. He carefully compiled an inventory of the specific goods taken from each hotel, noting the date, time, and name of hotel. He signed it, and persuaded the Castro officers to countersign each sheet. No complaints were ever lodged.

Meanwhile, the American Embassy evacuation plan that Colonel Kail and Brandy had worked out months before was quietly taking effect. Runners were sent to spread the word that Americans from all the other hotels should assemble at the Hilton. By the end of the day, the Hilton housed about 350 American guests, and shifts of up to two thousand Castro troops in the lobby, banquet rooms, and some of the hotel rooms. For a few days the two groups rubbed shoulders, somewhat uncomfortably.

The *barbudos*, Brandy remembered, tended to be well behaved by comparison to some of the tourists. One group of tourists, frustrated that Castro had ordered all bars closed for the duration of the crisis, broke into a locked liquor supply cabinet, committing the only actual physical damage to the hotel during the revolution. Meanwhile, at the other hotels, mobs ransacked the casinos, tearing out the slot machines and destroying them in the street. The motive was mixed. Of course, the machines contained coins that were easily picked up from the wreckage. But the slot machines had become symbols of the corruption of the Batista regime—the Las Vegas-owned company operating the machines had been a direct source of revenue for Batista's wife, who reputedly received fifty percent of the slot revenues.

While Brandy moved forward with the plans to evacuate Americans, he ordered the feeding of troops in the coffee shop and tourists in the dining room. An open buffet was set up with soft drinks, and the hotel maintained strict records of the meals served through these days

On 2 January, Brandy arranged the evacuation of a number of guests, focusing first on sending the sick, the elderly, and families with children back to the States. He organized a caravan of about twenty-five cars in the parking garage by short-circuiting their ignitions. In the first batch, he loaded some 120 Americans into the cars.

Philippe de Vosjoli, who had observed Brandy confronting the rioters in the lobby of the hotel on 1 January, approached Brandy and introduced himself. Brandy immediately liked the straightforward, pro-American, and strongly anti-Communist French agent. De Vosjoli explained his dilemma. He believed a leak somewhere in the French security arrangements might cause the Communists among Castro's forces to target him personally as a potential enemy. He wanted to evacuate without attracting notice. Brandy believed he should do a favor for a fellow Allied officer, especially one in the same line of business.

He included Philippe de Vosjoli and his wife in the group of American tourists. A number of harried, inexperienced, and sometimes rude clerks from the U.S. Embassy processed documents in the hotel lobby. In the confusion, the presence of two non-Americans in the American-sponsored evacuation went unnoticed, as Brandy simply waved aside minor questions and moved the French couple to the caravan. De Vosjoli would remember Brandy's kindness in later years, and would share with him many confidences and insights into the problems of Communist penetration of security agencies in the Western democracies. The friendship later grew, based as it was on mutual respect and the memory of the shared risks during the Castro takeover.

While assisting the loading of older guests into the cars, a young, loud-mouthed guest started to push aside the others and force himself into a car. Brandy went over and told him to stop it—women and children first, followed by the older folks. The arrogant and muscular young man tried to push Brandy aside. With lightning speed, Brandy decked him with a punch to the chin. The entire elderly group gave Brandy a round of applause. The loading procedure, from that moment on, flowed smoothly.

With the bellboys hot-wiring and then driving the cars, and with both Cuban and American flags flying from some of the fenders, the little caravan departed for the waterfront, with Brandy sitting on top of the hood of the lead car. On the way to the docks, they witnessed that fighting was still in progress, but the shooting stopped as the American flags went by. Brandy felt like Moses at the Red Sea, as the firing closed back around them as they passed. The caravan arrived at the docks, and with the help of militiamen, the group loaded aboard the ocean-going ferry *City of Havana*. Off shore, by pre-arrangement through Colonel Kail, three U.S. Navy destroyers cruised in international waters, to provide protection and an escort for the ferry across the ninety miles to Key West and the United States. Later caravans took another 350 American tourists to the ferry and the airport for chartered flights out of the country.

Later, many of the tourists evacuated in this manner wrote letters of appreciation to Brandy, with several sending copies directly to Conrad Hilton. Some first realized who he was from a news item in the *Chicago Tribune* describing their exodus, while others had known him well. Among the New Year's party-goers who wrote in appreciation were Dr. Curtice Rosser of Dallas, who was Brandy's friend and Barbara's personal physician; Ernest Dumler, an industrialist from Pittsburgh; John Thompson, a military reporter for the *Chicago Tribune*; and Frank Sherman, an attorney from New York City. In several cases, Hilton himself responded to the grateful guests.

Meanwhile, the local general manager of the hotel, José Menéndez, went into hiding. He surfaced a few days later, on 5 January, and with the help of his very loyal personal secretary, prepared a number of reports for the Hilton public relations office. These few clippings amused Brandy. They were created hurriedly to redeem the reputation of Menéndez, a man now viewed as a coward who had abandoned his ship. Although his absence was detailed in the *Chicago Tribune*, his self-prepared news clippings introduced him as a cool manager of crisis, when in fact he had not been present at the hotel during the whole tumult of the first four days of 1959.

For the first week of the revolution, Castro remained in Oriente province, finally moving into Havana on 8 January 1959 as order was restored by his troops. The motorcade proceeded directly to the Hilton. As Castro and his entourage entered, Brandy introduced himself and explained that the Conrad Hilton Suite was at the disposal of the Castro party. Brandy had taken the trouble to freshen up the suite with flowers and stock the refrigerator with soft drinks and beer. Castro and his group took a quick look, then declined to stay because the facilities were "too plush." However, a few days later the group returned, and Castro and his senior officers moved into the suite.

Brandy was summoned by Castro's security and bodyguards to taste the first meals brought by room service, to ensure against poisoning. Brandy did so, and then arranged for Fred Lederer, the food and beverage manager, to do the tasting, as the job became a tedious interruption of his own schedule.

For a few weeks the Conrad Hilton Suite was converted, just as Brandy had planned, into the Castro forces' command post. During this period, Brandy met many of the *barbudos*—the leaders of the various brigades who had fought against the Batista forces. He came to recognize the truth of what Manuel Ray had suggested—that many of the Castro men were devout Catholics, farmers who wore crosses and were genuinely concerned with reform. Among the early appointees to the new government were a wide variety of anti-Batista leaders. The labor unions were purged of pro-Batista flunkies, and some devoted non-Communist labor leaders became officials in the new union structures. A circle of men surrounding Castro, however, was indeed ardently Communist. The revolution, Brandy believed, could go either way, and the non-Communist leaders needed encouragement.

Brandy had an opportunity to explain to Castro that the casino business, which was closed down and had been a target of much of the revolutionary wrath, was a mainstay of the tourist trade. Casinos had become legal in Cuba in 1956, and the rapid rise of the tourist business from then to 1958 could be attributed to them. On 10 January 1959, Castro issued a statement designed to woo back some of the lost tourist business. His press release, signed "Dr. Fidel Castro Ruz" to reflect the fact that he held a J.D. degree, was designed to play down the revolutionary atmosphere. He also signed an English version of his pronouncement, which Brandy kept in his files.

> I wish to invite the American tourists and the American businessmen to come back to Cuba with the assurance that they will be welcomed by all citizens of our country. We are back to normal in Cuba, a Cuba where there is liberty, peace and order; a beautiful land of happy people. Our hotels, shops and offices are open and we want our friends from the United States to come and see this beautiful land of Cuba, which can now be counted among the countries where freedom and democracy is a reality.

Castro worked with officials of the American Automobile Association to spread the word among the American public that tourism would be welcomed. Brandy contacted the AAA representative in Miami, Robert Binner, in hopes of including the Hilton in summer package tours planned by AAA for 1959.

Frank suggested to Colonel Kail at the embassy that it would be a good idea to arrange for an American news organization to conduct a full-scale television interview with Castro, so that more could be learned about him. Although full assessments of the Castro forces were available, little was known about Castro, the man. Brandy also suggested that the ACSI approach General David Sarnoff, U.S. Army, ret., and Chairman of the Board of RCA (which controlled NBC), as someone who could be trusted. Sarnoff had served as General Eisenhower's communications officer during the Second World War. Sarnoff recommended that Jack Paar, host of the "Tonight Show," conduct the interview.

In Cuba, Colonel Kail worked with Brandy to arrange the event. Brandy approached Castro at the Hilton, suggesting that the interview would result in favorable public relations. He also developed a list of questions that avoided military and political issues. Castro read over the list, adding a few questions of his own and deleting others. On the whole, he accepted the list.

When Paar arrived, Brandy gave him the list of prepared questions and insisted that he stick with the script. Paar agreed, for the questions focused on Castro's personal background, his family including his son and daughter, and matters of general human interest. Castro understood English quite well, and Brandy would be available to provide translation services only if needed. The questions, although innocuous, were exactly the sort needed by the U.S. Army to build a more complete picture of the human side of the new leader of Cuba. Brandy thought back to his days in the Field Intelligence Detachment, in which interro-

Jack Paar arrives in Cuba to interview Fidel Castro in 1959. Brandy served as interpreter during the interview.

gation had always yielded more when the interrogator knew the personal background of the individual being questioned; the FID methods of building strong human intelligence might still have value, he believed. Brandy, standing quietly behind the sofa between Castro and Paar during the televised interview, appeared only briefly on the film.

The show aired on 2 February 1959, and several of those who had evacuated from Cuba a month earlier wrote to Brandy, noting that they had seen the interview. The show was repeated the next day on the "Today Show," a relatively rare crossover in those days between the entertainment side and the news side of NBC's offerings. Paar was pleased with the outcome and dropped Brandy a personal note, thanking him for his help in arranging the television interview:

> Dear Frank, I cannot tell you how grateful I am for all you did for me during my stay in Cuba. Everyone here thinks the film we got there is the best shot in Cuba. The Castro interview will be shown tonight on NBC and has been picked up by the Today Show to be shown tomorrow morning. As soon as I get the film returned to me, I shall ship it off to you as I promised, and it is your property. I've been singing your praises to everyone I meet. You are one helluva guy. My warmest regards to Mrs. Brandstetter.

A few days later the film arrived as promised. Brandy promptly turned it over to Colonel Kail at the U.S. Embassy, and Kail sent it from Cuba by diplomatic pouch for ACSI's evaluation at the Pentagon. In later years Brandy wondered if the film was still housed in the U.S. Army G-2 archives. The film, with its perceptive questions, combined with the report which he and Kail had filed in June 1958 giving warning of the Communists in Castro's entourage, may have attracted attention at the Pentagon.

Meanwhile, Brandy dealt with other local crises. Errol Flynn had an apartment in the Hilton and one evening, after a party, his quarters caught fire. Losses to the hotel were over four thousand dollars; Flynn claimed his own property worth about six thousand dollars was destroyed. Brandy worked to keep the story out of the press, but one or two rumors leaked that a wild party involving heroin had gotten out of hand. Flynn complained to reporters that after the firemen, the firemen's friends and relatives, and the fire inspectors had finished trooping through his suite, he was unable to tell how much had been destroyed by fire and how much had been taken by souvenir collectors.

Brandy received a telegram through Colonel Kail at the embassy to report for his active duty in the Army Reserves on 15 February. Thinking that the time had come for a clean break, Brandy simply submitted his resignation to the Havana Hilton and made plans to rejoin the New York Hilton.

On 13 February 1959, Brandy left Havana with a small Pan American Airways flight bag and flew to Miami, ostensibly to see his dentist. Maintaining meticulous records and understandable caution, he filed a receipt for a one-way ticket out of the country. By previous arrangement he had shipped his trunks and valises by express to some friends in the States.

13

Crown, Semenenko, and Hilton

B randy served the 1959 session of his annual active duty at the Pentagon in the Office of the Army Chief of Staff, Intelligence (ACSI), working under his first ACSI "Big Brother," Colonel Bob Roth, in the Collection Division. Brandy arranged a leave of absence from Hilton in New York. The tour of duty at ACSI began on 15 February 1959 and lasted until 5 March 1959. This duty marked his change from Mobilization Reserve to a career over the next eighteen years of working directly for ACSI, sometimes on active duty, and at other times, after retirement, on a strictly unpaid and voluntary basis.

Over that time, the officer to whom he reported at ACSI would change almost every two years. In the ACSI office, continuity was provided by Mrs. Dorothe K. Matlack, a long-term civil servant and chief of the Exploitation Section of the Assistant Chief of Staff-Intelligence (ACSI-CX). Dorothe (pronounced Dorothy) personally knew Brandy and other officers who worked to supply a continuing stream of good quality "humanint," or human intelligence. Brandy could continue the work of "eyes and ears" that he had begun under Ridgway, knowing that his "Big Brother" in Washington, whoever he would be over time, would receive his reports and that they would at least be considered and reviewed properly. Brandy's standard operating procedure was to contact only one officer, his "Big Brother" from ACSI, thus protecting himself from possible exposure.

During his February and March 1959 stay at the Pentagon, Brandy was in demand as an officer who had seen the Castro revolution first hand, and he went through several debriefings. At one session, attended by representatives from the State Department, the U.S. Navy, the CIA, and other agencies, he recalled that his warnings that Castro might possibly turn Communist were "horse-laughed" by the representatives of both the State Department and the CIA. Like the report that he had earlier forwarded through Colonel Kail, such warnings were not politically correct in February 1959. All he could do was provide the information; policy would be left to others. Nevertheless, the memory rankled.

After departing the Pentagon, he visited the executive offices of Hilton International in New York City. He learned that John Hauser was no longer president of Hilton International, the position having been filled by Robert J. Caverly, a new executive. Caverly, with a supercilious tone, informed Brandy that Hauser was no longer in charge, and the promised position at the Berlin Hilton had been filled. Brandy decided to continue his leave of absence from Hilton International, in hopes that another job with the company would open.

At Hilton International, several executives were impressed by the flood of letters received from individuals evacuated by Brandy's caravans from the Havana Hilton. Despite the distorted, phony, or "manufactured" news flowing from the local manager, José Menéndez, Hilton management realized it was Brandy who had saved the hotel and the Hilton reputation in the hectic first week of 1959. Hilton executives forwarded to Brandy newspaper clippings stating the actual facts, together with some of the letters from guests who had witnessed Menéndez's absence and Brandy's rescue efforts. Caverly himself had received at least one of the letters commending Brandy. Even so, Caverly clearly reneged on a previously offered position and Brandy was disappointed. His work in Cuba, both for the Hilton organization and for American national interests, seemed to be unrecognized and unrewarded.

He moved back to Dallas to be near Barbara, who was in a sanitarium there. He retained both his status as a Hilton manager on leave of absence and his status as a reserve lieutenant colonel, with annual active duty to be served at the Army Chief of Staff Intelligence at the Pentagon. The rejections from both quarters were severe, but they were past. Brandy concluded that he should not look back.

Brandy now settled into work as vice president and part owner of an auto-leasing business, Continental Leasing. The company, based on a long-standing automobile-leasing firm operated by Dallas businessman Scott Walker, had been established in 1957. The headquarters of the firm later moved to Shreveport, Louisiana, where it maintained an automobile leasing and truck business, an automobile-rental franchise of National Rental, and cab and limousine services in several cities. Brandy bought shares in Continental Leasing, owning about seventeen percent of the stock, while Scott Walker and his wife owned slightly over sixty percent.

During this time, Brandy was developing a private plan that he hoped would affect the Cuban situation. He worked on a proposal to acquire used engines from the U.S. Army, particularly the large engines from decommissioned army tanks, refurbish and box them, and then sell them to Cuba for water irrigation pump purposes. As events moved rapidly in Cuba in 1959, however, it became clear that the Communist members of Castro's inner circle were beginning to dominate. Brandy's plans for trade with the regime were soon abandoned.

Meanwhile, he kept in touch with Colonel William Rose at the Pentagon office of the Assistant Chief of Staff-Intelligence. Rose arranged for Brandy to be assigned for training on weekend duties to the 488th Strategic Intelligence Team in Dallas. He contributed to a study of the capability of Soviet oil fields, working with oil and mining engineer Colonel Jack Crichton, MI and U.S. Army, ret., who was later to explore the oil and gas reserves in the former Soviet Union during the 1990s. Rose also researched the question of whether Brandy would be eligible for promotion to full colonel, an inquiry Brandy had initiated in November 1958.

That summer, Brandy finally received a phone call from Hilton headquarters. Effective 1 July 1959, there was an opening in Mexico, to take over as manager of a Hilton-supervised property in Acapulco, the Las Brisas. Upon acceptance, he was to fly to Mexico City on 28 June to meet with Arthur Elminger, the vice president of the Latin American section of Hilton International. Elminger would provide all the details. Scott Walker at Continental Leasing understood that Brandy might be leaving at any time, so his departure from the leasing company presented no problem. Brandy remained a member of the board of Continental Leasing and a vice president of the firm over the next few years.

He knew Arthur Elminger from the days when he had struggled to complete the painting in the Conrad Hilton Suite in Havana. It had been only a year before, but it seemed like another life. Brandy was to meet Elminger at the Hilton-managed Continental Hotel in Mexico City.

Brandy had heard about the Continental in Mexico City. Mexican President Miguel Alemán had used his personal funds to build it. While under construction, it had been partially destroyed by earthquake. Alemán had pushed for its completion, but had left another hotel in Acapulco only partially completed. Alemán put the Acapulco Hilton on hold, and the steel skeleton structure there simply rusted in the bright tropical sun, a monument to another unfulfilled dream. Part of Brandy's assignment in Acapulco, while temporarily managing Las Brisas until another hotel manager position opened in Europe, would be to determine the feasibility and prospects for finishing the construction of the Acapulco Hilton as well.

When Brandy and Barbara arrived at the Continental in Mexico City, he was informed that he had missed Elminger, who had been called away on business to Tunisia. They could stay at the Mexico City Continental before flying down to Acapulco to take up the new position on 1 July at Las Brisas. He would have to investigate the situation in Acapulco without the benefit of any advice or tips from Elminger.

As Brandy and Barbara sat down in the Continental dining room, Brandy noticed an overweight Latin American gentleman in a nearby booth who stared at him from time to time. The man had three young women with him, and he appeared quite drunk. Brandy could not remember where, or even if, he had met the man, and he discussed the possibilities with Barbara. Perhaps he had been a guest at the Havana Hilton, or possibly he was someone from Texas. Brandy could not place the memory, so he put the question out of his mind. They turned to their dinner, which appeared delicious.

They were just starting to eat, when Barbara mentioned in a low voice, "Don't look up, but Big Boy is right behind you."

In a string of rapid, and somewhat blurred Spanish, the man said, "Colonel Brandstetter, a pleasure to see you, a great pleasure." Then he plopped a bottle on the table with his pudgy, ring-clustered fingers gripped around its neck. It was champagne.

"My compliments," he said with a bow.

He kissed Barbara's hand, then weaved his way back to his own table and lady friends.

Then it all came flooding back to Brandy. The obese man was Major Ventura's boss, a general and head of Cuba's secret service under Batista.

He explained this to Barbara. She was stunned. This man, indirectly, had been responsible for having him beaten up by Major Ventura's goons. Certainly they would not drink the wine! Brandy shrugged. The officer was a military man and had simply been doing his duty by ordering his officers and thugs to do the physical work. Sure, they should drink the wine. After all, it was Dom Perignon, and it would be a shame to let it go to waste. With a laugh, they toasted each other. They would put it all behind them.

Brandy and Barbara moved on to Acapulco, where Brandy settled into a round of management issues to place Las Brisas Hotel on its feet. During the first months, he still hoped and half-expected that he might get the appointment to Berlin. He thought he had the opportunity when Colonel Henry Crown, a major stockholder in Hilton International, came to visit. Crown had made his fortune in cement manufacture in Chicago, and then became a hotel financier and member of the board of directors of Hilton International.

John Thompson, a military correspondent for the *Chicago Tribune* during the Second World War and a personal friend of Crown, had sent him a very complimentary letter regarding Brandy's rescue efforts and efficient management during the crisis at the Havana Hilton. He had always admired Hilton service, he said, but he never knew what service meant until the Havana trip. As a member of the board, Crown brought the letter to the attention of corporate executives at Hilton. Crown also provided Brandy with a copy of the Thompson letter as well as his own reply. He agreed, he said, that Brandy had delivered a "splendid performance under pressure at the Habana Hilton."

Crown visited Brandy's personal Las Brisas cottage and asked him what he thought of hotel opportunities in Acapulco. Brandy stated that the new Acapulco airport under construction to accommodate large jetliners would soon bring in more and more tourists. As a result, he believed, the hotel business would soon start to thrive. It made sense to finish the Hilton, but Alemán did not have the funding. "OK," said Crown, "what if you were to manage the new hotel?"

Brandy insisted that he wanted to go to Berlin or to some other locale in Europe.

"No," said Crown. "You stay here, and become general manager for both of the hotel operations, the Las Brisas Hilton and the Acapulco Hilton."

Brandy agreed that the prospects for the business were excellent, but pointed out that President Alemán had exhausted his funding to complete the Acapulco hotel, having poured his resources into finishing the Mexico City hotel after the earthquake. The Acapulco Hilton could be a great hotel, Brandy said, but it would have to be financed, and would take millions. "The job of manager isn't there at this point," he said, "because the hotel is just a skeleton."

"Look," Crown said, "if you will accept the job of manager of both hotels, I can get the financing. I'll do it now. I'll line it up. You have to be the general manager." Gradually, Crown wore Brandy down, and he agreed that if the hotel were financed, he would commit to be the manager.

Crown then proceeded to put together the financing. First he asked Brandy to put a call through to Boston so he could speak with Serge Semenenko, another hotel financier.

Crown said, "Serge, I'm here in Acapulco. I have met Brandstetter here, and he agrees to stay on and finish the hotel. I'll put up thirty-three percent. Will you go in for thirty-three percent?"

Semenenko agreed.

Then Crown asked Frank to call Conrad Hilton.

Crown said, "Connie. I am sitting here with Frank."

He listened a moment.

"Yes, Frank Brandstetter, and we were talking about the hotel structure. I would like to finish it up. I just called Serge, and he will go in for a third. I'll put in a third. Will you put in for the other third?"

Hilton agreed, and the deal was concluded.

Crown said, "Connie, call Don Miguel Alemán and tell him we are ready." Thus, the agreement to complete the Acapulco Hilton was born.

Meanwhile, Brandy had been busy with work at Las Brisas. In this fashion, what was started as a short inspection tour completely changed the rest of his life. He moved to Acapulco in June 1959, and he was still a resident there forty years later.

14

Acapulco, Trouyet and Las Brisas

B randy arrived on 28 June 1959 in Acapulco to take over for a short time the management of the 112 unfinished Las Brisas Hotel cottages *(casitas)* and to prepare his report on the prospects of the Acapulco Hilton, then simply an abandoned skeleton of a hotel.

His first impressions of his assignment at Las Brisas were a mixture of promise and disappointment. Despite the fact that he had informed the desk clerk that he was the new manager, the word apparently had not spread to the kitchen and restaurant staff. It appeared that the restaurant waiters assumed that he and Barbara were simply another American tourist couple staying at the hotel. That was all to the good, however, as he would be able to see typical service, rather than an attempt to impress the new boss.

At his first meal in the dining room, the food seemed surprisingly well prepared. The service, however, was clearly in need of improvement. The waiters slapped down the dishes, turned away, and took no further interest. With their rank body odors and pistols sticking from their belts, they could do with some training and refining, he thought.

The diners in the hotel restaurant gave him further concern. A collection of gaudy young women and their elderly escorts made it obvious that the restaurant, at least, was a hangout for ladies of the night available to the male guests. It would be a challenge to change that image.

He approved of the arrangement of the rooms—small individual cottages or *casitas* against the hillside with only a small front desk and dining room down at the level of the road, right above the Acapulco shoreline. He and Barbara checked into two adjoining *casitas* that were to be their quarters at the hotel. Once settled into the rooms, he proceeded to look at his new office.

Again, he had a mixed reaction. The office itself was comfortable. The books were laid out on several desks, so that he could examine them. A large desk, a good chair, four telephones, a nearby safe, and attractive furnishings—that was fine, quite positive. At least the general manager's headquarters would be a pleasant place to work. But the room reports revealed a few mysteries.

Many of the rooms had been complimentary—which would make sense for a hotel seeking to build up the trade. He understood from his long experience, going back to his earliest days at the St. Moritz, that complimentary rooms were an essential element of the hotel business. But the curious fact here was that many of the comps were granted mysteriously by someone with the initials "J.M." There was no one with those initials on the current or former staff as far as he could determine. Furthermore, there were a couple of other aspects of the books that he did not like. He noticed on the records that, from time to time, two men had checked in together without wives. That troubled him, as he had no intention of developing a hotel with a questionable reputation.

On the other hand, he could determine from the records that many of the customers were quite wealthy. When offering their credit cards, the guests inadvertently revealed that their credit limits were often in four figures, indicating that at least some customers were capable of paying more for their rooms and were accustomed to elegant service. This was food for thought.

He was immersed in the daily reports when, looking up, he was surprised to discover a large, well-dressed, and imposing Mexican gentleman standing in the room looking at him. Brandy assumed the man was a guest who had wandered into the office suite area by error, or was looking for some help.

In Spanish, Brandy introduced himself.

"Hello, I am Frank Brandstetter, the manager. May I help you?"

The reply was in the same tone and cadence.

"Hello, I'm Carlos Trouyet, the owner. May I help *you*?"

Brandy was pleased. Yes indeed, there were several questions that Señor Trouyet could clear up. For example, what was behind the business of the "J.M." comps? He learned a lot in answer to that question, more than he expected.

Trouyet explained that across the street, on the ocean side, Juan March had built a series of cottages as a personal development for his wealthy banker friends to bring their girlfriends and mistresses. There was frequently an overflow, so he had built the Las Brisas cottage colony, which Trouyet had purchased. Until the change in ownership, March had simply comped the rooms to his friends and their playmates. All of that must come to an end, and he hoped that Brandy would see to it.

Brandy was impressed. Trouyet was down to earth, yet clearly a man of power. He spoke softly, but with assurance. There was no arrogance, no false macho quality, but simply a sense that what he said was factual and could be counted on as the truth. Immediately Brandy sensed the other man's intelligence and honesty, and his quiet forcefulness. Only later would Brandy learn exactly how much power the owner had.

Carlos Trouyet, who had holdings as a principal in thirteen of the largest businesses in the country, was one of the wealthiest men in Mexico. "Don Carlos," as he was known, came from humble origins; his father was unknown. Without family connections, usually crucial to success in the tight world of Mexican business and government, Trouyet had climbed to the top by sheer intelligence. He had studied in Europe, where he learned six languages. He had become a close friend, financial adviser, and investment banker to Miguel Alemán, the president of Mexico from 1946 to 1952. Trouyet had built his own fortune into one of the greatest in Mexico at the same time that he managed the president's funds.

Brandy knew none of this when he first met with Trouyet. He had been pulled hurriedly from Dallas to Mexico to take over the management contract for Las Brisas that Hilton International had signed with Trouyet. There had been little time for a full briefing on the hotel, its

problems, and its principals. He had also missed Arthur Elminger in
Mexico City on the way to Acapulco.

Trouyet asked him his first impressions of the hotel and what could
be done. Brandy, who had only just begun to learn about the property,
had not even had time to meet all the staff and discover the problems.
Based on his background and sensing the need to give a straight answer
to a straight question, he produced a quick summary of advantages and
problems. He liked the basic concept of individual *casitas* and a single
dining room. The central problem would be cost control, but without
studying the books further, he would not be able to give an assessment
of the issues. He would have to look at the payroll, to see if there were
too many people in some departments, and weed out the deadwood.
He would need to study room occupancy and service, food and beverage control, maintenance, sales, and promotion. Trouyet agreed. The
books were all there, waiting for the Hilton management approach.
Brandy's summary of the basic categories and his admission that he
needed to learn more about each category sat well with the owner.

Trouyet had a few points to make to fill in the background of his
purchase of the hotel. Conrad Hilton, whom he knew personally, had
recommended Brandstetter to manage the hotel. Trouyet was unfamiliar with the hotel business as a whole, only knowing the financial side,
not the management. He personally knew Peter Amadeo Giannini, a
California banker and founder of the largest chain bank in the United
States, the Bank of America. Giannini had introduced Trouyet to Juan
March. A native of Spain, March had left when Francisco Franco took
over in 1939. He had married into the vast wealth of a San Francisco
family. Using access to Bank of America funds, but without Giannini's
knowledge, March had developed the residential area, *Propriedades de
Montes*, above the beach at Acapulco. The bankers who invested in the
beachfront properties were all friends of March.

Irreverent newspapers in the capital had called the group "Ali Baba
and his Forty Thieves," suggesting they were all using access to power to
build fortunes. The "Forty Thieves" had begun to buy the *casas chicas* as
personal getaways from Mexico City. Actually, by Mexican, or even American standards, the homes were hardly beach cottages, but elaborate residences with pools, servants' quarters, and luxurious appointments, all

costing over $100,000 in 1960 American dollars to build. The director of Pemex, the national oil monopoly, even bought one. Some of the wives of the "Forty Thieves," however, had heard rumors of the getaways in Acapulco, and would sometimes drive or fly in to look for themselves. It was then that March conceived of the idea of building a cottage colony across the street, which in time became a cottage colony-small hotel, where the mistresses could stay while the wives were in town.

The cottage colony began to attract outside business as more people flew into the new Acapulco airport that Alemán had built. By late 1958, however, problems accumulated.

In the first place, March had built the residences and the *casita* colony on borrowed money, and he was not meeting his payments. Furthermore, March was a terrible manager. Debts continued to mount and March could not get any help from his forty bankers. To help March out of his trouble with the Inspector General of Mexico, who had found that $800,000 was missing, Don Carlos Trouyet bought the cottage colony business for ten million pesos to cover the debts and leave some small profit for March.

The peso was stable in those years, which allowed Brandy to complete a rapid conversion in his head. Ten million pesos amounted to $800,000 American money in 1959. It seemed a tremendous amount to pay for a tiny group of cottages and a restaurant with a sleazy reputation as a hangout for illicit assignations. Acapulco itself was a backwater, a little coastal town that few Americans had ever heard of. Yet, for Trouyet to pay that amount and then bring in the Hilton management team to build on the basis of potential, suggested immediately to Brandy that he had encountered a man with more than ordinary business courage and vision.

Brandy spent the next days assessing the hotel in order to provide a fuller evaluation to Trouyet's questions and to report to Elminger, the Latin American vice president of Hilton International. He developed a more detailed list of advantages and disadvantages. Among the positive elements: the overall ambience of cottages along the hillside; the isolation from the pollution and bustle of downtown Acapulco; even the name, "Las Brisas," meaning "the breezes," suggested the fresh air at the southern end of town; and the convenient location on the road to the airport.

However, there were serious difficulties: the room service was practically nonexistent; the only bar was a small one in the dining room; and the hotel had too few *casitas* to be profitable. There was no direct access for hotel guests to the beach itself. Transportation to and from the rooms was terrible, as guests did not always want to climb up the hill to their little cottages. Too few cars were available at the desk to continue running the guests back and forth. In addition, there was no local golf or tennis, no hotel shop, and the nearby shopping was overpriced and under-stocked. While the kitchen staff performed well on the food, the service continued to be rude and untrained. The employees had no pride, perhaps reflecting the hotel's slightly sordid origins. There were too many undesirable guests. A profitable resort hotel for couples or families could not, at the same time, provide a haven for ladies of the night. A major shakeup was needed if the business was to succeed.

Brandy began to work with the existing staff. With a newly hired secretary to take notes, he began a pattern of early morning staff meetings with department heads. The first meetings were difficult. Clearly, the department heads did not like the idea of being summoned together; to build them into a team with a commitment would be a challenge.

Brandy at work in his Las Brisas office, 1960s.

He decided to begin on a positive note. At the first meeting, he gave a little talk about hotel uniforms. He did not like the idea, he explained, that every uniform reflected rank. Rather, it would be better if all personnel, including the manager and the front of the house staff, dressed neatly in identical outfits. A clean, white Mexican Guayabera shirt, with short sleeves for better hygiene, and white pants would set the tone. Everybody would need three outfits. Furthermore, he said, the hotel would pay for the clothes. There would be a similar, tasteful outfit for the female employees. Kitchen staff, maintenance crews, and others would receive outfits suited to their tasks, but without distinction as to rank. He wanted the guests to get the sensation that everyone was there to help, that the hotel was a relaxed place, and the staff, like members of a family, were all in the effort together. From the comments among the department heads, he realized he had won a small measure of approval.

The next reform was a little more difficult. Brandy announced that he did not believe in tipping at a resort hotel. First, it was annoying for guests, who were there to relax, to be forced to carry change with them to tip for every little service, especially when they were wearing their

The expanding Las Brisas development in 1964.

bathing suits. Second, it was harmful for morale when the staff were competing with each other to try to wheedle tips out of guests. Third, it was basically unfair for the largest share of the tip to go to the dining room captain or waiter, when the tip was really a reward for the whole meal and the ambience, to which everyone on staff had contributed, including the kitchen crew.

The department heads knew what he said was true, but they grumbled at hearing it. To cancel tips would be a disaster, which Brandy understood. He could remember his early years in New York when he often lived on the tips. As the muttering increased, Brandy continued.

In place of tips, he would institute a system of standard gratuity that would be added to each guest's bill. With permission from Arthur Elminger, Brandy decided that each guest should pay five dollars a day into the gratuity fund. Brandy would instruct the accounting department to collect the funds and maintain them separately from the hotel receipts. These funds would be divided among the staff.

Brandy also decided that the proportion of the fund divided among headwaiters, waiters, bell captains, and all other help should be determined by a committee of the department heads. Top management, including Brandy, would not share in the division. But everyone else, including the lowest-ranking help—even the maids who cleaned the rooms, the busboys, the kitchen crew, and the maintenance personnel— should all receive some share, to be established by the committee. Brandy had seen this system work at the Roney Plaza in Miami, where it had been introduced by the managing director, Captain Eduardo Jouffret, a former French cavalry officer in World War I, who had imitated some of the European resorts. Jouffret's military background, his strong discipline, and his attention to detail served as a model for many of Brandy's methods.

The staff understood the idea of dividing tips. It was common enough for a waiter to share his tips with the headwaiter or with the busboys. But to extend the share to all of the back-of-the-house personnel meant the cuts would be too small, they thought. In addition, there were other problems. There were always individuals who would not go along. For example, if a guest insisted on giving a tip to a worker, the tip could not be politely refused if the guest continued to insist.

Conrad Hilton and Brandy at the cornerstone laying of the Acapulco Hilton in March 1961. Las Brisas Hilton photo.

The Acapulco Hilton, under construction in the early 1960's, towers over an empty beachfront. Photo by Guillermo Ochoa.

Brandy replied that the policy would be announced and made clear to every guest: no tipping, but a five-dollar charge would be added to the room charge to represent a service charge for all the help. If some guest insisted on tipping and it could not be politely declined, then the employee should take the funds and report them by turning them in to the accounting office to be placed with the gratuity fund. A receipt for the money and a reminder of the policy would be sent by the management to the stubborn guest.

One of the staff asked what would happen if the waiter or bellboy just quietly pocketed the money and didn't report it? Brandy had an answer. He might get away with it once, but probably not. The guest would be tipping to impress people, and would very likely brag about it, so everyone would find out. Any employee hiding a personal tip in that way would be stealing from his fellow employees. He would get reported and would be dismissed, with previously arranged approval from the unions. The hotel was a family, and there were few secrets in a family.

Concerning the sufficiency of funds for all of the help, Brandy explained that he had calculated that the five dollar per day, per guest, at that time, was somewhat more on average than the guests were tipping already under the informal system. The fund, as a consequence, would be large enough to expand the benefit to many who rarely got tipped, including the room cleaning staff, the kitchen help, and other back-of-the-shop personnel. If necessary, the amount of the daily charge could be increased. The tipping system went into effect under the supervision and approval of the union.

Brandy warned the front desk staff that they should be careful of who they accepted as guests. They were hoping to improve the reputation of the hotel to attract honeymooners, older couples, and families with children, he explained, not hookers and their customers or single men and women traveling together.

Soon after he announced the no-tipping policy, one of the accounting officers presented a problem at a morning staff meeting. It concerned the continuing room service charges for ten particular guests. These young women, "public relations employees" of Juan March, were ordering meals for their male friends to be served in their rooms. Sometimes as many as three meals were served over the course of the night,

suggesting more than one male "companion" was in the room throughout the night. What should management policy be towards these situa-
tions? The question was phrased rather delicately, and all of the staff
waited to see what Brandy would say about the continuing presence of
the ladies of the evening.

The former owner should have ended the practice of comping the
casitas, Brandy said, when he sold the property to Don Carlos Trouyet
and it was leased to Hilton International. We expected him to do that.
As of now, he said, looking at his watch, we are terminating those privileges. Accounting should make up a bill for each of the young women,
and also should ask them for a considerable advance payment to cover
the charges expected over the next few days. If they didn't check out
immediately, he would be able to make sure they left shortly, without
ever having to say anything unpleasant to them.

In fact the young women soon checked out, but Brandy had a system which he was able to employ whenever a troublesome or undesirable guest somehow got past the registration desk with a confirmed
reservation. He called it "Operation Flit," thinking back to the bug spray
"flit guns" of the pre-war era. Since each hotel room at Las Brisas was a
separate cottage, with its own utility controls, it was very easy to turn off
the electricity or water to a particular room without disturbing any other
room. Similarly, the phone could be cut off. If a guest were subjected,
simultaneously, to the loss of power, plumbing, and telephone, the room
would soon become unbearable. In the tropical heat, a room without
air conditioning and without toilets that flushed was unpleasant, to say
the least. If the guest could not call the front desk to complain, it increased the frustration. If such a guest delivered the message to the
front desk by walking down the steep hill, the complaint could be taken
down and then, somehow, the necessary word would fail to get to the
maintenance people. Furthermore, beds could go unmade, the usual
complimentary fresh breads and fruits delivered to the room could be
forgotten. Perhaps, instead of fresh fruit, the delivery would contain
only bruised or old fruit. If required, service in the restaurant could be
slow, the wrong dish could be served, or hot food could appear cold.
Subjected to "Operation Flit," undesirable guests would rarely stay more
than a day, yet none would ever be asked to leave. If an obnoxious guest

raged and complained in English about the service, the desk clerk or other employee could simply act sympathetic, shrugging and agreeing in Spanish that something should certainly be done about it. Of course, after the guest checked out, the water, power, phone, and regular service could be immediately restored for a more desirable guest.

The staff began to appreciate Brandy's reforms. Getting rid of the uncomfortable, hot uniforms and substituting Guayaberas and white trousers was one step that everyone liked. It was especially noted that Brandy himself dressed in the same outfit, and that, at least in this respect, everyone was treated equally. Furthermore, with "Operation Flit" used from time to time to rid the hotel of the ugliest of the "Ugly American" type guests, the staff felt Brandy was on their side.

Some of his reforms did not sit so well. He learned that most of the male employees came to work carrying either a pistol or knife. He continued to think that the guests would be uncomfortable seeing the bulge of a large automatic stuck in the belt of a waiter or busboy. Furthermore, someone might get shot either in an argument or by accident. He wanted to ban the weapons altogether, but his department heads explained that Acapulco was a rough town. People felt uncomfortable without some sort of weapon to protect themselves on the streets before and after work, especially those going home after the late shifts. If weapons were banned, some of the best employees would simply quit. Brandy arranged for hotel security to set up an area where the employees could check in their weapons and check them out when leaving. Later he bought two buses to pick up and return employees to the center of Acapulco.

Brandy visited the employee's changing rooms to see if they could leave their weapons in lockers and discovered, to his dismay, that the quarters were terrible, with only one or two dirty basins for washing up and only pegs for placing clothes. He put the maintenance people to work establishing shelves, lockers, and showers for the staff, again winning some loyalty and support with a small improvement.

Brandy noticed one employee on the records with a job description he hardly expected: "Ron Urbanek—Teacher." Brandy called in Urbanek to discover what he taught. Juan March had recruited him to teach English and Spanish to some of the help on a part-time basis, using a room over the employee's cafeteria to hold classes intermittently. Urbanek politely explained the job and his background as a teacher in Mexico City, showing Brandy his resumé. During World War II, he had worked on the Red Ball Express, the truck line that had supplied ammunition and other supplies in 1944 and 1945 from the channel ports to Patton and the front in a massive operation. Urbanek expected that Brandy, with his reputation for correcting the inefficiently and poorly managed aspects of the Juan March era, would simply give him notice to leave.

He was surprised when Brandy insisted that Urbanek switch over to full time and greatly expand the teaching curriculum. There should be courses in personal hygiene for all of the help. The hygiene course should serve to reinforce the idea that everyone was to wear a clean, white uniform and use the new showers daily. If an outfit became soiled, the employee should change to one of his replacement outfits and immediately take the soiled clothes to the hotel laundry. The laundry would have instructions to give priority to the workers' white uniforms. If an employee was continually sloppy and could not keep up his appearance, he would have to be replaced.

Brandy wrote simple and clear how-to manuals for various phases of the hotel operation. He used a collection of army training manuals on every topic from fire safety to jeep maintenance and kitchen procedures, writing the texts in English. Urbanek then translated them into Spanish for use in the hotel courses. Brandy worked with a wide collection of other instructional material, including Lewis Hotel schoolbooks and Statler-Hilton guides, constantly gathering new materials. He set up standard operating procedures for every phase of the hotel, and Urbanek translated them into Spanish and taught them in regular classroom sessions.

With the increasing support and loyalty from the staff, Brandy instituted a number of practices that began to win repeat business. Each swimming pool was decorated daily with floating flowers. Every morning, a German-made thermos bottle with hot coffee was delivered to each room, together with a selection of sweet rolls and fresh fruit.

He found he had to follow through on his threat to fire an employee who was pocketing tip money, in this case a member of the Culinary Workers' Union. When the other employees complained that the punishment was too harsh, Brandy met with a group of them in Urbanek's classroom to explain his position. He asked how they could defend someone who had been stealing from *them*. They still grumbled that it was only a small theft, and to fire the man was a disproportionate punishment. After that experience, Brandy decided that the decision on punishment of workers caught pocketing tips should be left to the staff committee in charge of the gratuity fund and to the union representative. He would allow them to decide whether firing, suspension, or reprimand was appropriate. The system worked; even tips offered were not accepted.

Another reform that Brandy instituted was, like many of his ideas, a reflection of his military training. He tried to convince each department head that for every position needed, there were at least two backup employees who could step forward to fill the shoes of those who might resign, be fired, take vacation, or fall ill. As in the service, when a soldier fell, there had to be a backup. Furthermore, when one department had problems, other departments should pitch in and help for the overall good of the hotel.

Time passed swiftly from 1959 through 1964. Between supervising the Las Brisas Hilton and completing the Acapulco Hilton and managing it, Brandy was kept busy. In 1963, Alemán canceled Hilton's contract at the Acapulco Hilton. As a result, from 1963 to 1964, Brandy devoted himself to managing Las Brisas and increasing the cottages to 128 and adding new pools. On Brandy's fifty-second birthday, 26 March 1964, almost five years after he had arrived in Acapulco, Don Carlos called and said that he wanted to see him.

Brandy took the plane to Mexico City, first stopping to see the vice president of Hilton International, Arthur Elminger. There were rumors that Trouyet was going to cancel Hilton's contract, just as Alemán had done with the Acapulco Hilton. Brandy suggested that since Elminger was working for Hilton, he should go along with him to meet Trouyet. Under the circumstances, since Elminger was in charge, he should see what the owner wanted. Elminger told Brandy to go, listen, then return and see him. From a business and chain of command point of view, Brandy felt uncomfortable, but he went to meet Trouyet as Elminger instructed him.

Don Carlos was blunt.

"Frank," he said, "I am going to cancel Hilton's contract." Brandy thought, here I go again, out of work.

Don Carlos continued, "I have known you now for five years. I am going to sell the hotel, after Hilton is out of the picture, on 1 April 1964. I want you to stay on with me in Mexico. I will sell the hotel, and I will put you in charge of a company. You will have a life-time position."

Knowing that Don Carlos was a man of his word, Brandy started thinking. Then he turned to Don Carlos and asked how much he was asking for the hotel.

"I bought it for $800,000," said Carlos. "I will take a $400,000 tax loss and sell it for $400,000."

Again, Brandy made a mental calculation.

"Don Carlos," he said, "let's keep the hotel for two years. I feel I can turn it around. And if so, we will build additional *casitas*, each with its own pool. With 250 *casitas* it will become a gold-mine; the cash flow will be a perfect business."

Carlos said, "Frank, you're crazy."

"No, Don Carlos," said Frank. "You have my investment of $200,000 in hand. I will pay a balance of $200,000 from my income, totaling a $400,000 investment. Then we will become partners, as long as you give me a free hand in the operations." With some further conversation, they agreed. Carlos had Brandy's money, in the form of escrow, in his hands.

Brandy and Carlos shook hands, and thus Brandy became part owner of Las Brisas, effective 1 April 1964, after Hilton's contract was canceled. The Hilton contract would have expired in any case on 30 June 1964, a few months later. Brandy went back to Elminger and explained what had occurred.

Over the next twelve years, Brandy managed Las Brisas as a participant in the ownership, constantly building the business and converting it to fulfill its potential. He used his experience to build an *esprit de corps* among the staff and attract a steady clientele. Brandy realized that a considerable capital investment would be required to expand the number of *casitas*, complete the necessary promotions, and build a new bar, tennis courts, and other facilities. He knew the project could only go forward in several steps, each costing at least as much as the original investment. He developed the plans for expansion, with each private casita having its own pool.

He soon was able to take the first of several construction steps that would change Las Brisas from its status as an obscure group of *casitas* for the girlfriends of "Ali Baba's Forty Thieves" to the number one resort hotel in the world.

15

The International Set

During the 1960s, Acapulco began to flourish as a tourist attraction, and Brandy played a central role in that development through his work as managing director and vice president of the Las Brisas Hotel and as a participant in the operation, having invested $400,000 of his own money.

He personally supervised and pitched into the physical labor of building the La Concha Beach Club with its underwater retaining walls, using huge boulders as a base, then filling the openings with quick-drying cement bags. All of this work was accomplished using three scuba diving teams with three men each, every team working twenty minutes underwater, with thirty minutes rest. Brandy demonstrated the procedure to these scuba teams. For the construction of new *casitas*, each with its own pool, he used a similar technique of blasting out rock with low charges, and breaking the rock into manageable chunks. In effect, the building site became a quarry from which many of the building materials were obtained directly, representing a saving in construction and transport costs. The development, solidly engineered and sturdy, withstood several earthquakes and hurricanes over the following decades.

From 1966 to 1969 Brandy built "Fortress San Carlos," complete with castle battlements and dummy cannon pointed out over the harbor, commemorating the Spanish fortress that guarded against the British freebooter Sir Frances Drake in the sixteenth century. Within the fort, he built a secluded set of *casitas*, each with its own private swimming pool and controlled access, for celebrities and diplomatic guests who sought privacy.

Brandy took pride in the fact that there were no fatalities and few injuries on the massive construction projects that involved the use of tons of TNT. He worked sixteen- to eighteen-hour days, paying attention to every detail and constantly supervising the crews to complete the construction with safety in mind.

Through this same period, he worked diligently to keep the clients at the hotel happy. He joined many guests for lunch at La Concha, the hotel's private beach club, getting to know them personally, exchanging thoughts, providing solutions to their problems, and then following up with letters to them. His secretaries routinely turned out dozens of letters a day, replying to thank-you notes, responding to invitations, keeping current with old acquaintances from his days in the army, at the Orinda Country Club, from Sans Souci in Jamaica, and from Dallas, as well as with his many new-found friends and acquaintances from among the hotel clientele. The letters flowed continually, most in English or Spanish, with a few in German, French, and Hungarian.

From time to time newspapers and travel magazines picked up the story of the photogenic resort rising above the azure Bay of Acapulco. Clipping services in the United States sent everything they could find. By 1970, the newspaper clippings alone filled huge scrapbooks; the magazine reprints filled many boxes. As friends and former visitors read the items, they would often cut them out and send them on to Brandy, who would courteously reply with a personal note. This steady pattern of detailed personal contact through correspondence, combined with free publicity, resulted in a superb system of public relations.

Several larger factors were operating to draw visitors to Acapulco during the "Jet Set" era of the 1960s and 1970s. Eastern Airlines flew from New York to Acapulco; Western Airlines flew there from California; and Braniff Airlines from Dallas. Early in the 1960s, Eastern Airlines and Western Airlines worked out an arrangement to allow

Fortress San Carlos, Las Brisas, under construction and completed, 1960s.

passengers flying from coast to coast in the United States to travel via Acapulco. Travelers could stay a night or two, then continue at the same charge that it would cost for a direct coast to coast flight within the States. With the arrival of large jet aircraft and the reduction in price, the sleepy resort town boomed.

Acapulco had been noticed first by American tourists when Errol Flynn, accompanied by his bandleader friend Teddy Stauffer, visited the community on an extended fishing trip in 1940. Flynn sailed on to the Caribbean, but Stauffer stayed in Acapulco, opening a small night-club that attracted a theater and movie crowd from the States through the 1950s. By the early 1960s, when Brandy began to develop Las Brisas, a glittering international society, including a few famous American expatriates, began to emerge. Wealthy Mexican socialites, including Baroness Sandra and Baron Ricky Portanova, serving as honorary am-bassador at large of San Marino, joined the growing circle of friends in Acapulco. What had been an escape colony for the movie person-alities of the 1940s had become a mecca for "international set" travel-ers from Europe.

In addition, with the reduction in prices brought by larger jet air-craft and regular flights, even more Americans flocked to the new ho-tels opening along the beach. Through this period of growth, Las Brisas remained unique and rode the wave of popularity and excitement, con-stantly meeting the demand for high quality service and comfort.

The thorough procedures Brandy introduced paid off. The no-tip-ping policy, the clean white uniforms, the expertly-trained staff, the ex-cellent and safe food, a fleet of pink jeeps to provide transport up and down the hillside, and the use of pink and magenta color themes in flowers, decor, and letterhead, all added a flair of fantasy to the beauti-ful setting. Even if a bit studied, the magical atmosphere was tangible. Idyllic tropical nights, sea breezes, the privacy of individual swimming pools, and the erotic smell of night-blooming jasmine, would make ev-ery trip for a married couple seem like another honeymoon. Every vaca-tion would be a dream-like excursion to a world apart; every escape from the hectic world of Chicago or Los Angeles or Mexico City would be a chance to "recharge the batteries" and "get a new focus," to fully relax without interference from radios or television sets.

During this period, Brandy ran into an old friend, Peter Hope, at a restaurant in Mexico City. The two men immediately recognized each other. Hope was a former British intelligence officer whom Brandy encountered while in London during his British MI training period.

"What are you up to these days?" asked Hope.

"Oh," Brandy replied, not wanting to stress his success too much to the former military officer, "I'm running a little hotel down in Acapulco. And you?"

Hope replied, equally modestly, "Well, I am the queen's representative here. I'm the British ambassador to Mexico."

Brandy took a polite bow. "Pleased to meet you, your Excellency!" They both had a good laugh.

Over the next years, Hope became a regular guest at the hotel. With the rash of kidnapping and assassination attempts against diplomats during the 1960s, his position became nerve-wracking. He would often fly to Acapulco, staying incognito for several days, to fully relax so he could return to Mexico City refreshed. After the completion of Fortress San Carlos, Brandy would assign Hope to Room 469 for these hideaway stays because it was the most secure room in the complex, with its own indoor-outdoor swimming pool.

In 1969, Ambassador Hope realized that a British consul was needed for Acapulco, and asked Brandy if he knew of anyone who would be available to accept, as a permanent position, the tasks and duties that Brandy was already performing gratis. There would be very little compensation, but the honorary title might carry sufficient cachet to make the position attractive to someone with a nice home that could house the consular offices. Brandy knew that Derek Gore, the local manager of Qantas Airlines, was looking for a new position, as that company was cutting back on its service to Acapulco from Australia. When he contacted Gore, the young man was interested until he learned that the monthly "salary" was little more than an honorarium. "I won't even be able to afford a little apartment on that," he said, "let alone a consular office."

Brandy suggested to Hope that Las Brisas hire Gore as a public relations officer. That position would provide him a salary. Then Brandy could dedicate one of the *casitas* immediately behind the registration office to Gore, who could live there and maintain the consular office. There would be no charge to the British; Gore would meet all his consular obligations; and he would also put in a full day of work for the hotel. Hope accepted the arrangement, and for the next decade Las Brisas maintained the British consular office, complete with a plaque on the wall and the Union Jack flying in front, providing service to visiting British subjects and expatriates residing in Acapulco. Gore handled both the public relations and the consular positions well, and the panache of the consular office more than paid the hotel for any loss of revenue from the single casita. Visiting British tourists were bemused to note that their consular office was located at Las Brisas; some, like Peter Sellers, when writing an account of his stay for *Vogue* in July 1973, made special note of it.

Brandy succeeded in attracting and holding a repeating stream of guests, many of whom shared Hope's desire to stay out of the limelight. Although celebrities were shielded from public notice and interference from the press, other guests sometimes met or got glimpses of the rich and famous, adding to the glamour of their own stay. One *Miami Herald* item, dated 11 February 1968, reflected this element of attraction by association with the celebrities of the international set in its coverage of the resort:

> Acapulco is the mecca for migratory jet-setters, international financiers and corporation presidents, politicians, starlets and barons, dukes, counts and princes from countless countries. In the last few weeks the cast included George Hamilton, Tony Curtis, Millionaire Serge Semenenko, Herb Alpert, Bill Dana, Lizabeth Scott, Polly Bergen, Eva Gabor, Cesar Romero. Creature comforts ad nauseam add to the popularity of the city dubbed "La Dolce Vita West." Take, for instance, the pink all-over Las Brisas, a mountainside hotel that is really a collection of individual air-conditioned "*casitas*" (little houses), each surrounded with palms and hibiscus, each with a private or semi-private pool, each with a fully stocked bar plus bar guide and refrigerator full of fresh tropical fruits....

The news item continued for several more column inches with similar detail. With such news stories, one hardly had to pay for advertising.

Free publicity came in many forms. Graham Kerr, the gourmet chef of television fame with his own show, "The Galloping Gourmet," visited frequently. Brandy arranged a few public relations events for him, including a photo opportunity at La Concha. Brandy staged a humorous underwater scene in which an attractive woman and her companion sat down without face masks at the bottom of a swimming pool, at a table set with "food" created by Chef Rudi Walterspiel and Brandy, consisting of colored marzipan that would hold its shape and not dissolve. The pool had been built with a window in its wall from which guests could watch the swimmers. Through this window, a movie and still shots were taken. The film clip of this underwater scene, with reference to Las Brisas, brought humorous and repeated attention on television. One of Kerr's "Galloping Gourmet" cookbooks featured a picture of Kerr, Brandy, and a colorful parrot on the cover, as well as several Las Brisas specialties in the collection of recipes.

The little touches of hotel service proved important. At Easter, dozens of white rabbits were dyed pink with harmless vegetable dye and released around the hotel grounds to the delight of children staying with their parents. It was impossible to round up all of the rabbits, and some of them became wild, leaving descendants among the hills and gardens of that section of Acapulco.

In the mid-sixties Brandy organized "safaris," which foreshadowed the popular "adventure vacations" of three decades later. Often the guests would find the round of sunbathing, swimming, and cocktail hours somewhat dull after a week or so. The safaris used the pink and white hotel jeeps, which left in a caravan for a tour of Acapulco and a ride through the rough terrain of the coastal rural areas. Visitors could see how the locals lived and get a glimpse of the rugged interior immediately inland from the coast. One special touch reflected Brandy's knack for entertainment. After the hot and dusty drive, the jeeps pulled into a coconut grove, where by pre-arrangement, young boys would climb the trees and lop off fresh coconuts. The large green-encased nuts were brought to the jeeps and carefully examined by the guests. Then, with a slash of the machete, the nuts were hacked open. The guests drank from the coconuts through straws. To their surprise, they discovered the coconut milk was a strong coco-cocktail, laced with vodka. It was a trick, but one that everyone enjoyed. Brandy had instructed the boys to inject the vodka by syringe into the correct number of coconuts in the trees, before each group arrived.

In another demonstration of his flair for creative entertainment, Brandy set up a parasail operation. He ordered special pink and white parachutes from the United States, similar to those used to drop heavy equipment. These parachutes were designed with holes in them to slow their descent. The slow-descending parachutes allowed most of the guests, including women and teenage children, to enjoy the thrill of being towed into the air behind a high-speed boat. Several bright photographs of Brandy himself, the ex-paratrooper, cigar clamped in his teeth, fully clothed, and flying in a parachute above Acapulco Bay, found their way into hotel publicity and into his collection. Doing this, he demonstrated to the guests that it was a safe sport.

Brandy parasails in Acapulco Bay, 1972.

Often the visitors to the hotel opened new opportunities for Brandy. One interesting and tantalizing chance came very early, in 1963, when Josip Broz Tito, the president of Yugoslavia, stayed at Las Brisas. An official of Mexico's Foreign Office called and explained that Tito was coming to stay for a few days, under a news blackout, and that he should be provided with every comfort. Brandy had no idea how large the entourage would be, so he called the Yugoslav Embassy in Mexico City, requesting all the details from the chief of protocol, including a list of recipes that Marshal Tito and his wife liked, a collection of liqueurs and wines, and even a list of the favorite Yugoslav folk songs that the dictator preferred. He passed the recipes to Rudi Walterspiel, the head chef formerly of the Hotel Vier Jahres Zeiten in Munich, and the music to his bandleader, Freddy Guzmán. He had menus printed in Serbo-Croatian.

At first Tito stayed in his private residence, but as he learned of the food and music from home in the dining room, he joined the group there. Tito and his entourage enjoyed the trip so much that he extended the visit by an extra week. The prolonged stay presented a dilemma for the Mexican Ministry of Foreign Affairs; Prime Minister de Gaulle of France was due to arrive, and it would be inappropriate to have two heads of state visiting at the same time. When word came that Tito should move on, Brandy was perplexed. He could not very well evict a head of state!

Nevertheless, he had lunch with Tito, and the two chatted amiably in German and Hungarian. Brandy knew that his background had been checked because Tito called him "colonel." He invited Brandy to move to Yugoslavia and create a new international tourist industry there, utilizing some old fortress areas like Dubrovnik on the Adriatic. Brandy also met the Chief of Protocol, Dabor Soldatic, who was promoted later on to Yugoslav ambassador to Mexico. Brandy got to know him well, and together they shared memories of World War II.

Voluntarily, with no urging, Tito left before de Gaulle arrived. Brandy kept his photos of the Tito visit in his collection and maintained his contacts in Belgrade; years later, when he traveled to the region, the pictures and the contacts proved useful.

Brandy considered the opportunity to move to Yugoslavia and set up the resort program, but when he checked with ACSI, they "nixed" it.

Yugoslavian president Josip
Tito with Frank Brandstetter
at Las Brisas in 1963.

It was not acceptable to have someone with a Top Secret clearance working in a Communist country. Brandy thought the ACSI missed a great
opportunity to have a window on the Eastern Bloc through Communist
Yugoslavia, but he agreed to stay put, as ordered.

Through the 1960s Brandy corresponded with hoteliers, resort managers, travel agents, travel magazine publishers, and government officials concerned with tourism. In 1968, Las Brisas was selected by *Esquire*
magazine as one of twenty-nine of the world's most outstanding hotels,
only nine years after Brandy had become resident manager of the small,
bankrupt cottage colony. Consequently, when Brandy traveled that summer to Britain, he wrote to the managing director of Claridge's and
Connaught Hotels, also members of the twenty-nine. He reserved a room,
declaring that he did not want a special rate, but that he intended to
visit as a full paying guest. This sort of contact drew the attention of
other hotel men around the world and emphasized the ranking of Las
Brisas with its peers.

Brandy's excellent management attracted the international set, bringing sophisticated and accomplished European travelers, many of them accustomed to the first class resorts of the Mediterranean. As he succeeded in attracting such demanding guests, soon many others followed, often drawn by the knowledge that famous, talented, and titled people of great wealth stayed at Las Brisas. In addition to such members of the international set, thousands of more ordinary tourists began to flock to Acapulco. Brandy concentrated on winning the international set as customers; the tourists followed in their wake.

Brandy worked closely with George Walsh, an advertising agent in New York, who continued to place items, small and large, in the world press. The *Travel Weekly* magazine of 16 July 1968 carried an item featuring Las Brisas, drawing the attention of former friends and contacts in several nations. *Hotel and Motel Management* carried a sensitive and thorough treatment in its January 1970 issue. That particular article attempted to capture Brandy's philosophy of management, focusing on his system of providing incentives, training, and advancement to workers who were treated equally, without ranks. Each held a position of responsibility. The system would work anywhere, he claimed, including the United States. "There isn't anything a man can't do if he puts his mind to it," Brandy said in response to the interviewer's questions.

Esquire featured the hotel in its October 1971 issue. The *Miami Herald* Sunday supplement *Tropic* carried a cover story, dated 2 July 1972 and titled "The Pink Playground," by Richard Joseph, the travel writer for *Esquire*. Brandy collected reprints of these items for a "Las Brisas Information Kit," which also included colorful postcards, together with a swimsuit catalog featuring photos of models at Las Brisas, issued by Nieman Marcus. The possibilities for publicity mushroomed.

In 1972, the American Society of Travel Agents (ASTA) ranked Las Brisas as one of the top three hotels in the world. In the category of resort hotels, they ranked Las Brisas as *the first resort hotel in the world*. Former President of Mexico, Miguel Alemán, personally presented the ASTA award to Brandy in a ceremony at the hotel. The achievement itself was newsworthy, and became a featured item in articles about the hotel published over the next few years.

Brandy receives ASTA award signifying Las Brisas as the number one resort hotel in the world.

Repeat customers all received equal attention. Embassy and consulate staff, military officers, clergymen, industrialists, hotel men from the States, airline representatives, magazine and newspaper editors and executives, medical doctors, attorneys, and bankers received the same personal treatment and follow-up correspondence as did chiefs of state, relatives of presidents and monarchs, and world-renowned movie personalities. One correspondent after another testified to the dreamlike quality of their stay at Las Brisas, often explicitly referring to the sense of returning to reality when they reached home. Brandy's replies reminded them that their dream was, after all, real, and could be enjoyed again with another trip. On every sheet of the pink stationery he mailed out, a tag line at the top brought back the memories: 200 POOLS, 150 PINK JEEPS, 250 ROOMS, "The only Hotel in the World where every Room has a Swimming Pool, sharing or private."

The special attention and courtesies guests received inspired them to become unpaid promoters of the hotel, as evidenced continually in the letters sent to Brandy. Many of them mentioned that they had praised the hotel, its hospitality, and Brandy personally to prospective guests, including their relatives, friends, employers, co-workers, and associates. A tax commissioner in Texas noted good-naturedly that he would have to stop showing his home movies of Las Brisas, since it convinced everyone to visit. Time and again, one customer would yield two more; and each of those would become advocates and representatives. Growth by word of mouth was exponential; winter seasons were fully booked, and the summer was nearly as full. Journalist friends would constantly run stories mentioning Las Brisas; the clipping files bulged with stories from the *Los Angeles Times*, the *Miami Herald*, and the *Chicago Tribune*, as well as with articles from the international travel magazines.

When anything went amiss, Brandy was sure to carry out every effort to correct the situation. When in 1968, one of the Easter rabbits was found dead near a *casita*, concerned parents remembered that their daughter had been playing with the animal and had been bitten. They feared rabies. The rabbit was sent to a laboratory in Mexico for testing while the parents returned to Michigan. When inconclusive results came back from the Mexican lab, Brandy instructed a hotel staff member to fly the sample to Michigan and personally follow through with a laboratory test there to ensure there was no infection. All turned out fine. The extra effort and support provided by the hotel converted what could have been a tragic incident into yet another graciously handled detail and won the hotel another supporter.

Las Brisas was fun for staff as well as guests. One day Pepe Salinas, one of the assistant managers, relayed an account of a peculiar incident. Brandy had instructed all of the help to meet every guest's requests, no matter how outlandish, as long as they were legal. One guest asked the housekeeper for a "burro." She was puzzled, and relayed the message to her supervisor. He agreed the American might be a little eccentric, but the request was certainly legal and could be met. Accordingly, members of the staff hurried into town, purchased a burro in the marketplace, drove it back to the hotel in a truck, washed and dried it, and brushed out its fur. The animal patiently allowed the staff to decorate it with a hat, ribbons, and pink flowers, and then they led it by a halter, slowly and carefully, up the steep staircases that connected the *casitas* on the hillside. A small procession of onlookers followed, wondering what was afoot.

At the guest's *casita*, the head housekeeper knocked on the door. The American was astounded to see the burro there. "Per your request, sir," said the housekeeper.

The guest simply stared, dumbfounded. The housekeeper went on. "You asked for a burro this morning, sir. Here it is, as requested."

"No," the American replied, still working on his Spanish, "I wanted a *burro de planchar*, an ironing-board, not a donkey!"

The staff cracked up, and the story became an instant legend that spread through the hotel.

Brandy had an idea. "Pepe," he said, "why don't you ask the staff to get you all of these stories, all of the strange and funny little incidents, and bring them to me."

A couple of weeks later, Salinas supplied Brandy with a handful of anecdotes. In addition to the burro story, there were others: one guest, after a bout of overindulgence that caused a severe hangover, wandered out for a dip in his private pool. Staring at him across the pool was a pink rabbit. The guest rushed back in and called for the house doctor, assuming he had the D.T.'s. It took a sedative and reassurance to get rid of his case of the heebie-jeebies.

Brandy asked his public relations people to write the stories up as a skit, to be performed just for the staff. He hoped they would get a good laugh at themselves and at the amusing crises that arose from crossing the language barrier and meeting every whim of the clientele. When the skit was performed in the classroom over the dining room, the staffers roared with laughter. The little play was so much fun that it was presented several times. After adding some professional touches, it was performed at least three times as a public charity event in a large movie house, with the governor of the state, the mayor, and the area's commanding generals and navy admirals in attendance.

Important guests were singled out for special attention, and the files soon bulged with full folders containing "Special Attention" and "VIP" letters and instructions. When a couple like Mr. and Mrs. Sam Newhouse of the Newhouse publishing group, representing over forty magazines, came to visit, Brandy would alert the staff to block the rooms, make

The Las Brisas Theatre Group after a performance in Acapulco.

contact regarding special dishes to be served, provide a car with driver, and set up flowers for the room. The list of people receiving such special treatment became extensive; Brandy would mark the reservation request with a rubber stamp and forward it through the affected departments with the instructions indicated by a check against the terms:

• Special Attention
• Credit Okay
• Call on Arrival
• Flowers

Later the stamp was replaced with a neatly printed form, with all of the special instructions spelled out for checking. Soon the procedure generated bulky documentation, with entire mimeographed lists typed by staff to account for the special guests. One three-week period from December 1968 to January 1969 showed, among dozens of others, these guests:

Sam Houston Johnson	Brother of President Lyndon Johnson
John O'Brien	General Manager, N.Y. Life Insurance Co.

Sy Weintraub	Film maker; repeat guest
Jack Musick	President of Hiram Walkers
John Randal Hearst	Head of *Town and Country* Magazine
J. Franco	Ambassador of Morocco to USA
Von Haffner	Ambassador of Denmark to Mexico
Guillermo Budib & fam.	Personal aide to Pres. Diaz Ordaz
Joe Moran	White House Counsel
Charles Bear	Director of *Time* and *Life*
Maurice Stans	U.S. Secretary of Commerce
Buzz Aldrin	Astronaut; repeat guest
Jim Cernan	Astronaut
Hale Boggs	U.S. Senator, Louisiana

The presence of the astronauts among the guests was no simple co-incidence. As the space project got underway, with the Mercury, Gemini, and Apollo programs, Brandy contacted NASA and extended the hospitality of Las Brisas to the astronauts, their wives, and children. Many repeatedly took him up on the offer. He only required that they pay the gratuity charge of five dollars per day per room, but the rooms and all other charges themselves were comped. He arranged with Eastern and Western Airlines to discount the cost of the flight to the lowest fare possible. As a consequence, the astronauts returned repeatedly with their wives for seclusion, rest, and relaxation in the private *casitas*. Several noted the visits in their memoirs, published years later.

Brandy was particularly conscious of the stress that the space program placed on the marriages of the astronauts. The concept of providing secluded visits for astronauts and their wives, he believed, helped restore several of the marriages and keep many of the astronauts, increasingly in the public eye, from marital crises, separations, and possible divorces. Thus the quiet vacations were not only a nice, personal thank-you gesture to a group of genuine American heroes, but were an unobtrusive way of ensuring the public image of the program.

Many of the astronauts presented Brandy with autographed copies of photos of themselves, with shots of the moon's surface, and with other space memorabilia, including a few items they had taken into space. Several of the gifts from the astronauts had special significance. Before the Apollo 11 liftoff, the first flight to land on the moon, Brandy purchased six small gold crosses at the Mexico City airport as he was on his way to Cape Canaveral to watch the launch. He had the crosses blessed by a priest in front of Buzz Aldrin, and asked him to take them to the moon. The lunar landing capsule for the flight had been weighed to the ounce, and many requests for special commemorative items had been rejected, although an official medal, a postage-stamp cancellation, and other items were packed into the tight cabin of the lunar lander. Aldrin took the handful of miniature crosses and put them in his pocket.

After the flight, Nick Ruwe, a State Department official in Washington, arranged a reception for the Apollo 11 astronauts at the American ambassador's residence in Mexico City. Brandy and Ruwe became friends, and as Ruwe continued in government service, rising to become a close aide of Richard Nixon, the two men kept in contact. At the reception organized by Ruwe, Brandy greeted Aldrin, noting that his handshake was clammy with perspiration. Aldrin explained that he was overwhelmed by the attention he had received and confessed to Brandy that he hated appearing in public. Silently, he took from his pocket a facial tissue; in it were wrapped five of the crosses, which he handed over to Brandy. Brandy demurred, saying that three of them should go to the astronauts. He did, however, take two. One he gave to Don Carlos; the other he kept. He assumed the sixth cross was on the moon, and would be there forever. Later, during a congressional investigation of the Apollo 11 mission, Aldrin admitted taking crosses to the moon, angering Senator Jacob Javits, who argued that if one religion was represented, others should have been represented as well. Later, Aldrin spent several secluded stays at Las Brisas, recuperating from the emotional pressures of his celebrity status. Even though he was a decorated Korean War flyer, publicity was not his cup of tea. Brandy retained the single cross that had been to the moon, later placing it in his space museum at home.

Other astronauts gave him mission badges and U.S. flags taken to the moon and back. On maps of the moon, a small crater was designated the "Brandy" crater. All such items found their way, properly documented, into his collection. The intrinsic value of the gifts at the time was low, usually a personalized gift with a value less than five dollars. Of course, as the Apollo project acquired historic importance, and as the gifts became not simply ordinary items, but memorabilia of a momentous event, they would take on another kind of value, far beyond their intrinsic worth. But Brandy adhered strictly to his no-tipping rule, asking that gifts which cost more than five dollars not be offered to either himself or his wife, or to any of the staff.

Word leaked out that on one orbit of the earth, one of the mission commanders altered, ever so slightly, the orbit so the astronauts could pass directly over Acapulco and take a photograph, from outer space, of the resort city they had enjoyed so much. This deviation from plan also became a subject of congressional inquiry, suggesting that the sidebar trip had been unauthorized. Brandy eventually received a framed copy of the picture of Acapulco taken from space, adding it to his collection.

The lists of special attention and VIP guests often included many who were friends of someone else of significance, such as Serge Semenenko, Carlos Trouyet, and Diaz Ordaz, the president of Mexico. The papal delegate to Mexico, cardinals, bishops, ambassadors, business executives, actors, military officers, statesmen, and publishers fleshed out the long rosters. As the purple mimeographed lists of names

Astronaut Neil Armstrong at a New Year's Eve party at Las Brisas, 1970. Photo by Guillermo Ochoa.

in the VIP files grew, they provided an index, and perhaps a defining collection, for some future social analyst of precisely who represented the "International Set" of the era.

The technique of publicity through word of mouth, through influential guests, and freely placed articles, all recommending the genuinely unique and excellent service at the hotel, reflected a curious ambivalence and duality in Brandy's character and assignment. It was essential that the hotel receive favorable notices, and he was very good at achieving that. Despite his attempts to remain in the background, his striking personality often made him a central feature of the articles. Frequently, he felt that publicity about himself could interfere with his obligation to serve as a reserve intelligence officer. On the other hand, as more publicity became attached to his name as a hotel man, observers would have less reason to believe that he was also engaged as a volunteer in government service.

He continued reporting to ACSI through the 1960s, coming to realize that he was one of a small, select group of active Army Reserve officers reporting to the Pentagon. In fact, he learned of only three others: a Protestant clergyman in Africa, an industrialist in Brazil, and a colleague, a banker in the Philippines, with whom he communicated and met from time to time. As far as he knew they were the extent of the ACSI network, although, because such information was properly compartmentalized, there may have been a few others. He did not need to know, and he did not ask.

In any case, he did not want to endanger his value to the service by publicity that would reveal that he was, indeed, engaged in supplying information on a regular basis to his "Big Brothers" in the Pentagon. On his reporting trips to Washington, he would meet his contact either at his hotel or the National Airport, very rarely actually stopping by the Pentagon. This reduced the chance that some casual observer, who knew him from Acapulco, would connect him with officialdom.

In the Autumn 1972 issue of *Travel and Leisure*, the duality of his character and his ambivalence towards publicity reached a crisis. The nonfiction author and *New Yorker* staff writer John McPhee wrote a very interesting characterization of both the hotel and its manager. It featured a dazzling picture of Brandy, wearing a white shirt and broad-

Las Brisas was a resort haven for many celebrities. Included here are actress Debbie Reynolds (above) and television producer Sheldon Leonard (below).

Robert Kennedy and his family visited Las Brisas in the early 1960s.

Edward G. Robinson and friends chat over lunch at Las Brisas.

brimmed hat, looking enigmatic against the backdrop of the Las Brisas Hotel *casitas*, with Acapulco Bay and Beach in the distant background.

McPhee, despite Brandy's emphasis on the hotel staff in the interview, focused on Brandy himself. During an interruption, he browsed a bit in Brandy's library, noting the rich collection of signed and autographed works, including *Lamia* from Philippe de Vosjoli, with its printed dedication to Brandstetter. McPhee jumped to a conclusion which was near the truth, but factually inaccurate. McPhee hinted that Brandy was working for the CIA. Brandy was irritated at this treatment for several reasons: it came uncomfortably close to identifying his actual intelligence role, which he had labored to keep quiet, and wrongly associated him with the Central Intelligence Agency. Like many in army intelligence, Brandy had his doubts about the efficacy of the "Company," even though he had great respect for many individual officers and station chiefs with whom he had worked. Yet he always remembered how CIA staff in Washington had scoffed at his warning in 1959 that Castro would turn to the Left, unless Americans directed resources to Camilo Cienfuegos and his Christian revolutionary *barbudos*.

When Brandy saw the proofs of the *Travel and Leisure* article, he was distraught. He offered to place a major schedule of advertising, worth tens of thousands of dollars, with the magazine if the article was changed to give emphasis and credit to the staff of the hotel as originally agreed. The editors refused to eliminate him from the article and ran it as written.

The article in *Travel and Leisure* brought over nine hundred letters to Brandy from old acquaintances, former guests, and potential visitors. A few noted in passing, and with some humor, McPhee's hint about intelligence activities, but most simply congratulated Brandy on the excellent coverage that the hotel and his management received. Over the years, however, rumors founded on McPhee's article persisted that Brandy was an "undercover station chief" for the CIA. From time to time visitors would insist that they knew the "real" story behind the enigma, based on nothing more than a memory of the article or hearing a version of it from someone else.

The ASTA ranking of Las Brisas as the best resort hotel in the world was well earned. The management and flair of Las Brisas echoed what

Brandy had learned at the St. Moritz with its international clientele, at the Roney Plaza with its concern for excellent service and its European flavor, and what he had observed in other first class hotels around the world. Brandy, drawing on his rich resources of experience, managerial systems, army methods, emphasis on continuous training, and his own personal qualities of charm, focused energy, hospitality, creative thinking, and certitude, had succeeded, in slightly more than a decade, in taking Las Brisas from obscurity to first rank in the world.

But it was not enough. He would next turn his attention to building a secluded villa for himself and a church that would bring other dimensions to the *dolce-vita*, the sweet life of Acapulco.

16

A Villa in Paradise; A Chapel in Gomorrah

randy worked with Carlos Trouyet in the late 1960s to develop the mountainous land on the rocky slopes behind Las Brisas into a residential development, Club Residencial Las Brisas. Using the same construction techniques employed in blasting the roads into the cliffs for the hotel *casitas*, he opened a luxury development at the end of the 1960s. As he had with the *casitas* at Las Brisas and with Fortress San Carlos, Brandy created his dream by working as his own architect, engineer, and general contractor. He ordered the materials to clear the roadways and the construction sites. He also supervised the subcontractor, Señor Vázques, and Juan Martinez, a recent university graduate in architecture. His direct handling of all phases of the contracting saved the operation hundreds of thousands of dollars that would have been spent for a prime contractor's fees and markup. The completed homes in the Club sold for prices ranging from a few hundred thousand dollars to over a million. The Club Residencial Las Brisas soon filled with lavish estates.

Barbara needed constant care through this period, alternating between visits to a nursing facility near Dallas and stays in Brandstetter's two-room *casita* at Las Brisas. Brandy conceived of the idea of building his own villa, overlooking the rest of the Residential Club and Las Brisas

Hotel *casitas* below. As he designed the house, he blended together several considerations: security, self-sufficiency, entertainment, comfort for Barbara, a magnificent view, and the demands of the terrain. The villa which emerged from these interwoven demands was unique, and bore Brandy's personal stamp. His plan at first was to construct a small, two-room cottage, much like the double *casita* he had at Las Brisas. But as the construction began, he decided to make the place more comfortable, adding rooms and expanding their size.

Above the road, a massive, curved forty-five-foot retaining wall of stone, strengthened by buttresses, provided the terraced area for the house. Like all the walls throughout Las Brisas and the Residential Club, they were one-third as thick at the base as their height, providing tremendous stability. A sixty-foot-long, kidney-shaped pool, with a blue mosaic bottom, dominated the area in front of the house, with ample space around the pool to accommodate dozens of guests. During construction, a huge boulder, about ten feet in diameter, blocked the building work. Instead of blasting it away, Brandy incorporated it into the design. It became a centerpiece of the covered portal or interior patio. Floors of onyx surrounded the boulder, and two holes were drilled in it

Boulder in foyer of Brandy's home, Casa de la Tranquilidad.

to allow a running fountain of water to play over the rock and cascade into a shallow pool immediately around it. Evaporation from this boulder and pool cooled the open portal area.

Facing this open portal, to the left, were three connecting rooms with two baths. The master bedroom was light and airy, with white marble floors and a fourteen-foot-high ceiling, a cheerful room for his wife. Through one door was a study and library; through another was a room for a nurse, who could easily enter should Barbara need her on short notice. At the end of the pool nearest the bedroom, very shallow and gradual steps led down into the water, so that Barbara would have no trouble lowering herself into the pool. The risers in all the steps throughout the villa were kept low, making it easy and safe for an invalid.

On the other side of the interior portal, to the right, a large dining room and a well-equipped kitchen, with pantry, provided for entertainment. It was the dining room that Brandy later converted to a museum for his photos and artifact collections, with ample closets behind it for storage of costumes and party equipment.

Beneath the main rooms he added an entirely self-sufficient complex of subterranean quarters. Included were bedrooms for household personnel and guests, a massive kitchen for cooking on a larger scale, and an assembly room or theater for films. In later years, the theater served as a command post for the White House Communication Center and Secret Service detachments, and even later, as a storage room for Brandy's overflowing archives. Brandy had thought it might serve as an emergency hospital, in time of need.

Behind the covered interior portal, a winding flagstone path with steps led down to the interior parking area; a flagged driveway inclined steeply down to two massive wooden doors set in the outside wall, a copy of a cathedral's doors. One servant's room was directly over the gate; in the traditional style of European castles, the gatekeeper could literally be on watch at the door should there be a need.

With the large underground kitchen and assembly area, the house would have been quite secure had there been a problem of nuclear fallout from an international war, a concern of many homebuilders around the world in the 1960s. Brandy had calculated the direction of fallout from a possible nuclear attack on Los Angeles, and based his concern on those estimates. Later, as weapons of greater megatonnage were produced, he realized that there would be no escape from fallout anywhere in the world. Noting that an earthquake fault lay forty miles off- shore, he built the walls and structure with possible quakes in mind.

Brandy, with mock-modesty, would sometimes refer to the home as his "little hermit cave," and to himself as "the hermit of the mountain." With its underground chambers and insured privacy, the villa could indeed serve as a retreat from the world; yet few hermits had ever possessed such beautiful and luxurious quarters.

"Casa de la Tranquilidad," or House of Tranquility, as Brandy named the home, represented a culmination of many different, and sometimes conflicting, elements of Brandy's character. On the one hand, the home was a perfect place for entertaining. He was able to host large international backgammon tournaments in the home in the mid-1970s, with scores of people in attendance. On the other hand, the home could be intensely private, with full seclusion from the outside, complete control over access, and security at a level matching that of Fortress San Carlos at Las Brisas. Both features of the home—comfort and security—would come into play as he welcomed a variety of guests over the following decades.

The home captured other elements of his life as well. His concern that Barbara be provided a comfortable place where she could share her life with him, despite her physical condition, reflected his loyalty to her and his concern with her well being. The open, roofed-over portal facing the pool contained elements from the *casita* designs at Las Brisas, in which a private pool and patio in front of every room faced the view of Acapulco. The library, study, growing archives, and eventually the museum, served to capture mementos of his travels, adventures, and contacts, and provide a display for his growing collection of awards. Specially-constructed furniture, including onyx backgammon tables and glass-topped dining tables, allowed for entertainment at a lavish, yet intimate, level, reflecting his years of experience in first-class hotels.

Brandy completed the home in 1971 and promptly moved in. Next door, he constructed a home intended for Edgar Bronfman, the president of Seagrams. When Bronfman and his wife visited the home as it neared completion, they decided that it was too small, and later had a pair of homes constructed for their children and guests in Acapulco. Brandy was able to arrange the sale of the next-door villa to his million-aire friend, W. Clement Stone, who had earned a fortune combining an international insurance firm and an inspirational self-help institute. Brandy met Stone at the 1968 Republican convention; Stone was the largest individual cash contributor to the presidential campaign of Richard Nixon. Stone was charmed by the villa and happily bought it, living there as Brandy's neighbor over the next two decades.

The Club Residencial thrived, and profits from the land sales accu-mulated rapidly. Yet there was a quality of the carefree life in Acapulco that dissatisfied Brandy through the mid- and-late 1960s. As the jet set flocked into the resort, the *dolce-vita* reputation of the city ran counter to his policy of attracting families and married couples to the hotel. He had made it a rule to quietly refuse service to guests known to be using dope or marijuana. Yet despite such efforts, the city had acquired a he-donistic reputation. He hit on an idea to offset that reputation: he would set aside some land at the crest of the hill, purchased with profits from the Residential Club, for a nondenominational chapel that could be seen from most of the city. As he thought through the concept, he re-membered the occasion when Buzz Aldrin presented him with the crosses that he brought back from the moon. This presentation inspired Brandy to visualize a large cross next to the chapel. Perhaps, Brandy thought, we could create in Acapulco a symbol of decency.

Although Mexico is famous for its hundreds of churches and doz-ens of cathedrals, many of them magnificent examples of ecclesiastic architecture, few churches had been built there in the modern era. The anti-clerical nature of the Mexican Revolution of 1913–1919, and the position of the PRI government since that time, had strongly discour-aged the influence and power of the Church. Priests were not permit-ted to wear vestments outside of church; and the properties of the Church had been confiscated by the state. In this political environment, to build a church could be a controversial step.

Carlos Trouyet, his partner, at first had mixed feelings when Brandy broached the idea to him. Although concerned about possible opposi-tion or retribution from the government, several events over the next few years won Don Carlos's full support for the chapel and cross project.

Don Carlos had four sons, of whom the oldest were Carlos, Jr., and Jorge. When Don Carlos and his wife, Millie, found it difficult to discipline their sons, they would send them to Brandy, who put them to work in the various construction projects at Las Brisas. In the mid-1960s, Brandy encouraged Carlos, Jr., to take up the study of Portuguese bullfighting, in which the bull is not killed and the bullfighters work from horseback. Carlos, Jr., traveled to Portugal and, with his father's blessing, returned with a stable of horses and a master trainer. He later performed in Mexico City and Acapulco and drew large crowds. Some of the American hotel guests found this form of bullfighting much more to their taste than the traditional Spanish and Mexican *corrida*, in which the relatively helpless bull is slaughtered and its bloody body then dragged from the arena. Although the Portuguese-style show was a curiosity and attracted attention, no regular support for horseback bullfighting could be developed in Mexico.

Young Carlos moved into the management of the Trouyet businesses with his brother, Jorge, traveling regularly between Acapulco and Mexico City. They often flew back and forth in their own twin-engine Piper.

Standing to the right of Brandy are Carlos Trouyet, Jr., and his brother Jorge at Las Brisas. Photo by Guillermo Ochoa.

On 13 November 1968, Brandy met with thirty-year-old Carlos and twenty-nine-year-old Jorge, discussing business late into the afternoon. They explained to Brandy that they would be flying back to Mexico City that night. Brandy tried to talk them out of it, urging them to stay over at a *casita* at the hotel. He was planning to fly to Mexico City himself the next morning by commercial airline, and they could all go to the airport together. No, they insisted, why not come to the airport and fly home with us? Brandy agreed, picked up his overnight bag, and drove the group to the airport.

The small plane could hold three passengers and the pilot. Brandy, Carlos, Jorge, and Carlos's girlfriend squeezed into the seats and Carlos started the engines to taxi the plane to the take-off runway. At that moment they spotted Trouyet's engineer, who was in charge of building Sanborn's store in Acapulco. He was running across the tarmac with his briefcase, hailing the plane. When the plane stopped, the engineer breathlessly explained that he had to get to Mexico City immediately. Since Brandy still had his reservations for the morning flight on Mexicana Airlines, he gave up his seat and waved the four off, then returned to his office at Las Brisas.

At seven that night, working at his desk, he received a call from Don Carlos, who asked whether the boys had decided to stay over. No, Brandy explained, the plane took off nearly two hours before. Clearly it was overdue. A round of hectic telephoning followed. Brandy soon discovered that the air control tower at Mexico City Airport had reported a private plane that had simply stopped transmitting by radio as it approached the city earlier in the evening. A search was mounted the next morning with helicopters and chartered planes. Brandy participated, flying with Manuel Arrango, a friend of Carlos and Jorge. Eventually, the four-seat Piper was spotted, crashed on a mountain slope near Mexico City. All the passengers had been killed on impact. Brandy went to the site and assisted in the sad process of identifying the bodies, as he was the only person alive who had seen the final seating arrangement.

The two Trouyet brothers were interred in a cemetery in Mexico City. When Brandy visited the gravesites a few months later, he found them unkempt and neglected, and he urged Don Carlos to transfer the remains to a more suitable place, a crypt below the proposed chapel.

Don Carlos agreed that the bodies could be moved there when the chapel was ready. The grief of Don Carlos, his wife Millie, and Brandy became a driving force to bring the dream of a chapel to reality.

On 19 March 1969, Brandy and Fr. Peter Nicholas Kurguz climbed above Las Brisas to choose the site for the chapel, scratching a cross on a granite rock outcropping. Kurguz gave a blessing to the site, and the two men sat for several hours visualizing the chapel and its magnificent view over Acapulco and down the coast.

Brandy asked Brother Gabriel y Chavez, a church architect, to design an A-frame chapel to be erected at the crest selected by Brandy and Fr. Kurguz, overlooking the Club Residencial and Las Brisas Hotel. Actual construction and cutting of the roads began in August 1969, and the chapel in May 1970. Following the wishes of Brandy and Don Carlos, the chapel, unlike many churches in Mexico, was to be nondenominational. It was to be a church of all faiths, open to scheduling of Catholic masses as well as to various Protestant services and individual meditation. Eventually, there were Jewish and Moslem ceremonies conducted there as well. The design was inspirational, taking advantage of the site with open vistas over the bay and small flowing ponds and cascades of water to cool the surrounding grounds.

Brandy asked the church architect to design the chapel to include 120 burial crypts beneath it to be offered free of charge on a first-come, first-served basis to anyone who wished to be buried there. Brandy ordered a cross to be erected next to the chapel. Illuminated with floodlights from below, the cross became a beacon over the city at night.

It was the wish of both Don Carlos and Brandy that the site of the chapel and the cross should be turned over to the public of Acapulco as a donation from them both. They also agreed, at Brandy's suggestion, that the total cost would not be deducted from Mexican or American income taxes, the cost being covered from their own personal funds as a gift to the people of Acapulco.

During the construction of the cross, Brandy took a trip to Rio de Janiero and realized that the great cross overlooking Ipanema and Copacabana Beaches was the approximate height above sea level as the one being built in Acapulco. On his return, he ordered that the cross

Frank proposed a chapel and cross atop the hill of Club Residencial to counter the *dolce-vita* reputation of Acapulco.

The lighted cross above the city of Acapulco provided inspiration and encouragement to many who beheld it.

under construction be extended by about ten meters; making it 170.5 feet above its foundation, a few feet higher than the one in Rio. After another trip to Paris, Brandy bought a small copy of the Rodin sculpture of praying hands. He then found an artist in Guadalajara, Mexico, and ordered a large eighteen-foot model. It was cast and placed next to the cross and chapel.

Millie Trouyet, the wife of Don Carlos, provided encouragement and suggestions for the design. During the final days of construction, on 29 April 1970, she died and never saw the completed building. She was buried next to her sons in the cemetery in Mexico City.

At the unfinished chapel, Brandy turned on the lights for the cross for the first time at a candlelight mass on Christmas Eve, 1970. Grieving and weakened by cancer, Don Carlos visited the chapel only once, in February 1971, to see the final resting-place of his sons, his wife, and himself. Brandy supported him as he stared, with a quiet stoicism, at the open crypts. Don Carlos died a month later, in March 1971, and Brandy personally lowered the caskets of Millie, Jorge, and Carlos, Jr., into the crypt. He placed Don Carlos's ashes there as well, fulfilling his wish of February. The first official funeral mass and burial was conducted in the chapel on 20 April 1971.

In 1974, Pope Paul VI honored Brandy with the papal award, "Pro Ecclesia et Pontifice," which was presented at a ceremony at the chapel, the Capilla de la Paz. It was presided over by Jose Quezada Valdez, the bishop of Acapulco, Fr. Peter Nicholas Kurguz, O.P., and Fr. Angel Martinez Galena. The award, created in 1888 by Pope Leo XIII, was granted over the years to secular individuals who were great benefactors of the Church. The Pope conferred the award to Brandy in recognition for "the good work which he has accomplished through his Christian zeal and efforts in promoting and directing the construction of the Chapel of Peace and Cross" in Acapulco.

Father Kurguz, during his sermon accompanying the award, pointed out that the cross, illuminated at night, had served as an inspiration to many individuals in Acapulco. Some tourists had told him that they had been considering taking their own lives, but upon seeing the cross, they had turned their thoughts to God for strength and courage, and "they received it." Father Kurguz fell ill after the church was opened, and stayed intermittently for two years in a small apartment below the chapel. He credited his recovery partly to the inspirational surroundings.

Padre Angel Martinez Galena, who had set up an orphanage in Acapulco, often officiated at chapel services. Brandy was an avid supporter of the orphanage, conducting charity events and making monetary contributions to the facility. The cross was built, Padre Angel said at a sermon at the chapel, to serve as a beacon for all Acapulquenos— the humblest construction worker or fisherman could simply lift his eyes and be inspired by the gleaming white symbol at the crest of the hill.

The message of the white cross above Acapulco was apparent to many visitors; Christian clergy sometimes noted it with feeling. Dr. Allen Lee, General Secretary of the World Confederation of Churches of Christ, wrote in the August 1973 issue of the *Christian Advocate*: "Here in this lap of luxury, in this haven of greed and grandeur, I was reminded of the source of my spiritual strength, the magnetic Master of men and the proper place and value of material things."

The cross and chapel continue to carry their message to this day. Rising above the bay, visible from miles around, they serve as monu-

Frank Brandstetter receives the "Pro Ecclesia et Pontifice" in a ceremony at the Capilla de la Paz in 1974.

ments to religious faith; immediately below them is Brandy's personal monument to his evolving philosophy of life, Casa Tranquilidad. Over the 1960s and 1970s he continued to reach for the twin elusive goals— peace and tranquility—even as his adventures in business and intelligence work took him far afield.

17

Philippe Thyraud de Vosjoli, Leon Uris, and Topaz

By the early 1960s, Las Brisas began to attract, on a regular basis, a wide variety of celebrities. The magnificent setting, combined with Brandy's excellent management that provided quality services and attention to all his guests, not only the rich and famous, began to pay off. The Special Attention Reports brought to Brandy's eye anyone who had international standing as an actor, writer, businessman, statesman, or military figure. From time to time he would introduce himself to such people, occasionally joining them for lunch. His charm and conversation soon made a few such acquaintances into friends. More than once, the friends from one sphere of celebrity would be quite surprised, and often elated, at the contacts they made with talented people from other spheres. For such people, the dream-like world of Las Brisas often yielded new adventures and contacts that seemed almost magical when they returned home.

Individuals Brandy had met over the years, including some from his days at the Havana Hilton, would show up occasionally. Early in 1961, he was surprised to be approached by Philippe Thyraud de Vosjoli, whom he had assisted in leaving Cuba in January 1959. Although he only met de Vosjoli hurriedly during the evacuation, Brandy had immediately sized him up as a strong anti-Communist, a French patriot, a good soldier, and a friend of America. At Las Brisas, de Vosjoli approached him and explained that he was troubled, hinting that he wanted to unburden himself about his knowledge of the penetration by Soviet agents into the highest circles of the de Gaulle government in France. As the two men chatted, Brandy realized that de Vosjoli was dangerously close to revealing classified information to him.

"Wait," he said. "You know I am still in the U.S. Army Reserves, and you and I speak the same language. You know that if you tell me anything, I'll have to report it back through channels. If you want to spill your guts, you have to resign first. My advice is: quit your post, then, out of loyalty to France, you can make your information public. But while still in the service—you've got to keep quiet—you cannot be a traitor."

De Vosjoli's suspicions focused on a French cabinet officer and other members of de Gaulle's staff. Although de Vosjoli was not specific, Brandy learned enough to relay hints of a possible major scandal and subsequent crisis to his "Big Brother."

Brandy flew to Washington, D.C., to report to ACSI, knowing that the telephone lines and the mails were too insecure for anything of this nature. Meeting his contact from the Pentagon at National Airport, Brandy explained what he knew. Two years later and after several trips, he was surprised to receive oral instructions not to pursue the subject further. The impression he got was that the U.S. government, at "the highest level," did not want information that would prove embarrassing to France. Brandy suspected that the pro-French attitude of President Kennedy went beyond the traditional political alliance with that nation to include a deep emotional linkage.

Brandy's attitude, however, was to forward through channels whatever information he obtained. What the government did with it was another matter. His duty was to relay what he learned. So he ignored the suggestion, noting that he was gathering information strictly on a volunteer basis, not under orders. He was later informed that this independence of mind might have cost him a promotion. His time in service as a colonel would have made a promotion to brigadier general appropriate and his name was on a list for a brigadiership. It had been quashed at the White House, he heard, because of his continued passing of additional information he uncovered to his "Big Brother" regarding Soviet penetration in France.

Brandy continued seeing de Vosjoli. On his next trip to Acapulco, de Vosjoli arrived with documents that Brandy requested to see as proof of Soviet activity. Brandy then put the documents in the hotel safe. He later photocopied the documents, which indicated the names of the individuals whom de Vosjoli suspected. He kept the originals in the safe and took the copies, flying to Washington D.C., to see his ACSI contact and to turn over the top-secret papers. He knew that de Vosjoli understood. The documents he supplied were turned over by ACSI to the CIA, where they fit into a growing picture regarding France.

The next round of developments surprised Brandy. In the spring of 1962, the CIA called de Vosjoli to participate in the questioning of a Soviet defector code named "Martel." Martel was the French cryptonym, or code name, for Anatoly Golytsin, one of the most controversial defectors from the Soviet Union to the United States during the early 1960s. In the shadow world of espionage, it was extremely difficult for analysts to determine whether or not Golytsin was revealing factual information or whether he was a plant by the Soviets, spreading disinformation. As the interrogation of Golytsin proceeded, however, the CIA came increasingly to trust this defector as genuine. As detailed in several works on the history of espionage through this period, James Angleton, the agency's lead "molehunter," placed implicit trust in the revelations of Golytsin.

When Martel (as de Vosjoli always referred to Golytsin) provided details, he showed that the KGB had penetrated de Vosjoli's own agency, the SDECE in France, much as the KGB had infiltrated the British MI-5 and MI-6 agencies with a "Ring of Five." The KGB ring inside SDECE, Martel claimed, was code named "Sapphire" by the Soviets, suggesting a whole string of jewels. Using a technique similar to one they had employed in Britain of using long-standing and secret sympathizers with the Soviet Union, the KGB placed several agents at the very highest circles of French security. One had been at the near-ministerial level since 1944.

De Vosjoli was shocked to learn from Martel that the KGB hoped to use one of the SDECE's own operations to gain information about the

United States. Martel claimed to know that a special branch of the SDECE had been created to penetrate American scientific and military secrets; the KGB planned to acquire information about the United States through this French agency.

With these latest documents that Brandy supplied in hand, the CIA insisted that a letter be sent directly from President John F. Kennedy to President Charles de Gaulle, warning him of the penetration. De Gaulle reacted by assuming that the allegations were designed to spread distrust against members of his administration, and perhaps had even been planted by the CIA. The SDECE and de Gaulle knew that their own effort to penetrate U.S. secrets had been mounted *after* Golytsin defected, fueling French suspicion.

Through 1962, de Vosjoli continued working with his Cuban contacts, building a network of informants there. His information in the summer of 1962 confirmed that the Soviets were bringing offensive missiles to the island. De Vosjoli relayed this information to the CIA, who then stepped up U-2 flights to spot the missiles on the particular plantations where de Vosjoli's sources had located them. During the October 1962 "Missile Crisis," President Kennedy quarantined the island and secured the removal of the missiles, after the historic stand-off which brought the two superpowers to the brink of a nuclear exchange.

In December 1962, General Paul Jacquier, who had been warned of the KGB penetration in France, ordered de Vosjoli to Paris. There, de Vosjoli was reprimanded for having provided the information regarding Cuba to the Americans without clearing it through France first. Furthermore, Colonel Marieul, who worked under Jacquier, ordered de Vosjoli to provide the names of his Cuban sources. Considering the fact that this information would very probably be forwarded through the KGB leaks directly to Moscow and then to Castro's security forces, de Vosjoli refused. Marieul also instructed de Vosjoli to begin collecting information on the United States. De Vosjoli was outraged. This was exactly what the Soviet defector had claimed would happen.

When de Vosjoli returned to the United States that December, he was severely depressed. He did not know who to trust in his own government. It appeared that no matter to whom he complained, he would only run into plotters, and possibly, Soviet agents.

As Christmas neared, Brandy received a telephone call from de Vosjoli. Brandy could tell that his friend was depressed, as if caught between two loyalties. He flew to Washington and talked with de Vosjoli, reassuring him, telling him to honor his commitments as an officer and follow his conscience as a patriot.

In the summer of 1963, some of the KGB ring members in France were rounded up. Kim Philby, the notorious "Third Man" in what Golytsin claimed was the KGB's British "Ring of Five," defected to Moscow. Two French government officials implicated in the Sapphire ring committed suicide, and Georges Pâques, a French KGB agent who was leaking information from NATO to the Soviets, was identified and arrested. Still, de Vosjoli believed the French Sapphire ring remained, so he refused to spy on the United States for his government in light of the continuing possibility that information would be relayed back to the Soviets from France.

On 18 October 1963, de Vosjoli submitted his resignation. With his diplomatic passport no longer valid, de Vosjoli had to travel on a tourist permit in the United States, requiring that he leave the country at least once every six months and then return. He believed he would be in danger if he returned to France. Accordingly, he and his wife left for Acapulco and a stay at Las Brisas.

Brandy and de Vosjoli had lunch at La Concha, the private beach club at Las Brisas, and de Vosjoli explained many of the details of what he had been through and why he had been so distraught over the past year. Brandy understood and admired his colleague for making the tough, ethical decision to resign and serve the West.

As they chatted, looking off the patio across the wide expanse of the bay, they both noticed a ski-boat circling the La Concha Beach Club. There was no skier behind the boat, and the men in sunglasses seemed to be eyeing the outdoor restaurant. De Vosjoli looked hard at the boat as it neared, then bowed his head.

"I know those men," he said.

They belonged to the secret "Action" section of SDECE, the group engaged in sabotage and assassinations. De Vosjoli suspected that they were in Acapulco looking for him. It all fit together and Brandy believed his friend.

"Philippe," Brandy said, "you've got to hide out until this blows over. Let me work on it."

Brandy had befriended a group of Mexican *campesinos*, or farm workers, who had taken up residence in a squatter section of Acapulco known as La Laja. There, where few houses had running water or electricity, the police and outsiders rarely penetrated. An early effort in 1958–59 to evict the squatters with army troops had been fought off with small-arms fire by the settlers. As the settlement became more stable, President Lopez Mateos had granted small plots to the squatters, and Brandy had supplied some construction materials such as cement and occasional food and medical shipments to them. The leader of the community, "Lupita" Cisneros, knew Brandy well and trusted him. Brandy had even been invited to annual celebrations of the anniversary of the "battle" of La Laja. Brandy arranged for Philippe de Vosjoli and his wife to hide out in this community for two and a half months over the winter of 1963–64, in one of the better-appointed houses at the edge of the barrio that had electricity and running water.

Later, the CIA provided a "safe-house" for de Vosjoli in Miami, complete with plain-clothes guards. De Vosjoli also obtained two Doberman guard dogs to protect his wife and children.

Through 1965 and 1966, de Vosjoli and his wife, Monique, would return to Acapulco to visit with Brandy and Barbara, often joining them on the terrace of Brandy's dual cottages at Las Brisas, numbers 328 and 329. Barbara and Monique grew fond of each other, perhaps finding some mutual identification in their roles as wives of dedicated patriots and committed intelligence officers.

During one of the de Vosjoli visits, Brandy happened to be lunching with another celebrity, the author Leon Uris, who had already become quite wealthy from the royalties on *Exodus* and *Armageddon*, two thrillers that had made the best-seller list. As Brandy and Uris were having lunch, the writer was drawn away to take a phone call. It was his agent in London. A contract had just been offered for the book *QBVII*, which he had completed while staying at Las Brisas.

Brandy had a thought. Uris was an excellent writer with a worldwide reputation. De Vosjoli, who was struggling to capture his memoirs, had a remarkable story to tell. Since Uris was ready to move on to a new subject, perhaps the two should get together.

Brandy introduced Uris to de Vosjoli at Las Brisas, making clear that if any collaboration resulted from the meeting, he would not have any financial part in the operation. As an officer in the U.S. Army's ACSI, Brandy did not accept gifts, monetary compensation, or royalties. Any arrangements would be theirs to make.

After discussing the matter, Uris told de Vosjoli to continue with his notes. He would be able to put him in touch with publishers if the ideas worked out.

Later, when both had returned to their homes, de Vosjoli in Miami sent to Uris in Aspen, Colorado, a draft and précis of his work, which he tentatively titled in French *Le Reseau Topaz* (The Topaz Network). Uris immediately called him to come to Colorado to discuss the idea in greater depth. They agreed that Uris would do the writing as de Vosjoli told him the story, which Uris would embellish a bit to make it more suitable for fiction. They would split any novel and motion picture royalties fifty-fifty, as suggested by Brandy. Uris went to work on the novel immediately, and

Brandy was responsible for bringing together author Leon Uris (far right) and Philippe de Vosjoli.

it was soon completed with the title *Topaz*, a veiled reference to the actual gemstone code name (Sapphire) of the Soviet spy ring in France.

The outlines of the real story are there. De Vosjoli is renamed "Devereaux" and is the central figure in a James Bond-like adventure, in which Golytsin or Martel is named "Boris Kuznetzov." The book is full of sex, torture, and narrow escapes, yet includes the outline of facts regarding Soviet penetration of the French government and the discovery of the Soviet offensive missiles in Cuba. The novel describes an extended flashback which summarizes some of de Vosjoli's adventures in the French Underground during World War II.

Leon Uris's agent worked on securing a publisher for the manuscript. Uris later told Brandy that he had negotiated a deal with Harper's, but when the publisher checked with the CIA and the State Department, he was informed that the story was too hot and too close to the truth, and possibly would anger the French. To convince Harper's to drop the book, so Uris told Brandy, the CIA offered to arrange for Stalin's daughter, Svetlana, to publish her memoirs through Harper's. Uris provided Brandy a proof-copy of *Topaz* run off by Harper's, with an inscription ironically noting it as "Harper's Folly." In any case, Uris continued his effort to publish the novel, and soon McGraw-Hill issued *Topaz* with a copyright date of 1967 and Leon Uris as sole author.

The book rose to the top of the best-seller charts, and remained on the list for some thirteen months. Uris provided de Vosjoli with about $65,000 as his share of the early royalties. Somehow, during the first year, the spy and the author had a falling out. Perhaps it was the fact that the book focused on "Devereaux's" love affairs; in actuality, de Vosjoli was quite devoted to his wife and the marital separation and torrid affair with a Cuban heiress in the novel were entirely Uris's inventions. In any case, de Vosjoli wanted to see a more literal version of the truth published. Uris stopped sending the royalty share.

When de Vosjoli informed Brandy of the problem, Brandy agreed that indeed, de Vosjoli was "up a creek." Another contact of Brandy's was a writer and editor for the international edition of *Life* magazine, Steve DeClerque. As de Vosjoli explained the situation of the terminated royalties to Brandy at his home in Acapulco, Brandy decided to call DeClerque.

Brandy explained how the real subject of *Topaz* was being denied a share of the royalties from his life story; and how the actual story was even more dramatic than that in the novel. Again, Brandy made it clear that he did not want any financial compensation from *Life*. In fact, he introduced de Vosjoli to DeClerque over the telephone, and then asked them to contact each other on another line. He did not want to be involved in any way, or have either individual indebted to him as a result of any arrangement they might make.

DeClerque remained faithful to the facts. He put together a short lead-in story, together with a long autobiographical account written by de Vosjoli himself, and another, shorter analysis, of the impact of the Martel revelations contributed by John Barry, a writer on the staff of the London (Sunday) *Times*. The special section was printed in the U.S. edition and international editions of *Life* on 29 April 1968, as the cover story: "The French Spy Scandal." The story provided detailed documentation of the revelations of Martel, a clear justification for de Vosjoli's resignation from SDECE, and an explanation of his acceptance of CIA protection in Miami.

DeClerque inscribed a copy of the Atlantic edition of the magazine and sent it to Brandy for his collection, noting that without Brandy's help, the story never would have been published.

With DeClerque's help, de Vosjoli hired an attorney and brought suit against Uris for his share of royalties. Meanwhile, de Vosjoli returned to putting his own memoirs in shape for publication. Little-Brown, which at that time was a property of Time-Life, published the memoirs a year later, in 1969, under the title *Lamia*, using the same dramatic photo of de Vosjoli from the *Life* cover on the dust jacket of the book. "Lamia" had been de Vosjoli's code name in the French underground in World War II, apparently derived from the name of a traditional figure in French folklore. Written with less sensationalism than *Topaz*, and closer to the facts, *Lamia* had much slower sales than the fictionalized work.

Just before *Lamia* went to press, de Vosjoli wrote to Brandy to ask him if he had any objection to having the book dedicated to him. There was no problem, Brandy said, now that he was retiring from active Reserves, as long as the book did not discuss any items except those that were already in the public domain.

When he received a copy and read it, he was proud to see not only the dedication on the frontispiece, but other details of his life. It included the full story of his standoff of the Cuban revolutionaries in the Hilton lobby on 1 January 1959, and information about the Devizes POW escape plot of 1944. A few friends and guests of Las Brisas sent Brandy notes commenting on de Vosjoli's description of the Hilton incident that they read in *Lamia*, and noting the dedication of the book.

Meanwhile, as the lawsuit dragged on, Brandy kept up a correspondence with both de Vosjoli and Uris, trying to be impartial and friendly to both. During this period, he hoped to get de Vosjoli further publicity in his efforts to market *Lamia* and other writings he was developing. When an edition of *Lamia* was published in French in Montreal, Brandy received a copy and wrote to congratulate his friend. He also obtained a copy of the Spanish edition, brought out by Plaza y Jane in Mexico City. He collected clippings about de Vosjoli through the Copley newsclipping service during the late sixties and early seventies. From time to time, as Brandy visited Florida to attend Apollo launchings in the late 1960s, he would arrange to meet Philippe and Monique in Miami for dinner or drinks to talk about old times, and they would return the visits in Acapulco.

De Vosjoli wrote another book, published in Brussels, titled *Le Comité*, (1970, Brussels, Editions de L'homme), which detailed the operations of the assassination squads of the SDECE. He also worked on an exposé of the drug trade operated by Corsican gangsters through prostitution rings in Europe. Brandy was impressed with this idea and put de Vosjoli in touch with Peter Sellers, in hopes that Sellers would find an outlet for the work. Sellers later replied that the concept of the work was too similar to "The French Connection" to be published. Perhaps it was so similar because, like the famous film, it was rooted in facts. Brandy also wrote to President Richard M. Nixon's press secretary, Ron Ziegler, hoping to arrange for de Vosjoli to address a variety of Republican groups, particularly Cuban-Americans, on the topic of drug addiction.

During this period, Brandy contacted another friend, the owner of a chain of radio stations in Texas, Gordon McLendon, encouraging him to examine the de Vosjoli story as a possible feature for a radio program. One of McLendon's aides visited de Vosjoli in Miami and misinterpreted the security precautions with which de Vosjoli surrounded himself as a sign of exaggerated self-importance or paranoia. This resulted in a disparaging story in the *Dallas Times-Herald*. In Florida, however, the *Miami Herald* periodically picked up on the de Vosjoli story, running features and shorter notices on how the retired spy made a living in his new-found home.

Finally, Brandy received word early in 1973 that de Vosjoli had won his lawsuit against Leon Uris, who was ordered to pay over $352,000 as his share of the royalties on the book and movie. Uris admitted that he had agreed with de Vosjoli to share royalties, but claimed in his defense that de Vosjoli had broken the agreement by proceeding to publish his own nonfiction treatment as well as magazine and newspaper articles.

Over the next twenty years, Brandy kept in touch with de Vosjoli, who would return to Mexico on vacations. De Vosjoli raised two sons and sent them to college and graduate school in the United States. He continued to write both espionage works and guidebooks from his homes in Miami and in Geneva, Switzerland. The signed volumes, published in three languages, and the dedications and clippings, all found honored places in the growing Brandstetter collection of memorabilia.

18

A Democrat as Commander in Chief

The facilities for privacy which Brandy developed at Las Brisas not only served to protect Ambassador Peter Hope and others who were in hiding because of concern for security, but also could be used to protect celebrities who did not want publicity. Many of those who wanted the experience of visiting Acapulco and sharing in its tropical charm could not pay the price of public exposure and constant harassment by *papparazis* and gossip-journalists. Even before he built the special Fortress San Carlos, with its particularly secure facility for diplomats, Brandy had hosted astronauts, actors, and politicians, as well as several heads of state and their relatives.

When Lynda Bird Johnson, daughter of President Lyndon Baines Johnson, was dating George Hamilton from 1963 to 1965, she often sought a retreat for vacations. She stayed for extended periods in Las Brisas during her senior year in college. As a consequence, Brandy became acquainted with the director of the White House Communications Office Mike Howard, who would come as a member of the small Secret Service detachment that was detailed to protect Lynda Bird on her vacations. Hotel security worked with Howard to set up radio communications with the White House, or with the LBJ Ranch in Stonewall, Texas, when the president was there.

Once Brandy overheard a telephone conversation between George Hamilton and some of his friends in Las Vegas. Hamilton made what Brandy took to be indiscreet remarks about the actor's relationship with the president's daughter. Brandy conveyed the remarks to Howard, suggesting that if statements like that were made public, it would reflect very poorly on the president.

"Mike," he said, "this is not good." Howard agreed that Hamilton was using his relationship with Lynda to advance his career, and doubted his sincerity.

Brandy's discreet handling of Lynda's visit impressed LBJ, and soon the president sent his brother, Sam Houston Johnson, to stay in the secure facilities at Fortress San Carlos. Sam Houston, who suffered from alcohol addiction, was accompanied by a nurse, as well as by a Secret Service detachment for a short period. Brandy had taken care of his own invalid wife for years, and was sympathetic to the problem. He kept Sam Houston Johnson comfortable, and struck up a friendship with him.

As Brandy talked with him, he learned that LBJ's brother sometimes resented the president, and that he had dictated a set of tapes to be converted into a book. This exposé of Lyndon Johnson would contain details about his private life. Brandy tried to reason with Sam, explaining that the exposé touched on sensitive issues, representing a threat to national security while the president was in office. Brandy convinced Sam Houston to place the tapes in the hotel safe.

He then called Mike Howard to explain what he knew about the tapes. He received a call from the LBJ ranch that evening. It was the president.

"Colonel Brandstetter? I want you to fly up here right away. I want to talk to you. Bring those damn tapes with you."

"Yes sir," said Brandy, stiffening at his end of the phone line.

Brandy regarded a request from the president as an order. He knew, however, that it would be hard to obey. It was the height of the tourist season, and all the airplanes out of Acapulco would be booked. He checked with the airport and found there was not a seat out to Texas for days. The next flight was on Braniff, at 7:00 A.M., but it was booked solid. Brandy sent the head of hotel security out to locate the local manager of Braniff.

Brandy converses with Sam Houston Johnson, brother of Lyndon Johnson, at Las Brisas.

"You tell him to call me," said Brandy, "and stay there on the telephone while I talk to him."

Soon the call came in. The Braniff manager was calling from a nightclub where he had been tracked down. Brandy explained that he had received orders to report to the president in Texas and had to have a flight.

"Listen," said the manager, "we are sold out. Maybe next week."

"You listen to me!" Brandy shot back. "Lyndon Johnson is a major stockholder in Braniff, and he is president of the United States! I am not asking. I am telling you to be at the airport, and to see that I get on that airplane." He hung up. The next morning at 6:00 A.M., he took his ready-packed valise and drove to the airport. The Braniff manager met Brandy and arranged for him to travel in the copilot's jump seat. Brandy expected to fly to San Antonio, making a short stopover to deliver the tapes, then return on the same plane as it flew from Dallas via San Antonio to Acapulco that afternoon.

When he arrived in San Antonio, Mike Howard was there to meet him and whisk him in a presidential limousine to the ranch at Stonewall, about sixty miles northwest of San Antonio. Brandy was shown in to meet President Johnson, and he stood at attention, reporting in.

"At ease, colonel," said LBJ, picking up on the military nature of Brandy's stance, with a bit of a smile. Brandy liked the president. He had met him briefly before, once in the Oval Office concerning the de Vosjoli case. This occasion was far less formal, and LBJ's down-to-earth, hearty manner appealed to him.

"Colonel, what exactly is on those tapes of my brother's?"

"Sir," said Brandy, "I'm not sure. I only heard him dictating a little, and it seemed to me he was getting into sensitive areas."

"OK. Give them to Mike here, and he will go off to listen to them, and see if you're right."

Brandy handed the tapes and Howard left the room.

"Now, colonel," said LBJ, "I want to hear the whole story of the Philippe de Vosjoli case." Brandy had sketched the outline of the case in a short report for the president months before at the Oval Office, but this informal setting would let him get into more details. Brandy fully reported what he had learned from de Vosjoli, detailing the KGB penetration of the French secret service, the SDECE, and the requests from France to spy on the United States.

LBJ was fascinated, and asked a few pointed questions to clarify the facts. When Brandy had finished the report, the conversation relaxed, and they talked about Mexico, and then about more personal matters.

"Colonel, I appreciate what you did for Lynda Bird, and what you are doing for Sam Houston. Now, tell me exactly what Hamilton said about Lynda Bird."

Brandy did so. LBJ invited Lady Bird in, and asked Brandy to repeat the story for her. Brandy searched for the right words to express the implications of what he had overheard in a manner appropriate for a mother to hear, and both Lyndon and Lady Bird understood. Brandy later believed that LBJ and Lady Bird decided that Hamilton was "persona non grata" from that moment. Lady Bird, in her published diary, explained that she sought to let Lynda have her own independence, but she also wondered whether the relationship with the handsome actor might not reflect on the presidency. Without interfering, the parents agreed with Brandy that Lynda could do better.

"Come on in the other room," said the president. "I have a few presents for you." Brandy stood by the fireplace, while LBJ watched him from his rocking chair. An assistant brought some packages, making it seem like Christmas. Brandy set the packages down and began to unwrap them. There was an LBJ lighter, a tie clip, and a pair of gold cuff links. Brandy started to thank the president, when the assistant came in with another round of boxes, including autographed pictures and a memento of the Johnson-Humphrey electoral victory of 1964. His hands full and the thank you partially said, he felt a little foolish, and LBJ burst out laughing.

As Brandy unwrapped the gifts, LBJ said sternly:

"I understand you are a Republican, colonel."

Brandy slowly set down the gifts, almost as if, as a Republican, he would be reluctant to accept them unless ordered to do so. Brandy stood at attention again and gave a military salute.

"Sir," he said formally, "you are my commander in chief."

"Sit down, colonel, and have a bourbon," said the president.

They both had a big laugh, and LBJ poured out two stiff drinks while Lady Bird had a cup of tea. The brief meeting stretched on, and there was no possibility Brandy could make the return flight on the Braniff plane. He stayed overnight at a hotel near the airport and flew back to Acapulco the next day.

He never heard any more about the tapes from Howard. Later, Sam Houston Johnson published *My Brother, Lyndon*, based on his reminiscences, which included many personal references but no breaches of sensitive issues. On 10 August 1967, Lynda Bird explained to her parents that she had dropped Hamilton, and had fallen in love with Marine officer Charles Robb, a military aide who was, at times, her bridge partner at the White House. The wedding was set for 9 December 1967.

That September the engaged couple took a quiet trip to Acapulco, to stay at Las Brisas. While they were there, Hurricane Beulah struck the Mexican coast, causing landslides all along the cliff roads of Acapulco and isolating many communities. Las Brisas itself was fully booked with a round of guests from the Gibson Refrigerator Company. Power to the hotel was knocked out, and Brandy had the auxiliary generators turned on.

The only phone link to the United States was via the White House communications room in a Las Brisas residence, where the radios were powered by small auxiliary generators that Brandy salvaged from the construction equipment collection. In the room, incoming voices were amplified with several speakers to overcome the static.

Brandy took Lynda Bird there so she could talk to her family. "Daddy," she explained, "we are going to be stuck here a few days. It's really bad. Lots of the coast and Acapulco is completely isolated, and there are no flights in or out."

Brandy could hear LBJ's voice over the speakers.

"What can we do from here?" the president asked. "What do you need?"

Brandy replied, hoping Lynda would relay the remark, "Helicopters!"

"Colonel, I heard that," the president said. "We'll see what we can do."

Over the next few hours, Johnson called Díaz Ordaz, the president of Mexico, and repeated what he had heard from his daughter in Acapulco. Helicopters were needed for rescue and relief there, and he wanted to send some down. President Ordaz explained that the Mexican constitution prohibited foreign troops from operating on Mexican soil. Johnson, in his persuasive way, pointed out that this was an emergency, that American troops could operate under Mexican control, and that the law was probably not intended to allow Mexicans to starve when relief could be provided. He would not allow publicity in the United States about the operation, and he assumed Ordaz could handle publicity there.

Accordingly, on President Johnson's direct orders, General T. J. Conway, Commander in Chief, United States Strike Command, MacDill Air Force Base in Florida, launched the rescue operation that lasted over the period of 28 September to 9 October 1967. The Strike Command sent a flight of C-141s, a KC tanker, and a group of six Hercules helicopters, operated by the 101st Airborne under the command of Colonel Harold S. Fischgrund. The whole relief effort was code named OPERATION BONNY DATE.

When the aircraft flew in, the Acapulco airport itself was inundated. Only an old runway, partly under water, was available for landing. After

The effects of Hurricane Beulah in Acapulco, September 1967. Photo by Guillermo Ochoa.

U. S. Army Colonel Harold S. Fischgrund (left), Frank Brandstetter (center), and Mexican Army Lieutenanat General Juan Manuel Enriquez (center right) confer about the problems of relief in the hurricane-ravaged area.

Mexican villagers offload food supplies from a U. S. helicopter.

U. S. Air Force operational navigation chart, with Brandy's proposed sketch for OPERATION BONNY DATE, 29 September through 7 October 1967.

the aircraft personnel reported in by radio to the Secret Service at the hotel, Brandy raced out to the airport in one of the Las Brisas jeeps. He parked it on a dry spot above the accessible runway, with the headlights flashing to guide in the huge cargo craft through the downpour.

Colonel Fischgrund greeted Brandy. After the introductions, Brandy asked the Airborne colonel where the troops were going to stay.

"I don't know," said Fischgrund. "We don't even have a point of contact here. The strike force got its orders directly from the White House. We're here."

"How big a group do you have with you?" Brandy asked.

"About 110 men," said Fischgrund.

Brandy raised his eyebrows and nodded. Something needed to be done. With the colonel and his aide, Brandy drove over the back roads, around the coastal slides, back to the hotel. Since Las Brisas was filled with the Gibson convention, which had already overstayed their allotted week by a few days because of the immobilized airport, he had no rooms at all. There were some deluxe residences below the hotel, however, which were occasionally rented out to selected guests with full hotel service, with the prior approval of the owners. In this instance, with the phone lines down, the owners of the homes could not be contacted. With scrupulous accounting to be certain the rent would be paid, Brandy arranged with the Las Brisas housekeeping staff to put extra beds in several of the houses. He then set up a twenty-four-hour chow line in the banquet rooms above the dining room in the hotel. Busboys took a fleet of pink jeeps out to the airport to bring the strike team back. Meanwhile, Brandy took Fischgrund down to the naval base. There, word had just been received from Mexico City, over the naval radio system, that U.S. troops had arrived to help. Brandy soon arranged that the soccer field be set aside as a heliport for the six Hueys. The Mexican navy also provided two rooms for a small command post.

Over the next week, Brandy flew on the missions, usually sitting in the lead helicopter between the Mexican commander, General Juan Manuel Enriquez-Rodriquez and Colonel Fischgrund, providing liaison and translation services. American helicopters landed at remote and isolated towns, where Mexican troops supervised the distribution of food, blankets, and medicines. Then the sick, aged, or homeless young were evacuated by the American helicopters back to Acapulco, where they could be cared for at the naval base.

Brandy later found that the cost of the rooms, the chow line, and other hotel services were recorded on the books of the hotel as a charge of some $36,000. He arranged with the bookkeeper to deduct five thousand dollars a month from his own salary until the amount was reimbursed, posting it as a debit to his personal account. When Don Carlos, six weeks later, noticed the huge debit against Brandy's name, he was worried. What crisis had caused Brandy to run up a personal $36,000 tab? When Brandy explained, Don Carlos immediately took over half the debt; a few months later, a Mexican official arrived with a check. Brandy noted the curious fact that the check was only a partial payment of the amount; maybe somebody along the line had taken their traditional *mordida*, or fee. Nevertheless, the books were cleared as Brandy and Carlos paid off the balance.

Brandy kept a collection of photos of the planes and helicopters, as well as a thick file on OPERATION BONNY DATE in his personal archives. Later he was saddened to learn that many of the men who had served in the operation, in his old 101st Airborne Division, were killed in Vietnam.

After Lyndon Johnson's retirement in 1969, the ex-president, Lynda, and Lady Bird visited Acapulco and came to Brandy's home for a cocktail and dinner. As the group finished their meal, LBJ gave Brandy a look.

"Colonel, I see you have a cigar in your pocket. Let me see it."

Brandy handed it over. Like all of those he smoked, it had been specially made for him, and it had his name on the wrapper. Lyndon Johnson opened the cellophane and sniffed the cigar.

"Go ahead and light it," said the president, handing it back.

Brandy demurred, out of respect for the ladies.

"Light it!" said Johnson.

Brandy did.

"Now," said LBJ, "blow some of that smoke in my direction."

Brandy followed orders. LBJ liked the aroma so much that he asked Brandy to give him one to smoke. Lady Bird reminded him that the doctors had forbidden it, but he proceeded anyway, walking away from

Mike Howard, Barbara Brandstetter, Lynda Bird, Lady Bird, and Lyndon Johnson with Brandy in the Space Museum at Casa de la Tranquilidad.

the group. Together, Brandy and LBJ strolled around Brandy's "museum room," with its pictures and mementos on the wall. LBJ studied the artifacts and pictures, particularly impressed by Brandy's collection of memorabilia from the space program, assembled from the gifts provided by the astronauts who had stayed incognito at the comped rooms at Las Brisas.

"Damn you, colonel, you've got more of this stuff than I do, and I'm the one who signed the appropriation bills for the space program!" said Johnson, laughingly. "I want a photograph of this."

Brandy called down to the hotel and contacted one of the public relations staff. "I know it's after hours," he said, "but the president is here, and he wants a photographer, so get one." Somehow they did. The photographer came and took several group pictures of LBJ, Lady Bird, Lynda Bird, Mike Howard, Brandy, and Barbara in Brandy's museum room. Later, one of these photos was added to the very wall where it was taken.

During the early 1970s, President Johnson and Lady Bird visited Brandy's home again. Brandy hosted a small group that included Tom Frost, Johnson's friend and financial adviser, on the outside patio. Johnson explained that he was starting a business and wanted Brandy's opinion. "As you know," he explained, "former President Don Miguel Alemán has lots of ranch properties along the border. So do I. I thought we could combine forces and raise cattle. What do you think of it?"

"Mr. President," said Brandy, "the idea of raising cattle in Mexico is great. Experimentally a few years ago, I raised some cattle in Sonora, since we could not get good grade beef for the hotel. It can be done, if you have proper care and proper feed. My problem was transporting the meat to Acapulco. We could not fly it in refrigerated, so it didn't work out. But there is good cattle ranching in the north of Mexico. As far as you going into joint business with Alemán, that is great, as long as he is alive. But should he die, all the investment you have on the Mexican side, is gone."

"What do you mean?" asked LBJ.

"Mexican law is very clear on that. No foreigner can own any land. While you are together, it's OK; but when he dies, you are going to lose your investment."

LBJ asked Brandy to repeat what he had said to Lady Bird and Frost. The repetition reminded Brandy of experiences he had had with General Ridgway, who always had a junior officer repeat his observations, rather than endorsing the officer's views by repeating them himself. The others listened and were impressed.

"OK," said the president, "Lady Bird, Tom, cancel it. And, Tom, if the colonel ever wants anything from your bank, you give it. You hear me?"

Brandy never took advantage of the offer. He remembered his conversations with Johnson fondly. He liked LBJ, even if he wasn't a Republican.

19

Port of Call: The Navy to the Rescue

As an army man, Brandy thought of the U.S. Navy as a means of transporting troops and equipment, and providing offshore support to the army, as during the 1944 invasion of Europe. Developments in Mexico in the 1960s, however, convinced him that the navy could be a significant force in international relations. Consequently, the U.S. Navy could play a major political part in the Cold War against Soviet influence, by conspicuous and judicious use of ship visits. His enthusiastic support for this principle grew out of incidents in the construction of the La Concha Beach Club on Acapulco Bay, below the Las Brisas Hotel.

After the little cove had been blasted out of the rocks and a jetty and breakwater built there, Brandy gave a concession for a scuba-diving school to two brothers, Alfonso and Reggie Arnold. They taught Brandy aqualunging, and together the three would take recreational swims at Roqueta Island, at the edge of Acapulco Bay, sometimes teasing the sleeping sharks they found there. As scuba divers, dependent on each other for underwater safety, the three developed a close personal bond. Brandy assisted the brothers financially, so they could buy safe scuba-diving equipment and ski boats.

When a hurricane damaged La Concha's breakwater, Brandy recruited the two scuba-diving brothers to help him complete repairs. Borrowing

Brandy and his scuba-diving friends reconstruct the breakwater of La Concha Beach Club. Photo by Guillermo Ochoa.

from the German concepts of concrete and rock emplacements he had seen at Cherbourg, Brandy personally worked to build similar structures, laboring in diving gear. Alfonso and Reggie worked with Brandy in the same shift, helping to manhandle heavy rocks and sacks of quick-drying cement into place. The work was strenuous. Three teams of nine men would relieve each other, each team working for only twenty minutes at a time. One afternoon, as Brandy was emerging from the surf after an exhausting stint underwater, he looked up to see a dump truck above him, about to disgorge its load of rubble and rock directly on him. With a shout, Alfonso pushed Brandy aside and halted the driver. Alfonso had saved Brandy's life, making their bond even stronger.

When the work was completed, Brandy kept in touch with the brothers to watch the progress of their business. Soon afterwards, Alfonso had a diving accident. He came up too suddenly from a deep dive, developing a case of the bends. He was rushed to the Mexican naval base in Acapulco for decompression. Unfortunately, the decompression chamber maintained there was a primitive, concrete, coffin-like box, and Brandy and the Mexican naval officers at Acapulco doubted if it would pull Alfonso through. Brandy immediately called the medical personnel at the U.S. naval base in San Diego. President Alemán arranged for a private plane, and Alfonso was quickly flown up for treatment. He survived, although he walked with a limp ever after. Brandy's quick action may have saved the life of the man who had earlier saved his own.

While at the base in Acapulco, Brandy uncovered some interesting information through discussions with Mexican navy officers. They explained that soon they would be receiving some expert technical help; the Soviet Union was sending a team of trainers and technicians to work with the Mexican Navy in Acapulco. Brandy knew immediately what that meant. In the early 1960s, every Soviet military or civilian aid project was riddled with KGB agents, and they would use their foothold in any project as a base to build an organization and spread distrust of the United States. In 1961, in the aftermath of the Bay of Pigs incident in Cuba, there was already a great deal of anti-American feeling in Mexico. American tourists were often harassed, beaten up, and even framed with drug possession. Mexican-American relations and the tourist industry in Acapulco were already at risk, without the Soviets getting a foot in the door with the Mexican navy. Brandy realized he might never have heard of the Soviet mission unless he had made the emergency visit to the base to deal with Alfonso's crisis. Now that he knew about it, however, he decided something had to be done to offset the increase of Soviet influence among the Mexican military.

Brandy flew up and saw Secretary of the Navy Fred Korth. He respectfully suggested that the U.S. Navy immediately donate to Mexico, with a small charge, mothballed ships that were anchored in Port Arthur, Texas. Korth acted quickly to transfer the ships to the Mexican Navy. When the ships were delivered to Acapulco, Secretary Korth flew down. Through the donation of the ships, a "building bridges" plan was developed between the two countries. Acapulco was then designated as a port of call, and visiting naval ships made protocol calls on local military and governmental officials. This action was planned to offset the negative feeling and image of the United States, and to build closer relationships between the officers of both countries.

Accordingly, late in 1961, the program began, at first quite gradually, with small patrol vessels, tenders, and supply ships. As time went on, larger ships including destroyers, cruisers, and non-nuclear submarines, all put in to the harbor, and the officers made the indicated rounds of visits.

Brandy soon developed a routine, which increasingly came to be supported and recognized by the military attaché at the U.S. Embassy in Mexico City. The attaché would notify the ship captain that he was to contact Frank M. Brandstetter, the general manager of Las Brisas, who would help answer questions. Also, he was to pay courtesy calls to the commandant of the 8th Naval Zone at the Mexican naval base, to the commander of the 27th Military Zone at the army camp, and to the mayor of Acapulco.

On the arrival of each ship, Brandy or one of his assistant managers would meet the officers and help arrange the details. In the morning, the commanding officer of the ship would make a protocol call to the three Mexican officials, presenting each with a wooden and brass plaque of the ship's emblem. A small luncheon would be hosted aboard the ship, the number of guests depending on the size of the wardroom. Sometimes as few as six or seven guests would have lunch on the smaller ships or submarines; at other times, as many as fourteen or fifteen would be served lunch on the destroyers or cruisers. Brandy joined the visitors as interpreter. In the evening, Las Brisas would host a cocktail party for the ship's officers and invite some of the hotel guests as well as the Mexican service officials.

Brandy routinely provided a complimentary room to the commanding officer of each visiting U.S. Navy ship. Frequently, they arranged to have their wives fly in to meet them at the hotel to stay for three or four days. Other officers could rent rooms at a twenty-five percent discount. The resulting charge was less than forty dollars, relatively high for Mexico in the early 1960s, but still a bargain for the junior naval officers. In addition, Brandy provided a jeep for the commanding officer, gratis, and jeeps to others staying at the hotel at a reduced rate. In the case of ships with large complements of enlisted crews given shore leave, Brandy provided each ship with a Las Brisas jeep and walkie-talkie for use by the shore patrol to help keep watch on the sailors as they made the rounds of the local bars and hot spots.

The program became more polished with every visit and the increasing number of arrivals of naval vessels through the mid-1960s and early

1970s. Brandy's files began to bulge with gracious thank you notes from officers who had enjoyed the hospitality, the stay at the hotel, and the attention to detail. Brandy's assistant managers, who worked as liaisons, were often singled out for specific compliments as they helped the officers with problems of tours, supplies, harbor transportation, and translation services.

Brandy also began to extend similar hospitality services to occasional vessels from other nations, particularly to British and Canadian ships, and German and Iranian war vessels. A Peruvian school ship, *Independencia*, a squadron of four Japanese ships, and a ship from the Republic of China also received the red carpet treatment that Brandy had developed. Among the ships entertained were Military Sealift Ships, U.S. Coast Guard vessels, and the training ship, *Golden Bear*, from the California Maritime Academy. When the *Queen Mary* was on its last voyage, in 1967, cruising to its permanent display dock for exhibit in Long Beach, all the crew and officers were lodged at the hotel. Press coverage was extensive.

The U.S. Navy and its vessels, however, remained the primary focus of the program. Frequently, as many as three or four destroyers and two or three supply ships docked in the harbor at the same time, and sometimes the festivities could be held jointly. On one occasion in September 1968, Brandy arranged a cocktail party including the officers of both the USS *Taluga* and HMS *Fife*.

Over the fifteen years that Brandy supervised the program, most commanding officers presented a plaque from their ships to both the Mexican officials and to Brandy. As his collection grew, each officer wanted to add to it. When Brandy completed his own home in the Club Residencial, he put the growing array of plaques on the wall of his library. The collection eventually filled a space of about 225 square feet.

Brandy often invited visiting astronauts to attend the cocktail parties for the ships' officers. Alan Bean, Rusty Schweickart, and Wally Schirra each gave short talks with film presentations on separate occasions to the visiting naval officers. Although the astronauts' visits were not publicized, their contacts with the ships' officers were very impressive, and through word of mouth both naval officers and astronauts became loyal supporters of Las Brisas.

The comfortable way in which Brandy merged his different roles continued through this period. As a patriotic Reserve Army officer, he could act to cement friendly relations between the United States and Mexico by establishing and facilitating the contacts between American naval officers and their Mexican counterparts. As a hotelier, his decision to give complimentary rooms was very good business, as the officers themselves often returned as paying guests, and encouraged friends and relatives to stay at the fabulous resort. As an intelligence officer, Brandy found it useful to keep informed, through the network of Mexican officers and officials, of the latest hints of political change. As a promoter of Acapulco tourism, his efforts to make the naval personnel happy, convert some of them into return tourists, and engage the tourists already present in social meetings with the officers, all brought business to the city. The presence of U.S. Navy ships and personnel provided American tourists here, at least, with assurances that Americans were welcome. But above all, his charm and hospitality made the visits run smoothly, and literally dozens of naval officers had fond memories of their stays at Acapulco because of his efforts.

Informally, Brandy began to provide solutions to a wide variety of problems encountered by the ships' officers and occasionally large crews. Often the issue was as simple as purchasing fuel oil or supplies. Las Brisas paid for the supplies, obtained a receipt from the ship officer, and transmitted the bill through the embassy for payment. Usually, payment was forthcoming quite promptly. One early ship, which had no provision for local purchases, was advanced over one thousand dollars. Such mundane services as hauling off the ship's trash and providing ship-to-shore tender service in case the ship's own gig was missing or damaged, became regular and time-consuming duties of the Las Brisas staff. Also, submarines, as standard operating procedure, had their food stores replenished with fresh vegetables and tropical fruits.

Brandy became more involved in solving personal problems that arose with the crews and officers of the visiting ships. Injured or sick seamen, who had to be flown to the United States, benefited from the hotel's arrangement and payment of the tickets without immediate reimbursement. Brandy shipped one seaman, who was AWOL, back to San Diego with a letter of explanation, alerting the authorities to pick

Mexican citizens and U. S. Navy
sailors share some music in
Acapulco.

him up on arrival. A group of boys from a California training ship took
a jeep without authorization and wrecked it; the California academy
paid the damages and handled the discipline. Another seaman from a
naval ship, apparently intoxicated, repeatedly drove a rental jeep into
the surf until he demolished it. Brandy arranged that no charges be
brought in the local court, and that the jeep be replaced at the expense
of the sailor. At one party for officers from three U.S. ships, held on
Thanksgiving, 1966, housekeeping at Las Brisas presented a bill for 1,032
pesos (about eighty dollars) for 344 broken champagne glasses. Apparently someone had initiated the practice of smashing the glass after
quaffing the drink.

Dozens of small incidents were dealt with routinely, while others
took considerable time and effort, with phone calls to the embassy, sooth-
ing conversations with local businessmen or officials, and lengthy meetings. In each case, Brandy helped mediate the solution, working with
the officers to handle the situation discreetly. On serious as well as minor difficulties, his diplomacy was always greatly appreciated.

244 Brandy, Our Man in Acapulco

In effect, Brandy was conducting some of the duties of a consular office. The State Department offered to make Brandy U.S. consul in Acapulco, but he declined. He preferred to operate unofficially, focusing on hospitality services to the navy, and not getting involved in all the paperwork regarding ship lading and other details that fall to a formal consul.

As the military attaché changed in Mexico City, the fact that Brandy had become the established contact in Acapulco for visiting U.S. Navy ships became even more traditional and accepted. Looking through the files, the new attachés and assistant attachés realized that Brandy was routinely copied on correspondence with visiting ships, and they continued the practice.

Brandy and his staff were very thorough in managing the details of the trips, so the embassy's trust was well placed. Brandy or an assistant manager culled through the embassy announcements of forthcoming ship visits and prepared a mimeographed schedule for the next month, detailing each ship, giving the name of her captain and the size of her crew complement. All pertinent staff at Las Brisas received a copy of the mimeographed sheet.

Once in a great while, a fully booked convention or the high occupancy of a winter season would prevent the hotel from engaging in its usual round of hospitality to a visiting naval vessel. In such cases, Brandy would personally write to the commanding officer with an explanation and apology.

Some ships' officers worked with the Navy League chapter in Acapulco that Brandy formed and served with as its first president, to provide gifts and entertainment for underprivileged children. Father Angel's orphanage often sent groups of up to fifty children to a ship for a tour, a short entertainment, and some gifts. The Acapulco-Beverly Hills sister city committee arranged with Commander D. R. Brainerd of the USS *Sterrett* to exchange symbolic gifts between the cities. Vice Admiral Bernard Roeder brought the navy's Marine band down on the USS *St. Paul*, and Brandy helped make arrangements for the band to perform free onshore concerts, both indoor and outdoor. When the Marine band marched through the streets of the city, it was a "first" for Acapulco and for Mexico as a whole.

In 1962, a foreign military unit, in this case a U.S. Marine band, was allowed to perform on Mexican soil in Acapulco. Photo by Acapulco Hilton.

Early in the visitation program, in 1964, Brandy was pleased to host not only the commander of a squadron of ships, but a high-ranking naval officer traveling with them, Vice Admiral Fritz Harlfinger, who was head of submarine warfare in the Office of the Chief of Naval Operations. A few weeks before the admiral's visit, Brandy had visited Washington to report to his "Big Brother." In passing, the officer had mentioned that by the next time Brandy came to town, a new deputy director of Defense Intelligence would be in place, one Admiral Harlfinger. When Harlfinger arrived in Acapulco, Brandy knew in advance of the admiral's next posting.

In Acapulco, after the routine parties, Brandstetter invited the admiral up to his *casita* for a brandy with a few of the other officers. The *casita*'s small patio looked out over the harbor; in the distance, the U.S. naval ships, with electric lights decorating their rigging, made a beautiful sight in the tropical night.

Brandy drew Harlfinger aside to the edge of the patio.

"Come over here, admiral, and take a look at your ships. What a sight!"

Drinks in hand, they looked over the city lights to the ships in the harbor. They were out of earshot of the other guests, who chatted behind them in the living room.

"By the way, admiral, congratulations on your new post," said Brandy, his voice low.

Harlfinger shot Brandy a look.

"What are you talking about?"

Brandy sipped his drink and stared at the beautiful lights. He went on, not letting the others hear.

"Yes, admiral, you should be quite comfortable. Even if the buildings are those temporary wooden ones. You'll be there on the second floor; there will be the status symbol of the green leather couch, right there behind the door on your right..."

Harlfinger had no idea that Brandy reported to Defense Intelligence, and indeed, his position and operation was rather quiet. To hear about the post on a tropical evening, under the stars, at the fabulous Las Brisas with drinks in hand, from the general manager of the hotel, was a bit too much.

Two months later, in Washington again, Brandy stopped by the admiral's new office to pay his respects.

Harlfinger waved him in and offered him a cup of coffee. Then, in old-fashioned hospitality, he reached into a lower drawer and brought out a bottle of bourbon to "sweeten" the coffee.

"So you really knew, didn't you, you old so and so," said the admiral, laughing out loud. Harlfinger and Brandy became fast friends, and the admiral frequently visited him after his retirement from the U.S. Navy, staying at Casa Tranquilidad as a house guest, after Brandy finished the home in 1971.

As the admiral grudgingly lost at gin rummy and backgammon to Brandy, playing late into the night on the outside patio, they would reminisce. They had many a chuckle over the night in 1964 when Brandy had sprung the news of the admiral's secret appointment.

20

A Party for a Prince

D uring the program of ship visits, Brandy received advance word of their arrivals from the American Embassy, from the British Embassy, and from naval authorities in Panama.

He learned through channels that Prince Charles of Britain was serving as communications officer during his eighteen-month-tour of sea duty in the Royal Navy, aboard HMS *Jupiter*, a British frigate. The ship was scheduled to stop in Acapulco in March 1974. A few days before the ship's arrival date, on 21 March 1974, Princess Anne, Prince Charles' sister, was the victim of an attempted kidnapping by a man outside Buckingham Palace. As a consequence of this assault, Scotland Yard immediately clamped tight security around all of the royal family, wherever they were in the world.

At the time of the attack, HMS *Jupiter* had just crossed the Pacific from Singapore to North America on a round-the-world cruise, and was at anchor in San Diego. After a weekend at the home of Ambassador Walter Annenberg, where Prince Charles met Governor Ronald Reagan, Frank Sinatra, and Bob Hope, the officers of the ship found shore leave restricted because of the enhanced security.

When the ship arrived off Mexico, the British ambassador decided, with the approval of Scotland Yard, that they could have a very small cocktail party on board to which only a limited group would be invited. Following the usual protocol, Brandy visited the ship on 25 March 1974 and met the officers.

Instead of setting up a party at the hotel as he had in the past with British and American ships, Brandy arranged a small private cocktail party at his own residence to be held two days later. When he cleared his plans with the British ambassador, Scotland Yard insisted that the house should be fully protected and the surrounding streets guarded. Also, they agreed that Casa Tranquilidad, with its high walls and controlled gate, was extremely easy to keep secure. After inspection, they assented to the little reception there.

At the introduction aboard *Jupiter* by the British ambassador, Prince Charles did not know who Brandy was. When he was introduced, Brandy said, "Your Highness, I look forward to seeing you again two days from now when I will have a quiet cocktail party for the ships' officers in my home overlooking the bay and the ship."

Charles looked at him. "Are you going to have any ladies?" Brandy was caught by surprise, and just swallowed. The British ambassador, Sir Galsworthy, was standing next to him. Later, Brandy drew aside the ambassador.

"Look," he said, "you heard Prince Charles. What are we going to do?'"

Galsworthy replied, "Provide ladies? That is not my department! But we should do something."

Galsworthy and Brandy discussed the problem—Scotland Yard, you know! They could not simply round up a list of invitees from the expatriate society in Acapulco. Finally Brandy said, "Why the heck don't you talk to Mrs. Galsworthy and see if she approves it, and then invite some of the ladies from the British Embassy, the secretaries and staff members? MI and Scotland Yard have already got all those people cleared. We can fly them down, they can stay at the hotel, and come to the party at my home. You and Mrs. Galsworthy can be there. Have them bring their bathing suits, and they can have the party around the pool. These young guys have been at sea for a while and it would be pretty nice for them to meet some British girls after all this time."

Galsworthy agreed and made the arrangements. On the afternoon of the party, 27 March 1974, the group gathered at Brandy's outside

Brandy and Prince Charles discuss
the image of royalty at a party in
March 1974 at Casa de la
Tranquilidad.

patio at Casa Tranquilidad. Brandy hosted the ambassador, the Mexican admiral, the ship's captain, and Prince Charles on a tour of his
museum room.

As the group walked around, Charles became interested in the brief
New York Times clipping and memorabilia about the Devizes German
POW breakout, posted in a frame in one corner. He asked Brandy about
it. Brandy explained the story, detailing the German plot to seize the
government, assassinate Churchill, and spread havoc, tying down troops
at the same time as the German offensive in the Ardennes, which attempted to push through Belgium to the sea. He explained his interrogation of Storch, the placing of undercover German-speaking British
and American officers in the camp to obtain more information, and the
dramatic nighttime arrest of the ringleaders a day before von Rundstedt's
assault in the Ardennes.

"Why have I never heard of it?" asked Charles.

Brandy explained that Churchill had the full story suppressed to prevent it from influencing his election, which he lost anyway, in June 1945 to Labour Party candidate Clement Attlee. The story remained suppressed after its initial publication on 11 May 1945 in the *New York Times*, and in the British and French press, he explained, simply because Churchill had the details classified at the time. After the election, the story was old news. John McDermott of the *Miami Herald* had collected information, but could not get the British to declassify the files. A short version had been published in May 1945, after European Theater censorship was lifted. Charles asked Brandy to send him materials and documents about the breakout.

Later, Brandy got a packet of documents from McDermott together with his original interrogation reports, photocopied the whole batch, and then sent them on to Charles, through the British Embassy's diplomatic pouch. Although he never heard more about the copies, he assumed the British Official Secrets Act had kept the story from being handled openly in Britain. He understood that the British view of security in these concerns was much more a matter of the political interests of the state as a whole, rather than the more narrow view of actual threats to national security officially held by America.

While the two men discussed further details of the Devizes case in Brandy's museum, the rest of the group hung back in another corner, looking at the space memorabilia.

"Your Highness," Brandy said, glancing at the ambassador and the admiral, "look over there. They're getting a little bit annoyed, since we're ignoring them."

Charles said, "Never mind that. I want to hear the rest of the story."

Brandy decided that, in his book, Charles was a man's man. They talked further about the rumored conservative group of military officers in Britain who had formed their own organization to "neutralize" the growing influence of leftists in Britain. It struck Brandy that it could get dangerous, almost like the Irish against the British, with possible bloodshed; this conflict would pit royalists against Socialist-Communists. Brandy said that conflict was not the answer, and Charles agreed. The rest of the guests continued to stay out of earshot. As Brandy and Charles talked, the formality dissolved into a conversation of an old military man with a young one, a sort of avuncular relationship. Brandy explained his philosophy of loyalty and duty to flag and country. Charles asked how he could fight for the cause in his time and position.

Brandy replied that Charles was being groomed to be king; not a leader, but a symbol representing the historic family of a historic nation. He would be a symbol, an image.

"However," said Brandy, "you have to make your own image."

Brandy expressed his opinion that the image could be enhanced if Charles took up military training in specialized areas such as commando techniques, underwater demolition, and aviation. He would be perceived by the people as a strong, macho figure and they would rally around him.

The party then shifted to the pool and began to heat up. Barbara Brandstetter was feeling ill, so she excused herself, and then the British ambassador's wife also left. Then the Mexican admiral left; finally the ambassador himself left.

As he departed the party, Ambassador Galsworthy said, "Frank, you look after things here."

"Yes, sir," he said, feeling that the ship's commanding officer would help provide chaperon service.

After awhile the party got a bit noisier. The British navy officers and the young women from the embassy began to have fun—laughing, joking, and swimming in the pool. Prince Charles was just a young man, thought Brandy. Why should he not have a good time?

Finally, when the commanding officer of *Jupiter* said he was excusing himself, Brandy stopped him.

"Oh no, you're not, I'm going to bed first. It's your responsibility to get your men back to the ship." Finally the two decided to designate the ship's executive officer to stay with the party and see that the officers all got back to the ship and the ladies to their hotel. Brandy went off to bed, hearing the party last into the warm tropical night and early hours of the morning.

A few days later, Brandy received a personal handwritten note from Prince Charles, five pages long, thanking him for the relaxing party and the advice. He later read in the press that on his return to England, Charles was soon ordered to undertake helicopter training. He thought back to the conversation in the museum room and wondered if he had influenced the decision.

Almost a year after the party at Casa Tranquilidad, Brandy and his wife were invited by Ambassador Galsworthy to a reception for Queen Elizabeth. The reception was rather formal, and Brandy attended in his dark suit. He noticed that all of the guests were British, many of them former military people who had served the empire in one capacity or another. He was the only American. What am I doing here? he thought to himself.

To his left, almost as if reading his mind, the gentleman asked him: "Are you British?"

"I'm afraid not," said Brandy, a little self-consciously.

The man continued, "Well, how come you are here?" There were only a limited number of invited guests—a lot of deserving British subjects resident in Mexico wanted to be invited.

"Sorry," said Brandy, "I just follow orders. I got an invitation from the queen, which to me, is a command. So I am here at her command." That seemed to quiet the questioning, but Brandy still felt a little out of place. He observed the procedures closely.

In the presentation line, about fifty people were lined up on one side of the room, and another fifty on the other side, arranged in a long horseshoe shape. The queen, accompanied by the ambassador, walked along one side, being introduced and greeting each guest in turn. Prince Philip, the Duke of Edinburgh, walked in the other direction, being introduced by the chargé d'affaires of the embassy. The protocol was strict, and each introduced guest took a formal bow or curtsy. There was hardly any conversation, only the murmured introductions and the greeting, and then the groups moved on to the next guest in the lines. The process was dignified, gracious, and well organized.

Queen Elizabeth simply shook hands with each guest and accepted the introduction given by the ambassador. However, when she came to Brandy, she stopped.

"So you are Colonel Brandstetter," she said.

"Yes, your Majesty."

"I want to thank you for what you did for my son, as a mother. Those poor boys really needed some relaxation, and it was a lovely party. My son came back and he raved, and as his mother, I appreciate what you did." Brandy simply nodded and said he understood that they needed

Prince Philip thanks Brandy in 1975 for his helpful advice to his son, Prince Charles.

some rest and relaxation. The queen continued, taking a few more moments. "Thank you," she said. "If you are ever in England, please be sure to contact us." Brandy wondered how he would arrange to "drop in" at Windsor or Buckingham, but he nodded his thanks.

"I was glad I could help, your Majesty," he said. Queen Elizabeth passed along, simply taking the introductions, making the greetings, and moving steadily and graciously. Next, coming the other way, the chargé d'affaires was introducing Philip to each individual in the presentation line. When Philip got to Brandy, he also said a few words.

"I heard with great interest about your mission involving the attempted POW escape at Devizes. Also, thanks for the advice you gave to Charles. As a father, I want to thank you."

Brandy realized then that they had invited him especially to say thank you, as parents, for helping their son. He thought their gesture was very nice; royalty aside, they were simply two parents thanking a stranger for helping out their son.

After the reception line broke up, everyone stood around informally for cocktail party conversations. Several people, including the two individuals who had been on either side of him in the line, approached. "We don't understand it," they said. "You are the only American here. Queen Elizabeth and Prince Philip both spoke to you! Why?"

Brandy answered only with a smile.

21

Seeking New Ventures

Brandy engaged in a constant round of enterprises, at first working with Don Carlos, and increasingly working with personal friends and contacts as investors and clients. Brandy's business ventures reflected his vision, talent for organization, and ability to bring together influential decision-makers. His experience, travels, and passion for gathering information enhanced the ventures. Some of the activities showed how he attempted to blend social and ideological goals into business planning.

A few of the early investments and business activities had revealed the same abilities and interest he used in bringing together his contacts, in creating a new kind of enterprise, and reflecting his social and political ideals. His plan to work with Continental Leasing to import tank engines to assist Cuba in its agricultural development had been just such an idea. His work in building Las Brisas into a major resort attraction for married couples, while improving the status of the employees, had exemplified his attempt to convert ideals into business practices. The chapel and cross project represented another effort to use business techniques for social goals.

Through 1968 and 1969, he worked with Don Carlos to manage a special firm, Mesones y Refectorios, S.A., which had ambitious plans to refurbish various ancient convents and monasteries in Mexico, and convert them into tourist attractions. The enterprise started with the monastery at Acolman, which is on the highway from Mexico City to the Pyramids of the Sun and Moon, near Texcoco. A frequent stop for tourists, either traveling individually or as groups, the sixteenth-century monastery was in fact an abandoned, ruined structure under the purview of the Mexican Department of Anthropology.

The plan of Mesones y Refectorios included the establishment of a restaurant in the refectory of the monastery at Acolman. Waiters and attendants, dressed in reproductions of sixteenth- century Spanish outfits, added to the atmosphere. In 1968 the restaurant opened with elegant shows, a moderately priced menu in two languages, and specially designed tableware and dishes following Spanish patterns appropriate to the era. Staff from Las Brisas managed the restaurant and the business received favorable press notices. Press releases and news stories drew attention to the fact that tourists, both Mexican and foreign, could experience fine dining in a true sixteenth-century setting, and get a feel for historic authenticity.

Brandy worked on a variety of ideas to increase the sense of history. He visited and gathered materials on Irish castles that had been converted to hotel-restaurant combinations, and collected photographs of the famous *paradors* in Spain, which he shared with the Acolman restaurant managers. Tlaquepaque, the ancient Mexican ceramic-specialty town, designed and manufactured an entire set of classic tableware. Brandy took part in some of the minute design decisions, aiming for an authentic look down to the last detail of table setting and costume.

Unfortunately, there were difficulties. Tour buses would not stop without special kickbacks or discounts. The number of customers diminished after the musical show finished its season. Soon, the enterprise was losing several thousand dollars per month, just in operation costs. Brandy and Don Carlos subsidized Acolman with funds from Las Brisas, which they also jointly owned.

Brandy hoped to raise funds to expand the concept. An ancient convent that the government would make available, Monserrat, on the corner of Isabel la Catolica and Izazaga Avenues in Mexico City, was a possible location for another "refectory" restaurant. In 1969, Brandy

The monastery at Acolman provided a historical site developed by Brandy and Don Carlos Trouyet in 1968 and 1969, to promote tourism. Top photo by Bon Urbanek.

wrote to Kirk Kerkorian, the majority stockholder in Western Airlines and a principal in the International Hotel in Las Vegas, introducing Father Pedro Kurguz. A young Dominican seminarian, Kurguz was a man in whom Brandy had taken a special interest. Kurguz had helped him select the grounds for the Chapel of Peace and had written several pieces on the incompatibility of Catholicism with Communism. Brandy had funded the reprinting of one such article, and hoped to be able to turn some of the profits from the operating firm at Acolman, Mesones y Refectorios, to help Fr. Kurguz establish his own seminary. It was on this basis that he appealed for help to Kerkorian. By mentioning William Green, a mutual friend, who was the Bishop of Las Vegas, Brandy blended his political, religious, business, and personal contacts, hoping to bring together the combination. Brandy's letter read, in part:

> Father Pedro N. Kurguz, in charge of Proyectos Intelectuales y Sociales, A.C., is on his way to visit you. The cause which he is representing, no need to say, is a very worthy one. The Las Brisas Hotel and Mesones y Refectorios, S.A. . . . is in the process of taking over the various old monasteries located on historical sites in Mexico so as to re-establish them as historical attractions. In the refectories banquets will be served so as to keep the atmosphere of sixteenth-century Mexico, in order to give the participants an intense historical knowledge of that period, tied in with Father Kurguz' program "KNOW AND ENJOY MEXICO". For background information, Don Carlos Trouyet, an international Mexican financier, is behind this and it is my responsibility to execute this program with the Las Brisas Hotel and Mesones y Refectorios, S.A.

After a very slow season in 1969, however, Mesones y Refectorios went out of business.

Meanwhile, Brandy worked with Don Carlos on two other projects. One was Trouyet's investment in El Tapatio, a planned luxury resort hotel south of Guadalajara on the highway towards Chapala. Trouyet was the largest single shareholder in the corporation owning the hotel, and Brandy's responsibilities included providing it with the same sort of

image that had elevated Las Brisas to world renown. He designed a ha-
cienda-type hotel that was built under his supervision. By transferring
several trained staff members from Las Brisas to El Tapatio, and ensuring a total concern for the guest, Brandy made sure the finished resort
began to attract and hold a clientele as had Las Brisas. After the death
of Don Carlos in 1970, however, his son Francisco Trouyet informed
Brandy that he wanted to sell his holdings in El Tapatio, in which Brandy
held a ten percent interest. The total value of El Tapatio was some $9.6
million, and the Trouyet interest was over one-third. Brandy began putting out feelers in the investment community to identify purchasers.

Through the mid- and late-1960s, another venture of Don Carlos
Trouyet engaged a great deal of Brandy's energy and interest. This was
the plan to develop Playa Encantada—Enchanted Beach—south of
Acapulco, near the airport. Trouyet and Brandy had purchased over
450 acres of beach property and land back to the lagoon behind the
beach, ideal for a resort, a community development, or a light industrial park. Brandy enthusiastically worked on all aspects of these plans.
At first the projects were to develop in several different phases: low-cost
retirement housing to attract both American labor unions and American corporations, a group of motels near the beach, a sports and outdoor activity area, and a luxury hotel on the beach. In addition, several
electronics firms would become tenants in a light industrial park, in
order to provide a stable base of employment not subject to the vagaries
of the tourist industry. The industrial park would be nearby, but away
from the resort operation. In 1967, however, Brandy developed a new
idea.

He heard about Eastern Airlines' plans to fly large 747 aircraft directly to Acapulco, and he learned that the airlines had set aside some
$31 million to invest into club developments in the Caribbean, Hawaii,
and possibly Mexico. Brandy worked up a concept for the ETC—the
Eastern Travel Club—to open a resort of its own at Playa Encantada. In
his vision, each week on Saturday, EAL would fly one plane in and one
out of Acapulco, filled with two hundred tourists, for a total of 1400
guest nights.

Using this number as the base from which to calculate occupancy,
Playa Encantada would work out a one-week total package arrangement

in which passengers would, for one price, get airfare, hotel room, sports activities, three meals per day, transportation to and from the airport, and all tips included. Brandy hoped to arrange matters with Mexican officials to allow passengers arriving for the ETC to clear Mexican customs and immigration in New York. On arrival in Acapulco, they could then get directly into large buses, similar to the "people movers" recently installed at Dulles Airport in Washington, D.C.

Without worrying about their luggage, the passengers would be taken directly to Playa Encantada, having pre-registered as they picked up their airline package ticket. Their luggage would be delivered directly to their rooms. For the budget traveler, those on incomes of around fifteen thousand dollars (1967 dollars), the plan would be attractive. All of the hassles confronting inexperienced international travelers—dealing with unfamiliar customs, immigration, baggage handling, and ground transportation—would be smoothed away.

The concept appealed to Eastern Airlines executives, and they asked Brandy to develop more specific plans, so he began to price out the cost of construction of a moderate-quality hotel, using some of the same construction principals and suppliers with whom he had grown familiar during the expansion of Las Brisas. Total costs would run about $8 million, U.S. currency. As he worked on the plans, he wanted to ensure that the buildings would have a Mexican motif, and that there would be no "barracks-style" housing in the complex. As he checked his contacts in the United States, he grew more convinced that there was a strong market for such a resort among middle-class Americans. He wrote early in 1967: "The results of my investigation have surpassed my expectations."

Don Carlos was very interested! He visualized putting up fifty-one percent of the funding himself, perhaps borrowing in the United States at favorable American rates, and having EAL put up the other forty-nine percent.

Brandy began to work on the local politics and authorizations. In order to obtain approval from the city for the development, a "donation" of six percent, more or less, of the land would have to be arranged. A delegation of wives of local, state, and national politicians, representing the National Institute for the Protection of Children, approached

Brandy and negotiated the gift in their name. Another parcel had to be granted individually to the National Director of Tourism, and legal papers were drawn up for that transaction. An engineering plan had to be developed, showing utilities and the impact of the development on water and power supply.

Upon the death of Don Carlos, the plans came to an abrupt end. On the same evening that Francisco Trouyet had asked Brandy to look into the sale of El Tapatio, he asked him to arrange the sale of the interest in Playa Encantada. Like many heirs of great fortunes, the young Trouyet brothers were concerned about liquidating their holdings, rather than building new ventures.

Brandy was distressed as he realized that the uncertainty about the future of Las Brisas was beginning to affect the morale of the staff. In the early 1970s, tourist business began tapering off in Mexico, and some of the competing hotels dropped to occupancy rates of thirty percent or less. Brandy was able to hold Las Brisas at about eighty percent, on an annual basis, in 1972 and 1973, but he grew more and more dissatisfied with the Trouyet heirs. Although Brandy and Don Carlos had rejected offers of $20 million for the property in the late 1960s, the younger Trouyet brothers, Francisco and Robert, now sought to find a buyer. Eventually Banamex, a major Mexican bank, purchased the hotel.

Meanwhile, Brandy began some personal investments, putting together funding from his own resources and from various friends. Together with a group of more than thirty others, he invested in Grapetree Bay and Grapetree Hotels, in the U.S. Virgin Islands, on the eastern tip of the island of St. Croix. The resort was in a beautiful location, and was, like the ETC, designed to attract resort travelers of modest means. Together, the investors raised some $450,000. Brandy personally invested $90,000 through a Mexican holding firm, and another $9,000, nominally held by his wife Barbara. Other friends of Brandy's who invested various amounts included Fritz Harlfinger and several members of the Lehman Brothers investment firm.

Grapetree Bay, however, was facing hard times. Occupancy rates remained low, and the management of the hotel had difficulty meeting its bills from utilities and vendors. The telephone system remained an incredible tangle, with over-billing and faulty connections. Return busi-

Although a beautiful resort, Grapetree Hotels became a financially impractical
venture for Brandy and other investors. Photo by Dukane Press.

ness, despite some lovely brochures, was insufficient, and the resort continued to lose money. In 1978 a new company, Exotic Resorts, headed
by Cornelius King, bought out the limited partners at about fifty percent of their investment; Brandy received a check for $45,000 and a
check for about $4,300 for Barbara's investment.

Brandy constantly looked for new opportunities for investment, often putting together groups of friends he had met over the years to
form a new venture or explore other possibilities. Working with Fritz
Harlfinger, Dominic Paolucci, and Bobby Burns, Jr., the four invested
in a Mexican gem mine in 1984 and 1985, which turned up several promising semi-precious stones, but no fortune for the investors.

In all of these investment operations, Brandy collected as much information as he could, organized it, thought through specific questions,
and took notes for his files on the plans. As late as 1990, he was working
on a concept of developing a new hotel in Moscow, right off Red Square,
for an American investment group headed by Michael L. Riddle of the
Dallas legal firm of Riddle and Brown. He prepared a detailed set of

questions for presentation at a meeting in Dallas in July. Was there already an agreement? What did it consist of? Do we have a right to build a hotel complex? Could Russian union pension funds be used to purchase or lease the land? Do we have a map, placing the particular site in reference to Red Square? Are the proposed buildings appropriate? Are they old or new?

Brandy answered most of these and dozens of other pertinent questions in his notes from the meetings, and added some concepts of his own. He thought it would be sensible to lease out the hotel complex to "Nordig" Corporation, a subsidiary of Finnair. There was an echo of the Eastern Travel Club arrangement in his thinking, as his contact at Finnair assured him that if the company operated the hotel, they would direct many of their air passengers to stay there.

Brandy, noting the changes with the end of the Cold War, suggested that the hotel might draw strongly on the ex-military officers now being retired, in order to staff the positions of hotel executives. Perhaps a closed military camp near Moscow could be used as a hotel training school, taught, if need be, by foreign hotel experts. As he had since the 1950s, Brandy thought of ways to combine positive social goals and profitable business, thinking ahead to the long-range consequences of the operation.

After he gathered the information, he reported back to Riddle on 13 September 1990. Riddle and Brandy concluded that it was not quite the time for investing in a hotel, and it would be a good idea to wait until the "air cleared" in the Soviet Union. He received a healthy, flat fee for his detailed investigation and full report, and the check was sent promptly to him in Dallas. At age seventy-eight, his consulting work was still valuable, his connections and his ideas still at work.

Through these same years, the other sides of his life continued to offer fulfilling experiences.

22

Stillwell and the Search
for the Legion of Merit

Through the early 1960s, as Brandy was developing Las Brisas, he continued to fly to Washington for active duty with ACSI, usually serving in Washington during the first two weeks of May of each year, and receiving briefings on current issues. Often, the informal contacts with Dorothe Matlack, who continued to represent the well-informed institutional memory of the office, and with former "Big Brothers," yielded a better sense of priorities in information gathering than did the formal training and briefings.

Brandy developed the code name "Crazy Horse" for himself through these years. The concept was that if he ever sent a message signed with that name, it represented a real emergency. Despite a number of close calls, he never invoked the code.

During the same period, he worked with the defense attaché and the legal attaché at the United States Embassy in Mexico. Increasingly, the American ambassadors and staff came to know that Brandy was an asset in Acapulco, and they relied on him not only for hosting the visiting naval ships, but also for information and assistance of a more sensitive nature.

His action of photocopying documents from Philippe de Vosjoli and forwarding them through ACSI channels, as we have seen, appeared to cost him a promotion to brigadier general. When, in the period 1963 to 1964, he sheltered de Vosjoli and protected him from possible retribution from the network agents in SDECE, he did so entirely on his own. It was a gesture of friendship and defense of a fellow-officer, simply doing what he thought was right, no matter what the political backlash might be in Washington.

Brandy learned on 22 November 1965 that official views were changing about his involvement in the de Vosjoli case. On that evening, the military attaché, Brigadier General Thomas Crawford, and his wife held a reception for approximately eighty guests at their home in Mexico City in honor of Lieutenant General Alva Fitch, who then served as deputy director of the Defense Intelligence Agency. Brandy attended, along with DIA representatives from U.S. embassies in Central America, members of the diplomatic corps, and a number of Mexican and American businessmen and their wives. Fitch drew Brandy aside at the party, inconspicuously stepping into a bedroom where they could chat beyond the hearing of the others.

"Brandy," said Fitch, "the army recognizes you did the right thing, protecting de Vosjoli. We can't publicize it, but we've arranged for the Legion of Merit. It's in the ACSI files." The "LOM," often bestowed on high-ranking officers in recognition of their service, was not among Brandy's awards to that date, although he had both the Bronze Star and Silver Star for his service in World War II. Brandy was pleased at the acknowledgement. He had not accomplished the work with recognition in mind, but it was gratifying to know that the army had come to understand the importance of what he had done.

Later, Brandy was surprised to receive the Legion of Merit medal in the mail. That was peculiar, as there were no documents presented with it, no statement of exactly what action had generated it, and no presentation ceremony. After thinking through the possible reasons for the curious procedure, Brandy simply put the medal away with his other decorations, including the navy's Meritorious Public Service Citizen award for his work with the naval ships. When he moved into Casa Tranquilidad in 1971, a handsome glass case in the study helped preserve the growing collection.

In 1988, more than twenty years after Brandy received the award,

General Richard G. Stillwell, ret., was staying at Casa Tranquilidad, touring the home as did most guests, studying the display cases and the
pictures and plaques on the wall. Stillwell noticed the "LOM" medal
and congratulated Brandy on it.

Casually, ribbing the general a little, Brandy commented that the
story behind that particular medal reflected how the army did things.
He never got the paperwork, and the medal had never been formally
awarded—probably because the action for which it had been granted
was too controversial or too sensitive, and because Fitch had passed away
soon after the orders were issued. So Brandy never knew, he said, whether
the award was really genuine, and thus he did not wear it, still waiting
for the papers. Probably, he said with a grin, as is typical of the army, the
papers were still in the file, waiting to be sent out. Stillwell thought the
matter should not be dropped, and he spent two years trying to uncover
documentation about Brandy's participation in information work, hoping to persuade the army to formally rectify the situation with a proper
award ceremony and formal recognition. Stillwell wrote to dozens of
current and former individuals in the intelligence and information community. These specialists included Deke DeLoach, former assistant to
the director of the FBI; Tom Polgar, former Mexico City station chief of
the CIA; former military and legal attachés; army officers who had served
as directors of ACSI and of DIA; naval officers; and intelligence historians and writers. Stillwell attempted to piece together a comprehensive
picture of Brandy's participation in intelligence work over the period
1962 to 1988. At first Stillwell kept the effort quiet, not informing Brandy
and hoping to surprise him with the final product. Within a few months,
however, word leaked back to Brandy of the effort.

The results of Stillwell's search were intriguing. Many of the individual actions Brandy had engaged in could not be discussed, as the
issues were still active. Several of the respondents to the Stillwell "campaign" to honor Brandy pointed out the problem in explicit language.
Often those who work in information fields cannot receive open recognition simply because their actions and communications, by their very
nature, remain closely held. One or two of the letters Stillwell received
could only be copied and sent to Brandy after having been "redacted"—
that is, censored—with particular pieces of information deleted.

Former Assistant Secretary of
Defense General Richard
Stillwell's efforts to document
Brandy's Legion of Merit medal
were intensive and far-ranging.

Nevertheless, there were several events and actions that could be discussed and written about openly, because the issue had closed, the sources had died, or the topic was no longer one subject to classification. Stillwell soon developed quite a catalog of incidents and a thick file of letters. His notes not only included events preceding Brandy's 1965 conversation about the LOM with Fitch, but episodes which took place over the years following, up to and after Brandy's retirement from the Reserves in 1972.

Brandy was interested in the material Stillwell gathered. As he received copies of letters commenting on his past activities, he put them into his growing archive of correspondence. In his files, the letters served several purposes. One was to let him know which topics he could talk about, since they were no longer classified. His store of anecdotes for recounting to close friends could be expanded, and the details could be made public. Secondly, the letters themselves sometimes served Brandy as *stich worte* ("stick-words"), which could start the flow of ideas and stories by providing a prod to his memory.

As Stillwell turned up bits and pieces, he sent Brandy a note in February 1989, asking for clarification:

1) When [were you] operationally involved with De Vosjoli? Who was principal action officer in Mexico? D.C.?
2) What was time frame (particularly short) of your efforts to block Soviet entreé to Mexican Navy? What was first USN countermove (SecNav action)?
3) Do the J.Edgar Hoover letters include any specifics on events which generated them? If not, can you give me a couple of clues which will help focus FBI file search?
4) When was Brandy caper that blocked Cornfeld's acquisition of a major interest in PANAM? [sic-Mexico]
5) What was operation that prompted Fitch to say that a classified LOM citation was being placed in file?
6) Beginning when—and for how long—was Raya K. a significant security and baby-sitting problem?

Brandy replied in detail, orally, to each of Stillwell's questions, first explaining point by point the details of the de Vosjoli story and the navy's program of ship visits. Then he covered the other questions. The stories ranged from nearly forgotten minor incidents to rich insights into the scandals, swindles, and subversive activities of more than two decades.

In 1963, J. Edgar Hoover had sent Brandy two letters, cryptically thanking him for his assistance in apprehending two of the most wanted criminals during that year: Boyd Frederick Douglas, Jr. and Bobby Eugene Booth. Douglas had been on the list of ten most-wanted fugitives. Brandy, at the Acapulco Hilton, had spotted both of the individuals as suspicious characters who did not seem to be a part of the usual run of tourists or international set visiting the resort. A quick check with the legal attaché in Mexico City had confirmed his suspicions in both cases; each was apprehended at the hotel and deported to the States, in U.S. custody.

The "caper" to which Stillwell referred regarding Bernie Cornfeld was a bit more complicated. In 1970, Don Carlos called Brandy at Las Brisas, telling him a potential buyer was coming to look at properties.

"Frank, I'm sending someone over to talk to you. Don't throw him out of the office."

J. Edgar Hoover's letter of thanks to Brandy for his assistance in the capture of wanted criminal Boyd Frederick Douglas, Jr.

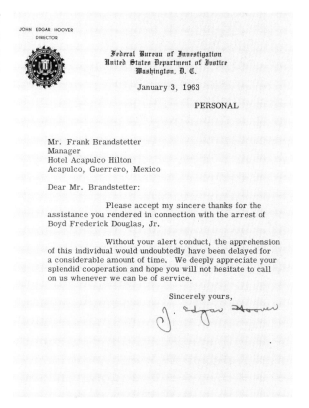

JOHN EDGAR HOOVER
DIRECTOR

Federal Bureau of Investigation
United States Department of Justice
Washington, D. C.

January 3, 1963

PERSONAL

Mr. Frank Brandstetter
Manager
Hotel Acapulco Hilton
Acapulco, Guerrero, Mexico

Dear Mr. Brandstetter:

Please accept my sincere thanks for the assistance you rendered in connection with the arrest of Boyd Frederick Douglas, Jr.

Without your alert conduct, the apprehension of this individual would undoubtedly have been delayed for a considerable amount of time. We deeply appreciate your splendid cooperation and hope you will not hesitate to call on us whenever we can be of service.

Sincerely yours,

J. Edgar Hoover

"Don Carlos," said Brandy, "if you tell me that you are sending someone to see me, of course I won't throw him out."

"Yes," said Trouyet, "but he is going to appear with long hair, a gold chain, and velvet pants. Just show him properties at Playa Encantada, nothing else." In 1970 Brandy had his own opinions about men who wore their hair long and sported jewelry and velvet pants, but, with a flinch, he agreed to take orders and be perfectly civil to the guest.

Sure enough, the next day, the man appeared. Bernard Cornfeld flew in to Acapulco in a private jet, and arrived with five young women in tow. As predicted, his hair was long, and he wore the flashy outfit described by Trouyet. The girls were dressed in Brazilian bathing suits, their sumptuous curves covered with little more than pieces of string in strategic spots. Following orders, Frank drove the jeep, showing the properties, while Cornfeld sat in the back seat, wedged among his girlfriends. Frank very properly explained the properties and answered Cornfeld's questions. After the tour, Cornfeld flew back to Mexico City. Something about the hyper-energetic little man raised Brandy's sixth sense that something was very wrong. The next Monday, Brandy flew to Mexico City and went to Trouyet's office.

"What are you doing here?" asked Trouyet, who usually communicated with Brandy by phone.

"Don Carlos, I don't know who the man is; I have never met him before. But there is something about him that hits me wrong. It is my duty, as a close friend, to tell you. That's all."

Trouyet was stunned.

"Do you realize that in two hours we have a meeting with the Minister of Finance? I am selling fifty percent of some of the Trouyet properties: the banks, the plastic companies, altogether about ten different companies. The half interest is some $300 million in cash. Cash. In order to formalize it, at two o'clock, we are having the meeting. So what makes you say this?" Trouyet was angry because the deal was within grasp, the papers ready.

"Don Carlos, it's only a feeling. With all respect, what I suggest is that you pick up the phone, and call one or two friends who might know something about Cornfeld." He suggested a contact at Lehman Brothers—Paul Davies—and another at Citicorp Bank, both of whom Trouyet knew from previous dealings.

Trouyet agreed. "All right, be back here at three o'clock."

Later that day, Trouyet explained that he delayed the signing for twenty-four hours while he waited for return information from the inquiries. Brandy concluded that $300 million in cash could only come from two sources: either the Soviet Union or organized crime. So Brandy called a journalist friend of his in Chicago who had written extensively about the criminal underworld, and then flew to Chicago to talk with him. Brandy asked him to check out Bernard Cornfeld. The journalist began making phone calls to his contacts during the afternoon. Contact after contact explained that International Overseas Services (IOS), the Swiss mutual fund controlled by Cornfeld, was under suspicion, even among underworld figures who had invested in IOS.

Brandy then called Deke DeLoach, the assistant to the director of the FBI, without informing him of what he had learned in Chicago. Brandy told him he had an urgent request and would fly to Washington

D.C. from Chicago on the next plane to talk about it. Deke had Dan Hanning, a fellow member of the American Legion and one of his closest associates in the FBI, meet Brandy at National Airport. Hanning took Brandy directly to DeLoach's office.

Deke said, "What the heck goes on?"

"We have to move fast," Brandy said. He described Cornfeld and the pending deal with Trouyet to acquire the Mexican holdings and control large businesses in Mexico.

"Whether it is organized crime or the Reds, we have to figure out who is behind this 300 million dollar cash offer to Don Carlos Trouyet."

For about five hours, DeLoach's men made calls to embassies and to contacts in the intelligence community. Considering time zones and delays, it would be hours before information began to come back. Brandy was exhausted from his trip from Acapulco to Chicago and Washington, so DeLoach sent him to a hotel, the Twin Bridge Marriott, to get some sleep. Brandy no sooner had settled into bed after a shower and a relaxing cognac, than there was a knock on the door. Hanning had come to take him back to the office.

DeLoach had reports coming in confirming what Brandy had learned from his journalist friend. Cornfeld and IOS were under scrutiny, and several police forces were investigating the organization. Under U.S. law, foreign investors and mutual funds could purchase U.S. securities, without themselves being subject to Securities and Exchange Commission (SEC) rules, and American specialists were growing concerned at the scale of Cornfeld's holdings in American companies. Cornfeld had become successful by associating prestigious people in both the U.S. and Britain with his company, and their names on the board of directors helped create faith among small investors that IOS was a reputable firm. Cornfeld first worked with American expatriates living in Europe, who served as salesmen of mutual securities to servicemen stationed in Europe, and later to middle class European investors. Cornfeld had built IOS into a huge investment empire, growing immensely rich by manipulating the stock in ways that would have been illegal in the United States. Nevertheless, Cornfeld was not charged with any crime at the time; in fact, he had recently appeared at a meeting of Wall Street brokers, where he denounced the SEC in a well-received speech.

Brandy flew back to Mexico City to see Trouyet. It would be a job to convince Trouyet of the dangers, with nothing firmly proven at this point. He went into Trouyet's office. Before he could begin his report, Trouyet cut him off.

"Frank, relax, I have already canceled it." Trouyet had called the banking contacts, and they too, had warned him away from dealing with Cornfeld.

There was no way of confronting Cornfeld in the United States in 1970. Soon, however, DeLoach made contact with the Royal Canadian Mounted Police, and the Canadians made Cornfeld *persona non grata* there. Cornfeld lost control of the company in 1970; in 1971 IOS was taken over by Robert Vesco.

During the liftoffs at Cape Canaveral, Brandy was surprised at one of the parties held there for the astronauts. John King threw a party with over one thousand people in attendance. Brandy, from his knowledge of the hotel and entertainment business, was astounded. With free liquor, caviar, and canapés, the expense for the party was well up in the six figures. Brandy asked himself why anyone would spend so much to "romance the astronauts?" Brandy looked into King's background, and discovered that he owned a large petroleum enterprise, King Resources, and that he sought to bring aboard several of the astronauts to add their prestige to his firm. The practice seemed familiar.

As Brandy dug a little deeper, he found that King was beginning to operate his company as a front for Bernie Cornfeld and the IOS with extensive investments in Canadian oil properties. Brandy then heard that King had given $1 million to the Richard Nixon presidential campaign in the 1972 election.

Brandy called his contacts in the Republican National Finance Committee. In particular, he got in touch with Bebee Bourne, the head of the fund-raising committee, and asked to talk with her. She knew Frank from his attendance at the Republican Convention in 1968, when he had sat at the same table with her and Clement Stone. Brandy flew to Washington and had dinner with Bebee at the Statler Hilton.

"Bebee," said Brandy, "you've got a surprise. You've got Bernie Cornfeld in the background."

"What do you mean!" said Bebee. By this time, Cornfeld's wheeling-dealing had become well known.

"You've got a contribution from King, and King is a front for Bernie Cornfeld. You'd better return it. If it ever comes out, it would be bad publicity." King Resources' connections with Cornfeld were not yet open information.

Later that day, Bebee got in touch with James Mitchell and Maurice Stans, and then called Brandy at the hotel. "We are returning the million dollars to King," she told him.

Although Wally Schirra briefly lent his name to King Resources, Frank Borman, on Brandy's advice, rejected the offer of $1 million to become a director.

In many ways, Las Brisas continued to provide Brandy with access to information and allowed him to offer services to the U.S. Embassy. Fortress San Carlos, the new development, had thirty-three *casitas*. To get to the *casitas* and suites, one had to cross a bridge; one or two guards at the entrance could provide full control over access. The location would be ideal for high-level meetings, and he notified his contact at the U.S. Embassy of the facility:

> I was delighted to show you the area of the new [casitas and suites] under construction, especially the fortress area, which has only one entrance over a bridge and will be ideal for private diplomatic meetings. On the upper level of the fortress we have fifteen luxury one-room cottages with their own bars and fifteen private pools. Below these cottages we have 18 rooms similar to the ones above. This layout gives complete privacy control and security for any Diplomatic group.

From time to time, the special *casitas* could be put to good use and provide a secure residence for return guests, like Ambassador Peter Hope, who needed both privacy and protection.

One case came to Stillwell's notice as he dug into Brandy's information work. During the period following the Fitch conversation about the LOM, an event occurred that proved Brandy's ability to provide a

safe house. In 1970, a young woman working at the Soviet Embassy in
Mexico City chose to defect to the West. Raya Kiselnicova held a press
conference in February of that year, providing information about the
Soviets' use of the embassy staff in Mexico City as a base for espionage
and infiltration of radical groups throughout the Western Hemisphere.
In her explanation of the events at the embassy, she made clear that at
least half of the three-hundred-person staff there was engaged in espionage and subversion; the size of the embassy was out of all proportion to the direct interests of the USSR in Mexico. By contrast, Mexico
maintained only a six- or-seven- person staff at their embassy in Moscow.

As Stillwell gathered information about Brandy, he received a long
missive from a former CIA agent who had served in Mexico. Without
even using a pronoun that would reveal her gender, the writer explained
how Brandy had played a crucial part in Raya's successful defection:

> In the early 1970s, an official of the Soviet Union sought
> asylum and was granted asylum in Latin America. As is of-
> ten the case with defectors adjusting to a new life this per-
> son needed employment, understanding, and sympathy. It
> was important to the Central Intelligence Agency that this
> person be available for a considerable time after the defec-
> tion for intelligence purposes as well as to be dealt with in
> this sympathetic fashion. In a manner typical of him, Mr.
> Frank Brandstetter stepped forward to carry out these tasks
> as a matter, for him, of what he considered to be a patriotic
> duty. This was not an easy job because of the problems the
> defector had in adjusting to a new life. Mr. Brandstetter
> handled his role in this—and his was the principal, day to
> day role—with patience, tact, and understanding. He not
> only helped another person in need but rendered great
> service to the government of the United States in doing so.

The author of this oblique reference letter also included a cover note to
Stillwell in which he explained his reason for writing such a carefully
constructed, non-specific commendation.

I have attained the unsatisfactory compromise of writing one of those annoyingly vague citations. I feel it must be this way for I know nothing of the present status of the person Frank helped and helped us with—he did both. I suggest that if it comes to DCI participation that someone still on board review the case to see if something more specific might be said in the citation.

He need not have been so careful. John Barron's book on the KGB had already discussed the case and Raya's sanctuary at Las Brisas was a matter of public knowledge. Frank had arranged that she take the job of one of the assistant public relations officers, and as time passed, she got better at the job, using her fluency in Spanish and English and her knowledge of international affairs to promote the hotel. Twenty-five years later, she still resided in Acapulco, having seen the world turn around many times. Through the 1990s, Brandy continued to see her at least once every month. She, at least, had come in from the cold!

23

Keeping an Eye
on Acapulco

I n several other ways, the year 1970 had been one of great activity
for Brandy in the area of intelligence and information services to
the United States. Brandy wrote to his friend Roy Loftin, explaining that he had several "trophies to nail to the wall." In addition to
uncovering the fact that King had fronted for Cornfeld, and taking in
Raya from the Soviet Embassy, he quietly played a role in blocking an
effort by American underworld figures who hoped to establish gambling resorts in Mexico.

Although the methods that Brandy used to discover the details of
the proposed gambling operation were never made public, the center
of surveillance over a number of underworld figures was the Acapulco
Hilton, where the men Brandy had hired and trained continued to
handle security.

In 1970, the Illinois Racing Board held an extensive hearing into a
pair of racing license applications, questioning the purchase of two race
tracks by a large corporation which had also recently purchased the
Acapulco Towers, a small hotel. The Acapulco Towers had a shady reputation, and the board needed more information. The hearing transcript
gave hints concerning Brandy's assistance in the probe.

In the course of the hearings, the board invited Illinois Bureau of

Investigation (IBI) agents to testify about the interlocking arrangements they had uncovered between Moe Morton, the manager of the Acapulco Towers for several years, and crime figures Meyer Lansky, Hyman Siegel, Moe Dalitz, and others. Much of the information had been gathered, the IBI said, through surveillance arranged at the Acapulco Hilton. It was clear that Brandy's security men had assisted in tracing the activities of the underworld figures in Mexico, although their role was not directly mentioned. The story that the Illinois board heard, a tangle of associations and incidents, is summarized here.

Over the period 1966 to 1968, Moe Morton had been engaged in building homes across the street from the Las Brisas development. In 1968, he was arrested by the Mexican authorities for defaulting on a $225,000 note to an American woman who had financed one home. Morton was slightly acquainted with the ex-president of Mexico, Miguel Alemán, and used this relationship to impress visiting Americans, who would advance him funding to build properties. Morton bragged about other friendships, including American underworld figures such as Mickey Cohen, Meyer Lansky, Bugsy and Hyman Siegel, and Moe Dalitz, as well as Hollywood personalities who associated with the underworld. In fact, Morton had been subpoenaed in a number of interstate gambling and racketeering investigations, including a scandal at the Friars' Club in California. The company that placed slot machines at the club was found to have rigged them to cheat the players. Morton was investigated by U.S. border Customs agents on 14 November 1968, when he crossed from Mexico carrying a check for $154,000.

Richard Gleibe, an agent for the IBI, traveled to Acapulco under the pretense that he intended to buy real estate, including the facility previously operated by Morton, the Acapulco Towers. In the course of this investigation, Gleibe interviewed the contractor who built the hotel. The contractor explained that among the problems he had with Morton was the illegal smuggling of hardware, locks, and plumbing items into Mexico aboard his fifty-one-foot yacht. Eventually, Morton was charged with smuggling and paid a hefty fine to the Mexican government. Furthermore, he constantly bribed Mexican officials to overlook infractions of local codes, against the advice of the contractor.

Between 1968 and 1970, Morton sold the yacht he had used to smuggle construction materials to Moe Dalitz, reputedly the "architect" of the system of skimming profits from the gambling casinos in Las Vegas for the mob. Morton bragged that he had been a "bagman" in those skimming arrangements.

Agent Gleibe also interviewed Morton himself to learn more details. The total cost of construction of the Acapulco Towers was about $640,000, and the land expense an additional $110,000. The hotel was completed in November 1967, and Morton then operated the building, not exactly as a hotel, but as a guest-house for a limited number of friends, mostly from the shadowy group owning gambling hotel-casinos, including Hyman Siegel and Meyer Lansky. Using a tangled series of holding companies, Morton took control of the company owning Acapulco Towers and cheated other investors out of their holdings. Eventually, he too, was pushed out of ownership, and the building was then sold to an international corporation that sought to establish the Illinois race tracks.

Brandy got wind of the fact that Canadian and American crime figures were planning a meeting at the Acapulco Towers in late February and early March 1970. He hoped to arrange a "roll up" of the individuals, such as had taken place at the famous organized crime arrest in Apalachin, New York, in November 1957, when fifty-eight men were arrested, including Carlo Gambino, Joseph Bonanno, Vito Genovese, and Joseph Profaci. From conversations with ex-President Alemán, Brandy concluded that the group visiting Acapulco in February 1970, many with gambling connections, hoped to establish a casino in Mexico.

Alemán had been interested in the revenue a casino could bring, but feared that a casino, if open to Mexican citizens, would drain away their hard-earned cash. If open only to foreigners, it would become a target for anti-foreign feelings, an insult to the Mexican people. It was the same problem which casinos had represented for Cuba, when they had become a source of income for organized crime, a drain on the resources of the Cuban people, and a symbol for the revolutionaries of international exploitation and foreign arrogance. Lansky and others from the American criminal world had been prominent in the Havana casinos on the eve of Castro's takeover; law enforcement authorities had assumed that the 1957 Apalachin meeting had been a planning session regarding participation in the Havana casinos.

Alemán and Brandy had discussed a number of proposals, including ideas to build a casino on Roqueta Island at the entrance to Acapulco Bay. If the transportation to the island was expensive, it might effectively exclude Mexicans who could not afford losing their money in the casino, yet it would not keep them out on the basis of national identity. Brandy's ideas to develop a Plexiglas underwater tunnel to carry trains from the mainland to the island caught Alemán's fancy.

From such discussions, Brandy was able to put two and two together. Clearly, Lansky, Siegel, Dalitz, and Morton were not arranging meetings in Acapulco simply for the climate. Brandy recommended to his friend, Alemán, not to get involved with them.

From the Acapulco Hilton, Brandy's security staff, all Mexican ex-secret services men, tipped the American Embassy that Meyer Lansky and his attorney, Moses Polakoff, were at the hotel, together with a Canadian crime figure, Ben Kaufman. Later, the IBI investigator examined the registration cards at the Acapulco Towers and found an extensive list of attendees at the Acapulco meeting, which was held in

Brandy chats with Miguel Alemán, president of Mexico from 1946 to 1952.

late February and early March 1970, including individuals from the Las Vegas casino interests, and others associated with organized crime in the United States. At the prompting of Brandy and his associates in the Acapulco Hilton security staff, Mexican authorities broke up the meeting and put everyone aboard airplanes that would leave the country at 3:00 A.M. on 4 March, in coordination with assistance from the U.S. legal attaché. Many of the individuals were stopped on arrival in the United States or Canada for questioning. Giancana's arrest on arrival marked the end of his career. Meyer Lansky was detained at the Miami airport on 4 March 1970, and was found to have a prescription drug (Donnatol, for his stomach ulcers) for which he had no prescription, and later was charged with the crime. He was acquitted of the charge in June 1970. While not exactly an "Apalachin Roll-Up," the surveillance and the information gathered at the Hilton and the Acapulco Towers put a stop to the mob's effort to establish a gambling base in Acapulco. The sale of the Acapulco Towers later in 1970 to a corporate investor marked the end of that effort.

Sometimes the contacts that Brandy made at the hotel led to insights into major operations of the international underworld, often years after the meeting. Through the 1960s, Brandy became acquainted as a personal friend with one unusual repeat visitor to Las Brisas, a man who unexpectedly and innocently gave him information about such issues. The visitor was Auxiliary Bishop Joe Green from Lansing, Michigan.

Bishop Green regularly traveled to Mexico with two or three monsignors for an annual vacation, all as Brandy's personal guests. Like Brandy, Bishop Green enjoyed gin rummy, and the two would play into the early hours of the morning, discussing all the problems of the world. Bishop Green had taken the lead in the Lansing area in persuading the Catholic schools and the parish priests to argue against the space-exploration program, on the grounds that funds devoted to space could be better devoted to social problems. Over gin rummy, Bishop Green explained his position to Brandy. One night Brandy took issue with him.

"With all due respect for your position, bishop, I have to disagree with you about the space program. Look, do you take out insurance on church properties, buildings, and so on?"

"Sure," said the bishop, puzzled.

"Well, think of it this way. Our space program is insurance. If we do not develop one, the Russians will. Then, with command of space, the U.S. will be at their mercy. So the space program is insurance for our whole way of life." Brandy then declared an eleven-card gin. The bishop had lost again. Although Bishop Green did not seem convinced at the time, later that year Brandy learned from one of the bishop's associates that the homilies against the space program had come to an end.

In 1966, Bishop Green told Brandy that just prior to his leaving for Acapulco, some of his parishioners had kidded him that he was traveling to the "sin center" of Las Brisas, with its *dolce-vita* reputation, private swimming pools and honeymoon *casitas.* The bishop and his colleagues almost canceled their trip. One of the reasons they continued to come was the perfect privacy that Las Brisas provided for its guests, not publicizing the comings and goings of famous individuals who preferred not to be followed by the press. Bishop Green remained a regular, especially admiring Frank's construction of the cross and chapel on the hill above his house. He often said masses in Brandy's small private chapel in the corner of the back patio at Casa Tranquilidad.

Bishop Green also developed a reputation in the Catholic Church for his ability to raise funds. He was transferred to Las Vegas, where, the church hoped, he could use his influence to obtain large contributions from the wealthy investors and businessmen of the thriving gambling community. Through the 1970s, Green continued to visit Las Brisas, maintaining his friendship with Brandy. After Brandy left the hotel in 1976, Green visited him at Casa Tranquilidad, where the late night discussions over gin rummy would continue.

In 1982, a massive scandal washed over the Catholic Church. The Vatican Minister of Finance, Archbishop Paul Marcinkus, an American by birth, became identified with several interlocking swindles. Earlier, American organized crime figures had attempted to sell nearly $950 million worth of stolen and counterfeit stock certificates to the Vatican Bank, controlled by Marcinkus, at a deep discount. Marcinkus, although linked to that arrangement, had not been indicted, nor had any proof of his complicity been established. Archbishop Marcinkus convinced authorities that he had been an innocent tool, and as such, had been used.

Then, Milan's Banco Ambrosiano, holding more than $1.25 billion in unsecured loans to Latin American banks, failed. With the bank on the verge of collapse, bank director Roberto Calvi disappeared, to be found later in London hanging under a bridge over the Thames, an apparent suicide. Italian police investigations uncovered more material. Banco Ambrosiano had been acquired by four Panamanian companies that were in turn owned by a Bahamian bank, Cisalpine Overseas Bank of Nassau. On the board of that bank was Archbishop Marcinkus. The Italians issued an indictment against Marcinkus, preventing him from leaving the Vatican for years, for fear of arrest.

Bishop Green had been selling bonds provided from the Vatican Bank in Las Vegas for the church. With the collapse of the Vatican Bank, the exposure of the Ambrosiano holdings, and further revelations that Roberto Calvi had possibly been killed by a member of Italy's organized crime and a leader of a secret Masonic lodge in Rome, Lodge "P-2," Green retired in disgrace. A broken man, he returned once to Acapulco and explained the details to Brandy.

The man accused of ordering the killing of Roberto Calvi was Licio Gelli, a reputed Italian crime figure and organizer of the "P-2" Masonic lodge. Strangely, Catholic Archbishop Marcinkus and other Catholic bishops were members of this very powerful Masonic lodge.

In the early 1980s, Brandy received a call from the military attaché at the U.S. Embassy in Mexico City.

"We are sending two guys down to talk to you, Brandy. See if you can give them any help," said the attaché at the embassy.

"Sure," said Brandy. "But you know, I'm retired. I am out of the business now."

The attaché replied, "Just see if you can help them out."

The next day, two young men from the CIA appeared and explained their problem. Licio Gelli, who was wanted all over the world for questioning in connection with the death of Calvi, was reputed to be planning to buy a house in Acapulco. He was said to be bribing officials to prevent his arrest, moving from one villa to another in several countries, including Uruguay. The agents needed assistance in discovering the location of his new home in Acapulco.

Brandy was nonplussed.

"Look," he said, "I'm just a private citizen. You guys have all the re-sources, all the millions, all the contacts. What can you expect me to do?"

"You have the local contacts. Wherever he goes, Gelli apparently builds a house with a parabolic antenna for satellite TV. He also likes lots of security. Maybe you can spot the place."

Brandy delicately declined.

"Look," he said, "I'm retired. I want to live quietly and in peace. The answer is no."

The two got a bit huffy.

"We have direct orders," one of them said. "Orders from the White House, President Reagan."

Brandy had met President Reagan and Vice President George Bush, and had supported them together with Gordon McLendon, making heavy contributions to the Republican Party. Furthermore, a presiden-tial order was a presidential order. His answer was simple.

"OK. If the president wants it, I'll do it. I'll assist in any way I am able."

The agents were satisfied. One of them brought out pictures of Gelli, both front and side views, which Brandy or his men could use to recog-nize him.

Still, Brandy thought the fellows were a little naive. Acapulco had become a huge, sprawling metropolis. There were literally dozens of neighborhoods where fugitives could hide out. But he agreed to give it a try. They provided him with their phone number at their office in Mexico City.

After they left, he thought through the situation, narrowing down the options. First of all, Gelli would probably choose a wealthy and ex-pensive neighborhood, so his luxurious and large house would not stand out. That led to two communities: the Club Residencial itself, where Brandy continued to serve on the board of the homeowners' associa-tion, and an older exclusive neighborhood near La Quebrada Point. A quick check of the records of Club Residencial Las Brisas revealed no suspicious transfers in recent months or years. That still left the possibil-ity that the house could be somewhere in the La Quebrada neighbor-hood of very private villas, most with high walls.

Another approach was the parabolic antennae. Although they were becoming popular in the 1980s, they were hardly on every home or estate. Brandy spread the word among his contacts, and soon, several properties were pinpointed as possible candidates. He looked at each.

One house in particular in Le Quebrada struck him as the most probable target. It had high walls and the required antenna. It was on a cul-de-sac street, with a second entrance on another street. No one knew the tenants, and the guards at the house carried automatic weapons. Furthermore, a stairway led down the cliff to a secluded dock, for a third possible protected access. Further examination showed that trees had been cut to give the home clear fields of fire down the streets to its entrances, providing even more security. Whoever had acquired the property understood security very well, and the date of transfer fit.

Brandy called the agents in Mexico City at the number they had provided.

"I think I might have your man's place," he said.

"Good," came the reply. "Now we need to set up surveillance."

"Fine," said Brandy, "come down and I'll show you the place and you can go from there."

"No. We are too conspicuous there. Please rent us a place nearby, and we will get three 'sports fishermen' to come for a few weeks' stay. You get the place rented, and set it all up, and we'll bring the boys down."

Renting a place in that neighborhood would not be all that easy, thought Brandy. However, it would indeed be easier for him than for a couple of young Americans from Mexico City with crewcuts, trench coats, and sunglasses.

Brandy checked the neighborhood. One of the houses a few doors away belonged to a former guest and friend from the United States who had stayed at Las Brisas many times. Brandy called him and told him he would like to rent the house for a short period. He could hear the silence as his friend in California did a double take at the other end of the line.

"Well, thanks, Brandy, but the house is not for rent."

Brandy had to argue, explaining that he would guarantee against damages, and that he would personally pay the first month's rent in advance, with a deposit. The "fishermen" would be very respectable, and would not be throwing any parties. So, he said, do me a favor, and let me have it for two months. Reluctantly, the owner agreed, and Brandy sent a check to cover the expenses for one month in advance, drawn from his own personal account.

Over the next few days, he transferred the funds, drew up the agreement, sent the check, got the confirmation, and lined up the house keys. When everything was ready, he called the agents back in Mexico City.

"Brandstetter here. I have that house rented that you wanted me to arrange," he said.

"Oh, well, we received word that the operation is called off. We got orders to drop the whole matter."

Brandy knew such things happened. Perhaps Gelli had been spotted elsewhere; orders were orders. But there was something bothering him.

"When did you hear about the cancellation?" he asked.

"About a week ago."

The agents did not offer to reimburse him for his outlay of cash. Information gathering had its frustrations. Brandy learned, one more time, how the young men at the CIA worked.

24

A Stay with Seagrams

I t had been in 1962 that Brandy met a young man who was to influence his future after leaving Las Brisas. During the hectic stretch
from just before Christmas to right after New Year's Eve, every
room in Acapulco was booked, and there was no room for unfortu-
nate couples who arrived without a reservation. One night, Brandy,
passing the registration desk from his office, noticed a loud commo-
tion in progress. He discovered a young man and his wife, the man
angrily confronting the desk clerk. He had a reservation, he insisted,
and the hotel had simply lost it. He was getting very upset and his face
was flushed.

Brandy approached, and in his most calm voice, inquired as to the
trouble. He checked the records, then rechecked them. There was no
reservation and no cash deposit on record for Edgar Bronfman, the
angry young man. Brandy explained that the travel agent, or whoever
had claimed to make the reservations, had not really done so. Something about the man's name struck Brandy, and he asked, "Are you related to Sam Bronfman?"

"I'm his son!"

Brandy carefully steered Edgar and his wife to the bar and ordered
them drinks. Meanwhile, he spoke softly in Spanish to the desk clerk.

"Have housekeeping go up to my *casita* and clear out all of my things from the living room, and make up the two studio beds there. Clean everything up and make it ready for two personal guests—clean up the bathroom, provide new soap, and towels."

At the bar, Brandy quietly soothed the irate Mr. Bronfman.

"Look," he said, "it is not our fault that your reservation was not properly made here. There are absolutely no rooms to be had tonight in Acapulco. But I can't stand the thought of turning you and your wife away, when you came all the way here for a vacation. I remember your father. Years ago, he did me a real favor." Brandy was thinking back to 1939, when the elder Bronfman had allowed Brandy and his partners to pay off their outstanding debt for the Champlain Hotel over an extended period. "You and your wife can stay in my own apartment tonight, and we'll see what we can work out tomorrow."

He took the Bronfmans up to his casita, and they were delighted. The next day, Brandy was able to fit them into a canceled reservation, and Bronfman's potentially miserable experience had been turned into a happy one, beginning a good relationship with a new friend.

Edgar did not forget Brandy's kindness. Year after year, he returned at Christmas, with correct reservations each time, always staying at Las Brisas and confiding with Brandy about his personal investments in the motion picture business. Brandy advised his good friend to concentrate on the liquor business his father had founded. Brandy was never a "yes" man and never sought anything from Edgar; thus he felt his words of advice were respected.

Edgar told his father about Brandy, and Sam Bronfman remembered the Champlain Hotel incident. Edgar eventually bought two five-bedroom residences in the Club Residencial Las Brisas established by Brandy and Trouyet.

In 1964, Sam Bronfman discussed a proposition with Brandy and Edgar. Seagrams was planning a major investment in Mexico to establish Seagrams de Mexico (SDM) and build a major distillery. Brandy could join as general manager and vice president of the company. In addition to a handsome salary, he would be given ten percent stock in the firm, representing a value of about $3 million, U.S. currency. Because at this point Brandy had recently agreed to continue at Las Brisas as general manager, had invested his own money in the hotel, and had become Trouyet's partner, the timing of Bronfman's offer was not right.

"Look," said Brandy, "I am fully committed here at Las Brisas. I appreciate the offer. I would be happy to be a consultant—to be your 'eyes and ears' here in Mexico—but I know nothing about the liquor business." Sam Bronfman understood, and Seagrams went ahead with building a multi-million dollar investment in Mexico, producing and distributing products and investing in tequila production in Guadalajara. For old times' sake, Brandy assisted in marketing all the Seagrams products, carrying them in the mini-bars and pushing their sales at Las Brisas.

In 1971, Sam Bronfman passed away, and after the company went through some reorganization, Edgar Bronfman emerged as chief executive officer and chairman of the board of Joseph E. Seagrams & Sons, Incorporated (JES), the parent firm in New York. Charles Bronfman, Edgar's brother, became vice president.

Brandy kept in touch with Edgar, as he continued to travel to Acapulco for holidays, staying at the family houses there. On 12 July 1976, after Banamex had taken over Las Brisas and Brandy was replaced as general manager of the hotel, he received a phone call from Edgar Bronfman.

"Brandy," said Edgar, "I hear you left Las Brisas. I want you to come to work for me."

Brandy was astounded. "How did you know?" he asked. "It only happened this morning!"

"I have my sources," said Edgar, imitating Brandy's own style. "Come to New York and we'll talk about it."

Brandy explained that he wanted some weeks to go into retreat, to think, and to relax.

"I'm on my way to Bohemian Grove," he explained, "in the Russian River country north of San Francisco. I've already accepted the invitation. I don't want to be involved in operations, in an operating capacity in any company. I'm ready to retire, do some traveling. But on the day I leave the Grove, I'll give you a call and see what I can do to help—perhaps I can be your 'eyes and ears' during my planned travels worldwide."

On 15 July 1976, Brandy flew to San Francisco, and drove out to Bohemian Grove for a stay at the 1976 Summer Encampment, hosted by his friend, the novelist Allen Drury, who lived in nearby Marin County. After a two-week round of parties and lectures under the redwoods, staying in the "Totem-In" camp section, he called Bronfman and made an appointment for 26 July. He flew to New York, arriving in mid-morning to see Edgar as promised.

The receptionist said that Edgar wanted him to come right in as soon as he arrived, so Brandy stuck his head in the office door. Seeing that Edgar was in a conference, he apologized. "No, no," said Bronfman, "come on in, Brandy."

As Brandy stepped in, he was astonished to hear Bronfman say to the group, "Gentlemen, I want you to meet Frank Brandstetter, the new general manager and vice president of our operations in Mexico."

"Hold on a minute," said Brandy. "I told you I want no part of operations. We need to talk this out, Edgar."

Talk it out they did. After less than an hour, Bronfman convinced Brandy to assume the general manager's position at Seagrams de Mexico for a year and a half to two years, as Brandy suggested to them, to get the company into shape. He would receive a substantial salary, with all social security and taxes paid in Mexico and the United States, together with a hefty expense account. Brandy could keep his house in Acapulco, work in Mexico City during the weekdays, and fly home for the weekends. After one or two years, he could switch to another role, less involved in operations, and serve as Edgar's personal representative, his "eyes and ears," on international trips. But first, he had to get the Mexican company in shape. Edgar gave him a bundle of materials to read that night, and the next day Brandy was to meet some of the other executives.

On the 27th, Brandy met with Harold Fieldsteel, executive vice president for Finance and Administration of JES; with F. Shaker, vice president, International Administration Division; and with James E. McDonough, who was president of Seagrams Overseas Sales Company (SOSCO). They gave him an extensive background briefing.

Despite optimistic business plans prepared by Shaker in 1966, the Mexican company had failed to move into the black during its nearly ten years of operation. In 1967, SDM had bought into La Martinena, a tequila distillery in Jalisco owned by the Ruíz family, from which Seagrams had previously purchased tequila. Seagrams hoped to establish a stronger position in both the domestic market for tequila in Mexico and the growing export market to the United States. In addition to the distillery, SDM had acquired fifty-one percent interest in Ruíz mescal plantations, over six hundred hectares, worth more than $1 million in American currency. Inter-company price agreements worked out between the tequila operation and SDM, which were supposed to guarantee a profit to the Ruíz family, led to a decline in their income from the days when they had been an independent firm. They grew restless with Seagrams and offered to sell out to them entirely, but nothing had been agreed. Then the Ruíz family increasingly began to sell their product outside the Seagrams family of companies. Seagrams, in turn, found that despite agreements among all tequila producers, some companies were undercutting the agreed prices and hurting the position of Seagrams exports to the United States. Some of the undercutting tequila came from distributors supplied by the Ruíz plantations!

It was difficult for Brandy to get clear cost figures because the books of SDM appeared to offer contradictory information. Rumors had spread of theft, mishandling, corruption, and general incompetence at various levels. Huge, unsold inventories carried on the books may or may not have been in the warehouses. Clearly the company needed a strong hand and some improvements in practices, personnel, direction, and morale. It would be a challenge.

On the second day, after the meetings with the managers, Edgar Bronfman, who seemed troubled, escorted Brandy to the elevator and drew him aside as they waited.

"Brandy, your first priority is to help me save my reputation with my family members. The Mexican company is your second priority."

Brandy took this as a mission to help his friend. As he learned more about the Mexican operation and Seagrams in general, he gained a clearer picture of what Edgar was talking about.

Early in August 1976, Shaker flew to Mexico and met with Brandy at Casa Tranquilidad to iron out details. Also attending were two men from Las Brisas, Felipe Chiu and Manuel Escalante, whom Brandy wanted to bring in as part of his new team at SDM, and a financial officer from SDM who had been appointed a few months earlier. Shaker agreed that, initially, Brandy could bring in as many as four new employees, and that some of the executive personnel at SDM would be let go. Shaker agreed to a budget of over $160,000 to cover the severance costs imposed by Mexican labor law, of those dismissed as well as those hired from other firms. It was agreed that for Brandy's health, he could get away from the air pollution of Mexico City and return to his home in Acapulco every week.

On 12 August, he took up his new position at Seagrams. From the beginning he faced several crises, involving completely unreliable book-keeping methods, poor morale, apparent theft and corruption, and personality conflicts among not only the management in Mexico, but also among those at the New York headquarters. Seagrams itself was undergoing internal dissension in the mid-1970s, as various factions jock-eyed for position in the aftermath of Sam Bronfman's passing. Glim-mers of the conflict surfaced in the trade papers and business pages of national newspapers during these years.

One of the first crises Brandy dealt with was a strike at the distillery plant in Jalisco. On 14 August, he flew to Guadalajara and negotiated directly with the union representatives. Brandy toured the plant and found that it was a mess, with inadequate and filthy bathrooms and lock-ers for the employees and unsafe working conditions. Assurances that the plant was not going to close and that conditions would be addressed settled the walkout. Over the next months, Brandy personally moni-tored improvements at the distillery, overseeing the work himself. In the warehouse, where the barrels were located, he discovered that some of them had a hollow sound when struck with a wooden hammer. They turned out to be empty or half-empty, but were carried in the ware-house computer as full stock. There was obvious theft!

On 1 September 1976, only a few weeks after Brandy started, the Mexican peso was devalued. This immediately threw all Mexican busi-nesses, particularly those relying on imports, into a tailspin. Brandy ex-plained to Fieldsteel in New York that he had insisted that stocks of imported liquor be built up, but that the local accountants had com-plained that SDM could not get credit. Now, with the peso devalued, freshly imported products from overseas would be prohibitively expen-sive. Brandy began to suspect, in his first months, that someone in the company had been trying to ruin it in order to allow an outside purchase. He passed on his suspicions to New York, but received little sympathy there.

During September, he discovered that the Electronic Data Processing (EDP) system at Seagrams de Mexico was a complete mess. Completely different figures recording the amount lost over prior years would be generated from day to day, fluctuating wildly with each printout. Brandy recommended and began to implement personnel changes, getting rid of those he found incompetent and replacing them quickly. Over the next year and a half, he brought in more than twenty new executives, most of them former employees from Las Brisas. Slowly, the books began to make better sense, although the EDP system remained unreliable.

Brandy believed that one of the problems faced by Seagrams de Mexico was its lack of public recognition and public image. As he looked into the business, he found that the population in general, and most of the people within Seagrams in Mexico, failed to recognize the wide variety of products manufactured by Seagrams affiliates worldwide. Working with publicist Nicolás Sánchez Osorio, Brandy set up plans to celebrate the tenth anniversary of Seagrams with a gala event in Mexico City, and to use the event to display Seagrams products from all over the world.

Using his lists of contacts from Las Brisas, over 150 distinguished guests were invited to a party held on 4 November 1976 in Mexico City. Ambassadors, airline representatives, society notables, and travel agents attended the function. Displays of Seagrams products, including a collection of dozens of miniatures, decorated each table to be given away. Guests were provided with a handsome case containing miniature samples of scotch, gin, vodka, wines, and liqueurs from around the world, all products of Seagrams affiliates. Snacks of cheese and fruit accompanied the drinks and speeches.

Edgar Bronfman and executives Harold Fieldsteel, Jim McDonough, F. Shaker, and the Mexican officials of the SDM, Aarón Sáenz, Sr., and Aarón Sáenz, Jr., all attended. Nicolás Sánchez Osorio made certain that the distinguished company was photographed and written up for the society columns and the Sunday supplement, *Novissimo*, which he published. The attendance of so many luminaries gave the event wide coverage throughout the Mexican press.

Brandy, Fieldsteel, and Bronfman had a few private moments at the gala. Brandy told them that the company was in a dilemma; the way the books and the EDP system had been maintained amounted to gross negligence. Bronfman turned to Fieldsteel and smacked his fist down. "I knew it," he said. "I knew it all along." From that moment on, Brandy felt he had made an enemy of Fieldsteel. This feeling became a certainty later on. Fieldsteel did not agree with Brandy's harsh assessment of the Mexican company, perhaps because many of the problems had developed over the last ten years when he had tried to manage the widespread international holdings of Seagrams. Brandy realized that his comments and suggestions had not been getting to Edgar, and that he would have to report personally and fully. He felt he had to tell the truth, no matter how much it hurt. Furthermore, he believed he had a special mission to work for Edgar and be totally honest with him.

After the tenth anniversary party in November, the problems continued. Brandy flew to London to attend a meeting of the board of directors. In the complex world of Seagrams, the holding company for SDM was a British corporation. There, Brandy explained the progress to date, and had a chance to renew his friendships with a few contacts, including the Prince and Princess of Liechtenstein, some of his old friends at Scotland Yard, and at MI-5 and MI-6.

At the end of the year, after working for about six months, Brandy wrote an extensive and private report to Edgar Bronfman, spelling out the sorts of problems he encountered. Seagrams de Mexico, he came to believe, would be an ideal case study for the Harvard Business School on how *not* to run a company. One of the most severe issues was the problem of money supposedly owed to the Mexican government for tax stamps. According to the Secretaría de Hacienda (Mexico's equivalent of the Internal Revenue Service), the company was over $1 million in arrears, including fines for overdue payments. A review of the files finally revealed the canceled checks for the amounts, all properly sent and deposited. Brandy suggested that the company should file suit with the government to set aside the tax claim. He was advised not to do so by members of the "24 Club," of which he was a member, made up of presidents of large international businesses who managed plants worldwide, including Mexico. "No one wins against the government," the members told him.

Brandy, however, insisted on moving forward. Working with a law firm, the company presented its case. The Secretaría de Hacienda placed an "impost" on the firm as the case proceeded. The case seemed clear cut—somehow there had been a mistake. As government investigators dug deeper, they found that one or more employees in the tax office, working with cohorts at the government's bank, had cashed the checks and transferred the cash to their own pockets, not crediting the company. Apparently, other companies had also been affected by this massive theft. The claim against Seagrams was dropped and the impost lifted. One battle won.

Working with Sánchez Osorio, Brandy developed further publicity efforts for Seagrams, including the convening of "Seagrams International Backgammon Tournaments," held at his home in Acapulco. Sánchez Osorio, who had served on the management team for a backgammon tournament held in Monte Carlo funded by Philip Morris Company and also had organized an international backgammon tournament in January 1976 for Brandy held at the Fortress San Carlos section of Las Brisas, worked out the details and gathered an international group to attend. It was the first backgammon tournament held in Acapulco. Sánchez Osorio was well connected with the international backgammon set who would participate. In December 1976, Brandy hosted another tournament, attended by over 150 guests at his home. Only Seagrams products were served, and the backgammon tournament provided Sánchez Osorio with colorful copy for issues of *Novíssimo*. Among the guests were backgammon players from Britain, France, Greece, Spain, and the United States, as well as from Mexico. Registration fees, supplemented with a small amount from Seagrams, allowed for cash prizes of several thousand dollars to the winners and runners-up at different levels of play. Sánchez Osorio arranged for five beautiful models to present a poolside fashion show, as he had for the Las Brisas tournament. Between the attractive models clad in bikinis and the various rich and famous attending as players or onlookers, the December event at Casa Tranquilidad received front page coverage all over Mexico. Edgar Bronfman and his wife were among the guests.

Brandy hired Felipe Chiu, formerly of Las Brisas, to become director of Marketing and Public Relations for Seagrams. Chiu organized a number of other events through 1976 and 1977 that kept Seagrams in the public eye. In December 1976, SDM sponsored a Silver Fair in the mining city of Taxco. A special dining-club car was placed in a parking lot, where Seagrams products were served and where the Seagrams logo and name were prominently displayed. From 25 February through 27 February 1977, Seagrams sponsored a Grand Golf Tournament, held at the Club de Golf, at Acozac on the Mexico-Puebla highway. The prize money, the prominent players, and the publicity releases got coverage for Seagrams in sports pages across Mexico, including the high-circulation *El Sol de Mexico*, in Mexico City.

Other events included a yacht regatta held in Puerto Vallarta, and a reception thrown by Brandy for his colleagues from the Seagrams Company in Argentina, held at the Princess Hotel in Acapulco. At each of these events the prominence of the Seagrams logo, the bars displaying

The first international backgammon tournament was held at Fortress San Carlos, Las Brisas, in 1976.

Seagrams products, and the press coverage all brought the company name to the public and to hotel managers in glamorous circumstances. The motto of the company, "quality and prestige," was amplified and echoed by the events.

In 1977, another crisis for SDM developed, this one originating in the United States. The U.S. Securities and Exchange Commission (SEC) conducted an investigation into the contributions made by Seagrams and by Bronfman to the 1972 and 1976 electoral campaigns of specific candidates. The SEC accused the firm of not properly reporting contributions and of having donated liquor to political party functions without properly recording the gifts as donations. Brandy was informed that SEC investigators would be visiting Mexico in mid-August 1977, and that they would be particularly interested in whether Edgar Bronfman himself had violated laws prohibiting U.S. firms from engaging in bribery in foreign countries.

At the Bronfman dual homes in Acapulco, some 121 cases of liquor had been supplied for use over the period 1975 to 1977. About sixty cases had been consumed, with some of the bottles given away as gifts. The SEC investigators asked whether any of the liquor had been used to pay off local or immigration officials when the Bronfmans had brought with them their Spanish nursemaid, whose papers had not been complete. Brandy was prepared for these questions, and had a fairly detailed account of the disposition of the household liquor cases, together with a legitimate account of how gift bottles were distributed without any intent to bribe. While he handled the interrogation perfectly well, he was suspicious. Someone in New York, Brandy believed, was trying to put pressure on Edgar, and he had his theory concerning the source of information that had led the SEC to question the private liquor stocks at the Acapulco houses. Only a few people had access to that information. Accordingly, he warned Edgar, in a private "eyes only" memo, what he thought was going on.

Brandy attended the fall meeting of the board of directors in London again, and received word that his replacement at SDM had been selected to take over the job as of 1 January 1978, as previously planned. Brandy felt that much work still needed to be done to get the company running smoothly, but with his new team in place, many of the problems were beginning to be resolved. He was gratified with the official statement of the directors: "The Board wished to record its appreciation of Mr. Brandstetter's efforts on behalf of the company over the last 18 trying months, when his strenuous efforts had kept the credibility of the company very much to the fore."

Brandy's next position with the company was director of Diplomatic and International Account Sales, with Seagrams Overseas Sales Company (SOSCO). He began working for James E. McDonough and Ed Deheny from the New York office. Brandy's real mission was to visit Edgar personally and pass on any unusual business transactions in the Seagrams empire.

Brandy found the new deal attractive. In addition to his salary, again with all taxes and social security prepaid, he would receive a strong travel and entertainment budget. He was to develop a plan for sales of Seagrams products, concentrating on luxury international hotels, international airlines, embassies, and other diplomatic facilities. Using his contacts and arranging trips around the world, he would meet with the chief executives of the companies and personally introduce them to the local Seagrams executives to arrange purchase of Seagrams products. This concept avoided kickbacks at the hotel chains by consummating liquor sales at central headquarters, rather than at the individual hotel or beverage manager level.

Brandy plunged into his new SOSCO activities with vigor, putting behind him the job at Seagrams de Mexico. He planned his campaign like a military operation, describing his mission as "OPERATION DOOR OPENER," with several phases. Phase I involved making contacts in the Western Hemisphere with a series of executives, at the correct level, in international hotel companies and airlines. Phase II would come later, traveling through Europe, and Phase III would involve an Asian trip.

He designed, and had Seagrams agree to print, a brochure showing dozens of their products, including not only the famous Canadian and American brands, but scotch, liqueurs, vodkas, gins, wines, and champagne from around the world. The brochures received immediate reactions as he gave them out at functions, parties, and scheduled meetings. People simply had no idea that such diverse brands as Israeli Sabra, Swiss Cheri Suisse, Dutch Vandermint, Scotch Chivas Regal, The

Glenlivet, Irish Bushmills, and Myers's Rum were all Seagrams products. Altogether there were over forty American products, more than ten from the United Kingdom, with groups of products from Brazil, Argentina, Chile, Venezuela, and elsewhere. People who read the brochure and talked to Brandy were impressed with the fact that Seagrams could sell, from its bonded warehouses in Antwerp, case-lot loads of dozens of brands, including wines, champagnes, liqueurs, and the finest whiskeys, at very attractive wholesale prices. Taxes would only be paid at the country of receipt.

Brandy offered his home to Conde Nast publications for a get-together of 150 people in August 1978. He also attended the American Society of Travel Agents convention in Acapulco. Through this period, because of Brandy's knack for public relations, both Seagrams, and his particular role in Seagrams, appeared in the press a number of times.

Brandy planned his trips and contacts through 1978, working from detailed lists in hotel industry directories and his own contacts. The travel budget had been set for four thousand dollars per month, but Brandy's expenses during 1978 led SOSCO officials to decide to cut the amount at the end of the year. Brandy soon discovered that there were several other difficulties. Apparently SOSCO had not paid the IRS, as had JES, even though they had agreed to do so. Brandy received a huge bill from the U.S. Internal Revenue Service. He also began to encounter delays and some diffidence at headquarters as he wrote and telephoned about arranging his 1979 travel plans.

Finally, early in March 1979, James McDonough wrote to Brandy, deciding to terminate the arrangement and pay him through mid-year. "These arrangements," wrote McDonough, "do not appear to be appealing or practical...the results do not justify expense or manpower involved." Brandy was disappointed that Edgar did not touch base with him and was hurt by this apparent neglect. He felt that his OPERATION DOOR OPENER had not been given a fair chance to succeed.

On taking the job, Brandy had been informed that he was not to clinch any sales, but simply to open the door for others to make the sales arrangements. He felt that when they did not follow up, he received the blame for the operation not leading to results. Furthermore, as he traveled, he had continued to report to Bronfman, by what he still believed were "eyes only" memos, concerning evidence of corruption or violations of the company's rules against conflicts of interest. He later realized that some of those reports had been seen by the very individuals he reported about, making his position increasingly less tenable in the hot-house of corporate office politics at New York headquarters.

Brandy tried to understand Edgar's personal and business problems, yet, for years he wondered just who poisoned the very close personal relations that had existed between the two of them. This relationship had at one time been so close that Edgar once told his wife, while the three were flying from Acapulco to New York, "If anything should happen to me, see Brandy. He is as dear to me as my father was. He will give you straight advice." Then Edgar rose and kissed Brandy on the forehead.

On 10 November 1998, Brandy received an inscribed copy of *Good Spirits: The Making of a Businessman*, by Edgar Bronfman. A mutual friend, who sent the book to Brandy in Acapulco, told him that Edgar did not have time to personalize any copies at the book signing. When he found out, however, that a copy would be sent to Brandy, he said, 'I love that man—please give him my love.' With that, he personalized the book. This anecdote made Brandy feel that his old friendship was re-established after nineteen years. In celebration, Brandy raised a glass of Chivas Regal, his favorite Scotch whiskey, and drank to Edgar's health and happiness.

Edgar Bronfman, Chief Executive Officer and Chairman of the Board of Seagrams had a close friendship and productive working relationship with Brandy.

25

Islands in Crisis: Cyprus, Malvinas, Corsica

By 1979, at the age of sixty-seven, Brandy was ready for some serious rest and relaxation, and looked forward to resuming his plans for international travel, with interludes at Casa Tranquilidad. Despite good advice from General Matthew Ridgway and others who knew him well, Brandy could not resist traveling to points of crisis around the world. He would combine his vacations, some to resorts, others to remote areas, with a quiet self-appointed mission to keep his "eyes and ears" open, and report back what he found to General Ridgway, to the ACSI, and later, to the Intelligence Community Staff under Vice Admiral Al Burkhalter.

He developed his own standard operating procedure. He traveled light, but always took along formal clothes in case he was invited to a reception. He did not go with prearranged contacts, preferring to develop his own on the trip. He took large amounts of cash, usually ten thousand dollars, together with a supply of travelers' checks. The cash sometimes came in handy. He minimized his contacts, only rarely touching base with the U.S. legal or military attachés in the countries visited, and then only if directly requested by the ACSI, DIA, or by Al Burkhalter. He carried a note that in case of emergency, one or two people should be contacted, usually General Ridgway or another friend who could contact his current "Big Brother" at the ACSI or Burkhalter. He remained a loner. The notes he kept were often cryptic, simply little reminders, often in several languages, which prompted his memory as to facts and figures. He needed no "cover," as in fact he would tell the truth: he was a hotel man—or later, a retired hotel man—looking into hotel invest-ment opportunities as he took a vacation. And in point of fact, he never traveled "under orders" for anyone at headquarters. His reports were voluntary. If they were used, fine; in his mind, he did his duty and passed on the information. If the information was not used, that was not his business.

Brandy's archives rapidly filled with detailed maps and expense records for each year, showing his routes around the world, often with as many as six or seven extensive separate tours. Many of the trips did not result in any startling information; on a few of the travels that hap-pened to coincide with a local crisis, however, he learned a great deal. Three of these trips took him to troubled islands.

Cyprus had been in turmoil since the mid-1950s, when a guerrilla war against British rule was begun by Greek Cypriots seeking unifica-tion with Greece, or "Enosis." The leaders of the Enosis movement had formed the National Organization of Cypriot Combatants (or EOKA), headed by Archbishop Makarios and General Grivas. The British de-ported Makarios, and then, in 1956, allowed him to return to become president of independent Cyprus, with British bases at Akrotiti on the south shore and Dhekela at the eastern end of the island.

In 1963, the Turks withdrew from the power-sharing agreement and a civil war between Turkish and Greek Cypriots erupted. The United Nations sent a peacekeeping force to keep the two sides separated.

Brandy, who had information that the Turks would attack Greece because of the oil deposits between Turkey and the Greek islands, de-cided in March 1974 that the situation was becoming very interesting. He flew to Washington, and contacted his current "Big Brother" there, explaining that he thought the Aegean Sea was about to explode into conflict. He was told that conditions appeared normal, and that no fol-low-through, in the ACSI's estimation, would be required. Neverthe-less, at a backgammon tournament held that year at his home, Brandy picked up further indications from some of the Greek shipowners in attendance, of the growing crisis in the region. He managed to obtain two different letters, one from the Turkish ambassador to Mexico, and one from the Greek ambassador to the United Nations, resident in New York, advising their government officials that Frank Brandstetter was visiting to consider building hotels.

In June he flew to Pittsburgh and chatted with Ridgway, who was well acquainted with the problems between the Greeks and Turks. He agreed that trouble might erupt. As Brandy flew back to Acapulco to make arrangements for the charter of the motor yacht *Beth* out of Piraeus, Ridgway wrote to Brandy, "You cannot settle all its [Europe's] problems, even with your energy. Don't try."

Brandy went in any case, arriving in Athens on 8 July. He visited the U.S. military attaché and told him of the information he had picked up regarding the forthcoming clash. The attaché "horse-laughed" at Brandy's remarks, as he had recently attended joint Greek-Turkish maneuvers with NATO, where officers of the two forces had gotten along just fine. However, the attaché said, do stay on the lookout for ships with the unusual antennas that the Russians use for their intelligence.

On 10 July, Brandy left Piraeus aboard the chartered yacht; on the 14th, at the Greek island of Rhodes, which lies some twenty-five miles off the Turkish coast, he sent back a guest who had traveled with him that far. On the 17th, some thirty miles southeast of Rhodes and headed for Antalya on the Turkish coast, the *Beth* was stopped by a Turkish patrol boat. Brandy argued with the Turkish captain for about forty minutes, explaining that he was on a fact-finding mission for the Turkish government. It was a dicey situation; the yacht had American registry and flag, but the crew was Greek. He showed the letter from the Turkish ambassador. He kept the Greek letter in his pocket. Finally, the Turkish officer released the yacht. The *Beth* then headed north through the intermingled Greek and Turkish islands in the eastern Aegean.

At the Greek Island of Kalimnos, less than twenty miles to the Turkish shore, Brandy observed both a civilian panic and the mobilization of troops. Hundreds of Greek residents tried to flee the island, and dozens nearly swamped his yacht at the refueling dock. With the aid of one of the yacht sailors who had a rifle, the refugees were put back ashore, one by one; but no fuel could be obtained. On the 19th, headed back through

the Cyclades Islands to Greece, the yacht captain was able to buy eighteen drums of diesel fuel from a smuggler in Astipalea, a small island
near Thíra. During a hectic night, in rolling seas, the yacht captain kept
dodging military patrol boats, not sure whether they were Greek or Turkish. On the 21st, in the early morning, Brandy returned to Piraeus, after
being stopped repeatedly by Greek warships.

Greek officers in Cyprus had deposed Makarios, who fled the island. Turks became alarmed and their leader, Rauf Dentkas, asked for
help from Turkey. The Turks sent troops, invading the island and taking control of the northern third of the land. The island became divided along the "Attila" line, which U.N. troops later took over as a
narrow buffer zone between the two ethnic sides. On 20 July 1974, as
Brandy's yacht neared Piraeus, five thousand Turkish troops invaded
Cyprus. The Greek-Turkish war had begun, just as Brandy had fore-
cast.

Brandy checked into the Hilton. There were few taxis available, no
communications, and the city was in an uproar. He visited the U.S. miltary
attaché, offering his services again. Once more, he was rejected, this
time with a slightly testy tone, Brandy thought.

Brandy found that all flights and ship departures out of Athens were
canceled, so he decided to leave Greece by ground transport. Through
the concierge at the hotel, he contacted a former law professor, who
was also a Communist gun smuggler. The concierge told Brandy that if
anyone could get him out of Athens to the Yugoslav border, this professor would be the one. Brandy met the professor, made financial arrangements, and bought an old, unobtrusive car, as no rental cars were
available. The next problem was to arrange an entry visa from the
Yugoslav government.

When he went to the Yugoslav embassy building in Athens, he found
a crowd of hundreds of people trying to enter to get a visa in order to
flee from Greece. He approached the Yugoslav guard, who was holding
off the crowd with his weapon. Brandy pulled from his briefcase the
photo he carried of himself and Tito having lunch at Las Brisas, fourteen years earlier. The guard was so impressed (or perhaps confused)
by this picture, that he immediately escorted Brandy past the crowds
and lines, passing him to another guard, also impressed by the fact that

Brandy had personally met Tito. He was taken directly into the consular office.

There, he explained that he was a friend of General Dabor Soldatic, who now served as assistant foreign secretary for Latin America in the foreign ministry in Belgrade. Brandy requested a call be put through to him. Soldatic was on a holiday, but his secretary knew Brandy through the correspondence he had continued over the years; so she instructed the consul in Athens to issue him a visa. His passport was promptly stamped, and he was free to visit Yugoslavia.

On the evening of 22 July, at 5:25 P.M., he was ready to leave the Athens Hilton with the Communist professor, pass through the arms cordon surrounding Athens, and travel over the mountains. Just as they were pulling away, a gentleman ran up and asked if Brandy could take him and his female companion along to the Yugoslav border. After a few minutes, Brandy recognized the man. He had a small air charter company which operated from Klosters, Switzerland, about sixty miles from Zurich, and he had done some "extra-curricular" jobs for the American intelligence community.

"OK," said Brandy. "Help me make space." After piling Brandy's luggage on the roof, they all squeezed into the small car. Heading out to the north that night, they went through country mostly under the control of Papandreaou's socialists. At the Greek-Yugoslav border, Brandy paid off the professor, and left the charter pilot and his friend with the old car, since they did not have Yugoslav visas. Brandy walked across the border with his luggage. Years later, the passenger ran into Brandy and thanked him for helping them get across safely that night.

Once across the border, Brandy rented a bus and took it to Skopje. From there, he flew on to Belgrade, then to Frankfurt, where he called General James A. Munson, who had previously been U.S. military attaché in Mexico. Munson now served as assistant division commander of the 1st Army Division, based at Frankfurt. Munson invited Brandy to stay at his home, where he learned about the situation in the Aegean and delivered the information and Brandy's observations to the ACSI.

Several years later, on 30 March 1982, at a cocktail party at his home, another chance conversation stirred Brandy's interest in a different trouble spot. A visiting banker from Argentina began discussing the situation in his country. He noted that the military forces in Argentina were feeling strong enough to recover the Malvinas (or as the British called them, the Falkland Islands) from Great Britain. Considering the fact that the British Prime Minister, Margaret Thatcher, was having domestic political problems, the time might be right for Argentinean action, he suggested. Another reason for military movement was Argentina's need for the oil that possibly lay off-shore. Also, a military victory could serve to unite the Argentines.

Brandy said that he might consider flying to Argentina to take a look for himself. The banker told him he would never be able to get down to the area of southern Argentina because the whole region was under strict military control. Of course, Brandy took that as a challenge, and it only whetted his appetite to go.

Another contact suggested that if Britain and Argentina went to war, Chile might assist Argentina since they, along with Taiwan and Israel, represented a strong anti-Communist independent block, a "fourth world structure." The idea did not quite make sense to Brandy. He was well aware that in 1980, Chile and Argentina almost went to war over three islands: Picton, Nueva and Lennox, located at the Atlantic mouth of the Beagle Channel cutting through Tierra del Fuego, south of the Straits of Magellan. Brandy, in any case, was resolved to go to Argentina to see what he could discover, and especially to detect whether the Chilean-Argentine frontier remained calm.

Again, Brandy flew to Pittsburgh to inform General Ridgway of his proposed fact-finding trip, and again, the general advised him to take it easy. A few weeks later, when Ridgway learned that Frank was on his way to Argentina, he sent him the following note that Brandy kept on his desk beneath a glass top in his library.

26 April 1982

Dear Frank
I would expect you to be where you are—where the action is.
But you don't have to be the lead scout, nor the bearer of
messages under a flag of truce.
CUIDADO! Y de me parte cuando regresa.
Votos caluroses de ambos aqui.

M.B.R.

On 1 April 1982 Brandy left for his Argentine trip, a journey which lasted fifty-six days. His first stop was Mexico City to get a visa for Argentina. The Brazilian ambassador to Mexico, a friend and frequent guest at Casa Tranquilidad, intervened and arranged the visa with the Argentine ambassador, thus avoiding a waiting period of several days. The visa was to be valid for over two years. Brandy then flew out of Mexico City on Linea Argentina, leaving on 2 April and arriving the next day in Buenos Aires. On board the plane, he ran into Curtis Lowell and his wife June. Lowell was the representative of Julius Baer, a private Swiss bank in Zurich.

As Brandy began talking with Lowell, he realized that he had been a member of the FID group during World War II at Broadway, England, later serving under Brandy's command. Lowell was visiting a mutual friend, Count Stefan von Tannstein, who was also a frequent guest at Casa Tranquilidad, together with his wife Marian. Von Tannstein was now director of Lufthansa in Buenos Aires for Argentina and Paraguay. Like Brandy, Marian had a German and Polish aristocratic ancestry, in her case going back to the Polish King Kazimierz Jagiellonczik. Brandy was struck by the double coincidence of meeting a fellow officer from World War II who was visiting a mutual friend, and conducted a small "reunion" on the plane.

Lowell and his wife insisted that Brandy come and visit with them at the Tannsteins. Brandy at first declined graciously. His usual procedure was to travel without local contacts and let no one know where he was, with the exception of General Ridgway and perhaps one other contact at home as a backup. In this case, however, he decided to change his plans and take up the invitation to visit the Tannsteins, but stay in a hotel.

On the day of his departure from Mexico City, Argentine forces seized the Falkland Islands. On 3 April, the day he arrived in Buenos Aires, Argentine forces moved on to take the South Georgian Islands, further to the east in the South Atlantic Ocean. Over the next three weeks, Britain mounted a task force to move to Ascension Island and plan the recapture of South Georgia and the Falklands.

During the days the British assembled their forces, Brandy met with the Tannsteins and other members of the strong German community there. He knew German protocol, always addressing people with their correct title. Even so, he was bemused to note that former German officers, long resident in Argentina, were still addressed as *Herr General*, or *Mein General*. Many had contacts throughout the Argentine military.

At a Tannstein dinner party during which Brandy's planned trip to the war zone was discussed, Countess Rixa von Oeyenhausen asked to come along with him. Brandy said no. Several of the men agreed with Brandy and explained that the trip would be arduous and she should not consider it, but she would not be dissuaded. After dinner, Brandy took her aside and spread out the maps of his planned journey to the war mobilization zone, pointing out the hazards.

Indignantly, she explained that she was a hunt-master, or *jagtmeister*, one of a very few women so ranked. She had crossed the Sahara in a car race and was a highly qualified car mechanic, held international medals in sharpshooting, and was fluent in German, Spanish, French, and English. Brandy was intrigued. In addition to all of those virtues, she was a very good-looking woman. However, his better judgment prevailed and he regretfully declined her offer. The mission would have to come first.

With Stephan von Tannstein's help, Brandy arranged a trip by air to the south of Argentina, the final point being Ushuaia on the Beagle Channel. He planned then to work his way north to the towns of Rio Gallegos and Rio Grande, the staging areas for the Malvinas campaign. Rio Grande was the closest point to the Falklands, about three hundred air miles due west of the islands, located in Tierra del Fuego. He asked von Tannstein to keep any mail or messages that came for him, and to advise General Ridgway in case of an accident. He left his formal clothes and tuxedo with von Tannstein, took five thousand dollars in American Express traveler's checks, ten thousand American dollars, and another three thousand in Argentine money, for traveling expenses. As always, he kept his trusty American Express card handy.

From Rio Gallegos, already in the military exclusion zone, he arranged a seat on a military flight south to Rio Grande, although what he observed at Rio Grande made it unnecessary for him to retrace his steps.

At the Rio Grande airport, the security officer asked him how, as a foreign national, he had gotten a seat on a military plane into the heart of the military district! Brandy patiently repeated the story that he was a hotel investor, scouting out locations for hotels in Argentina, and that he had planned his trip a few months ago, prior to the war. Indeed, that was all true. He planned to investigate the feasibility of a ski resort in Ushuaia. The officer heard out Brandy's story, then told him to take a seat and not to leave it, while all the facts were checked out.

Brandy sat quietly on his assigned bench. He was reading a German book, and his outfit suggested that he was a typical German business-man-tourist. He wore a long suede cape and a Tyrolian hat with an edelweiss insignia on it. His mustache was turned up, like a German officer's, and he carried a leather kit bag. "Just a lost German tourist, caught in their war," he thought to himself, getting into the role.

His perch on the bench was an ideal observation point, he soon discovered. The airport was a military base, and Brandy carefully noted the incoming and outgoing aircraft, their type, their numbers, and the units of the reservists being rushed through the facility. Directly in front of him, the air force troops were marshaled into groups: one containing the aviation mechanics, one the armament specialists, another, the signal communication group. Commanders of the units, with their jet pilots, went to each group to select the reservists to serve with them. The officers remained oblivious to the German tourist with his nose buried in his German book.

Brandy listened unobtrusively to the rapid-fire Spanish commands and was impressed by the serious, professional military demeanor of both the officers and the pilots selecting their crews. He decided that whoever confronted these pilots would have a good fight on their hands. They had been trained from 1964 through 1974 by German Luftwaffe aces, including Hans-Ulrich Rudel. They displayed all the cockiness, élan, and self-assurance that the Luftwaffe pilots in Germany had shown in 1941.

As the units formed in front of him, Brandy from time to time checked back with the security officer, asking what he could do to expedite his flight to Ushuaia so that he could get back to his business, as if bored to tears by the activity around him. Inwardly, he richly enjoyed the special opportunity, which he had not had since 1945, of witnessing firsthand a real mobilization of efficient, sharp troops. Finally, ten hours after his arrival, he was issued a military pass for the next military plane, a twin turbo jet, to Ushuaia.

He arrived at Ushuaia in the middle of a blinding snowstorm at 7:00 P.M. on 8 April. The airport, now run by the military, was under a blackout. Again, the military police would not let him leave the airport area. An officer finally arrived and Brandy showed him the three military passes that he had been issued: Buenos Aires to Rio Gallegos, Rio Gallegos to Rio Grande, Rio Grande to Ushuaia. The officer was impressed. Brandy secured a ride to a hotel, Las Lengas, which he had picked from a guidebook. According to his information, the hotel had forty-four rooms and was a "category three" hotel, directly overlooking the military airport.

On arrival he found the hotel dark, except for one light. When he knocked, the owner of the hotel answered the door to explain that the hotel was closed. Brandy asked, as a fellow hotel operator, if he could rent a room. The owner graciously opened the water line to a room next to his office and gave Brandy a candle and some blankets. Brandy then unloaded his luggage into the room.

Despite the desperate cold, the room was ideal. In the moonlight, he discovered that it also had a view over the Beagle Channel. Due west was the Chilean boundary. Across the channel, to the south, lay the Chilean island of Navarino; about eighty miles due east along the channel, were the three islands under dispute between Chile and Argentina: Picton, Nueva, and Lennox. If the Chileans were to use the Falklands War as a pretext to move on those islands, the room was the perfect strategic location to observe any action.

In order to obtain a meal, the owner of the hotel suggested, Brandy should walk to the nearby bistro, Tante-Elvira. It turned out to be a three-mile trek through twelve-inch snow, with a thick storm reducing visibility often to near zero. Not having eaten for over fourteen hours, Brandy plodded ahead.

The hike was worth it, for the meal at Aunt Elvira's was exceptional. He had an excellent, freshly caught large crab, a good bottle of Orfila wine, and a glass of cognac. As he drank the Orfila wine, he realized he knew it well, since it was grown and bottled by Bodega Orfila, S.A., a family-owned enterprise belonging to his friend Ambassador Alexandro

Orfila, later the Argentine representative to the Organization of American States in Washington. Alexandro and his beautiful wife Helga had often stayed with Brandy at Casa Tranquilidad. Musing over the strange coincidences, he finished the wine and cognac, then trudged back to his room. He slept until 10:00 A.M. the next day, 9 April.

The international boundary between Chile and Argentina seemed perfectly quiet in this remote corner of Tierra del Fuego, and naval forces were not present to disturb the peace of the channel. Therefore, after a few days, Brandy attempted to rent a car. The rental agent in Ushuaia informed him that he could only rent a car if he hired a driver as well. As they started their tour, Brandy suspected the driver was more than he seemed. First they drove around areas near Ushuaia, the Beagle Channel, the Islands, and the Chilean border in the southern part of Isla Grande, part of Tierra del Fuego. On the second day, Brandy "smoked out" the fact that the driver was a non-commissioned officer in the Argentine navy's intelligence branch. Brandy remained in his role as a hotel man, looking for possible resort sites.

On 15 April, Brandy was flown by military plane first north, then west, to the border of Argentina and Chile, allowing him to observe if the Chilean armed forces were moving on the offensive there. On the 19th, he returned to Rivadavia, where he was arrested. Somebody had tipped off the authorities about his border trips. He was then deported back to Buenos Aires on the same plane with the British women and children, and the elderly who had been arrested on Malvinas.

In Bueno Aires Brandy was contacted by Vice Admiral Burkhalter. He went out again over the next few days, taking little-used roads and sheep trails along the Chilean boundary. During the following weeks, the trip extended as he moved north, visiting the lake country near Bariloche. There was no evidence of Chilean mobilization. He even explored the frontier passes between the two countries, stopping to see the "Cross of the Andes" high in the mountains, standing with one foot on each side of the peaceful boundary as he posed for a "typical" tourist snapshot. Of course, a trained observer might note that the absence of troops at the border in the casual snapshot was itself a point of strategic significance. After traveling 5,760 kilometers, he concluded his journey on 15 May 1982 at the small town of La Quiaca, on the Argentine-Bolivian boundary.

During these weeks, the British counterattacked in South Georgia, and then in the Falklands. In what turned out to be one of the major air-sea battles of the 1980s, the Argentines lost the old cruiser, *General Belgrano*, with 350 men aboard. In turn, they sank the British air defense destroyer HMS *Sheffield* with Exocet missiles launched from their land-based Entendards, piloted by the very crews Brandy had observed assembling in Ushuaia. The Argentines also sank a tanker vessel, the *Atlantic Conveyer*, by Exocet missile after mistaking her, in the fog of war, for the British carrier *Invincible*.

After returning from the Bolivian border area, Brandy stayed in Buenos Aires from 17 to 26 May, and then flew out for Acapulco, arriving home on 27 May 1982. By the time the British moved on Port Stanley in the Falklands, reducing the Argentine forces there in mid-June, Brandy was looking around the world for his next mission.

At the end of the summer, which had started so eventfully in South America, Brandy made the first of two separate trips to Corsica, the large French island north of Sardinia and off the west coast of Italy. He traveled to the Mediterranean island by way of Rome, to investigate whether there had been Libyan agitation, weapons supply, or financial support for Corsican independence from France. On the first trip to Corsica, between the 2nd and 16th of August, 1982, he traveled with Oliver Giscard d'Estaing, the brother of a former president of France.

In the following year, Brandy returned to Corsica with Michel Francoise Rougenoux, chef du protocol, from the Quai D'Orsay—the French Foreign Office. Rougenoux continued to serve under President Francois Mitterand, and later was appointed the French ambassador to Romania. Brandy stayed at the Corsican villa of Gyula Balkany, director-general and owner of the internationally renowned Rety couturier shop, located at #54 Faubourg Saint Honoré, Paris. Later, he also stayed at the Sofitel Thalassa, near the town of Ajaccio.

Again, Brandy talked his way past checkpoints, here guarded by the Foreign Legion, to visit some of the prehistoric monuments in the interior towns of Petreto, Bicchisan, Porpiano, Sarene, and Aullene, taking photographs of the spots. On another drive, he passed through all of the interior valleys, stopping at most of the small villages along the way. The officials with whom he traveled, d'Estaing and Rougenoux, were a little concerned for their safety because Brandy was driving on back roads to the mountain villages in the interior of the island. He learned from speaking with the farmers in the villages and drinking glasses of wine in the small country bistros, that most of them were neutral towards the question of independence and wanted only peace.

He gathered materials explaining the interaction of the ancient clan system with modern politics in Corsica and describing the rise of terrorism on the island since the early 1970s. In September 1978, the National Front for the Liberation of Corsica (FLNC) dynamited an airplane at the Ajaccio airport. Plastique bombs in villages showed that the independence movement was alive through 1982, and continued into the regime of Francois Mitterand. Two regiments of the French Foreign Legion, including the crack 2nd Parachute regiment numbering a total of 2,284 troops, formerly stationed in the African colony of Djibouti, kept the peace and protected tourists along the coastal areas in 1982.

Brandy noted with interest a rumor that Muammar Al Kadhafi, who was born in 1942, was the son of a Corsican officer stationed in North Africa in that year. The Corsican blood in Kadhafi would explain his enduring interest in the movement for Corsican independence and his supposed support for the terrorists in the FLNC.

Despite the continuing conflict in Corsican politics, the island provided beautiful settings for hotels, resorts, and tourist excursions. Brandy's stay, as in all his travels, combined a quiet gathering of information with an enjoyable, often first-class, trip. He had long conversations with the French prefect of Corsica while having dinner with him in his home. As the prefect gave Brandy an informative background summary over after-dinner drinks, the stillness of the night was suddenly shattered by the sound of an FLNC bomb in the town of Ajaccio. After a pause, the prefect resumed his lecture on the complexities of Corsican politics, unconcerned, as if the nearby explosion was only the echo of distant thunder.

By this period, Brandy had made it part of his standard procedure to stop over in New York to visit Richard Nixon in his office in the Federal building and inform him of his observations. Thus, when he returned from Corsica, he passed on his information to the former president. Nixon later gave a speech using the information provided by

Brandy concerning the Kadhafi-led agitators' penetration of Corsica. Another mission completed.

26

Reports to Nixon:
South Africa

A s Brandy continued his travels through the late 1970s and the
1980s, the trips combined his many roles: tourist, hotelier, busi-
ness executive, adventurer, and voluntary intelligence officer.
In 1981 he attended Ronald Reagan's presidential inauguration with
Clement Stone. Soon after, he decided to visit the Republic of South
Africa.

During 1980 conservative writers and commentators, like those on
Gordon McLendon's radio stations, argued that American support for
the embargo of South Africa was extremely hazardous to the national
security of the United States. South Africa controlled the production of
three-quarters of the world's gold supply, together with a heavy proportion of strategic minerals such as molybdenum, tungsten, and cobalt.
Because of this, McLendon argued, the United States and her allies in
Europe increased the chances of potential Soviet involvement there and
a loss of those vital resources. Hints from Secretary of State Alexander
Haig of a new policy towards South Africa suggested the need for thoughtful information about that area of the world. As an intelligence officer,
Brandy could competently respond to that need.

Yet, all the other facets of Brandy's activities and personality were
reflected as he planned the trip. He had pledged himself to learn more

about the peoples of the world, and the life of the native peoples in South Africa remained a matter of personal interest. He had worked with McLendon in 1980 in London, helping him gather documents and information about profitable investments in the metals market and the purchase of metals contracts with orders from South Africa. Both of them had taken a two-week crash course in London from two strategic metals experts from Oxford University. McLendon had brought his ideas together in a book titled, *So You Want to Get Rich in the Metals Market* and acknowledged Brandy's assistance in this work. Further information, directly from South Africa, would be of significant interest to McLendon and would help his editorial comments in radio broadcasts.

Then there were the sights: Kruger Park would be interesting to visit as a tourist. As a hotelier, he was drawn to the fabulous chain of Sun Hotels in South Africa. He had met the chairman of the board of Sun Hotels, Sol Kerzener, honeymooning in Acapulco with his beauty-queen bride; Kerzener had invited Brandy to visit. A specific opportunity arose when Brandy's close friend, Nicolás Sánchez Osorio, now editor of *Vogue de Mexico* and still publisher and editor of *Novíssimo*—the full-color Sunday supplement published with Mexican newspapers—arranged a fashion photo trip to South Africa.

Just as he had when visiting Bratislava officially for Ridgway and unofficially for himself, Brandy comfortably mixed his motives, personal and public. The multiple aspects of his trip to South Africa allowed all segments of his personality to flourish, and each separate aspect of the complex mission was carried off with success.

In April 1981, Brandy flew to Los Angeles to attend a party for Grace Kelly thrown by Baron Ricky Portonova and his wife Baroness Sandra Portonova. Among the luminaries present were Frank Sinatra and his personal attorney, Mickey Ruden. After a brief appearance at the party, Brandy flew on to Dallas and then to Pittsburgh for a quiet visit and briefing for General Ridgway. Staying at Ridgway's home, Brandy explained he was headed for South Africa for a look around. Ridgway requested that he report back to him and, as always, Brandy accepted that as part of his mission. Furthermore, Ridgway had a contact in South Africa he suggested Brandy look up: Dr. Jack Penn, a plastic surgeon whom Ridgway had known since World War II.

Penn had authored a memoir, *The Right to Look Human,* for which Ridgway had written a preface in 1974. He had established a reputation not only as one of the world's leading reconstructive plastic surgeons, but as a progressive thinker and writer about issues of race relations in South Africa. He believed, as did many white South Africans, that the nation held great promise for advancement. The world's lack of patience and its mistaken effort to rush the country to full one-man, one-vote democracy, however, could only work against the efforts of moderates like himself, he argued. Ridgway suggested that Brandy contact Penn when he visited.

Brandy was troubled by the request. He always preferred to accomplish his reconnaissance cold, without contacts, because introductions from afar might tend to pre-shape his response. He could do better, he thought, by making his own contacts, talking to people he met casually and by accident, and using introductions only as a way of gaining access to new sources. Out of respect for Ridgway, however, he agreed to stop by and talk to Dr. Penn. As usual, he promised to deliver to Ridgway a copy of whatever information he gathered for the defense intelligence establishment.

On 27 April, he took his leave from Ridgway and traveled to New York, where he was scheduled to meet with Sánchez Osorio to finalize the details of the trip, see a South African travel agent to work out train schedules and car rentals, and get his South African visa. When he checked into the Helmsley Plaza in New York, he called his old friend Nicholas Ruwe, formerly of the State Department, now serving as chief of staff to Richard Nixon. President Nixon ordered Ruwe to offer Brandy his office at the Federal Building in New York City, when he was in town. Brandy declined the offer but accepted Nixon's invitation, through Ruwe, to visit him at his town house on 30 April.

He had met President Nixon before, and felt he had a long association with the former president. In 1948, as a young veteran, he had worked door-to-door in San Francisco for Nixon's congressional campaign against Helen Gehagen Douglas. In 1968, he had met Nixon while attending fund-raising dinners with Clement Stone. He encountered him again in 1972 at the Republican convention, and also at the inauguration.

A group of interesting people gathered for dinner in New York that evening: Hobart D. Lewis, a long-time member of Nixon's "inner circle" and editor-in-chief of *Reader's Digest*; James Keogh, who had served as a speech writer for Nixon and as director of the U.S. Information Agency; R. Strausz-Hupe, former U.S. ambassador to several posts including Morocco, Ceylon, Belgium, and Sweden, and now ambassador-designate to Austria; Cassius Daly, a banker from New Jersey; William Van Cleave, an advisor to President Reagan on technical questions regarding intercontinental ballistic missiles; and James R. Schlesinger, who had served as chairman of the Atomic Energy Commission, director of the CIA briefly in 1973, and secretary of energy. This small, informal brain trust met periodically with Nixon to discuss current issues.

Before dinner, Nixon offered to make drinks, insisting that they all have one of his special martinis. He took pride in mixing his own style of very stiff drink for everyone. He declined Brandy's offer to help. "Sit down, colonel," he said. "This is my task and my pleasure."

A regular kind of guy, thought Brandy, as he watched. And he was loyal, intensely loyal, to his friends. Brandy admired that quality, even though he believed Nixon's unrelenting loyalty to those around him was at once the man's greatest asset and his greatest liability.

At dinner, the conversation ranged over many subjects, but particularly over the world and domestic situation faced by the new president, Ronald Reagan, who had taken the oath of office seven weeks earlier. Nixon brought the conversation to a head by asking each person around the table what he planned to do for the new administration to assist President Reagan. When the conversation came around to him, Brandy explained that he planned to look into the mineral situation in South Africa and bring that information back through channels, so that the evolving policy towards the nation could be based on some current, fresh, and direct information. He echoed the concerns expressed in the conservative press that a cutoff of South African minerals, or worse, a take over by a Communist-controlled government there, would put the West in a difficult strategic position.

After dinner, Nixon leaned over and quietly asked Brandy to stay on and join him for a drink when the others left. Brandy complied, and over cognac, he and Nixon had a private chat in the library.

"Colonel," said the former president, "the day you get back from South Africa, I want you to report to me. I want to learn everything you find out, before you see anyone else."

"Yes, sir!" said Brandy. He realized he now had three commissions, or perhaps four—all taken on voluntarily. One was for General Ridgway, a second for Gordon McLendon, a third for President Nixon, and a fourth, of course, was for the director of the intelligence community staff, Al Burkhalter. For Brandy, these jobs were voluntary and informal, yet each represented a commitment. It was someone else's job to determine the importance of the strategic information he would supply to the four men and the defense community. As always, his mission was simply to collect the information and pass it on.

The next morning, 1 May, wearing his safari suit with cigars plugged into the loops designed for elephant-gun ammunition, Brandy headed around the corner from the Helmsley Plaza to meet Sánchez Osorio at Le Cirque restaurant. He knew that his attire was not quite what was expected at clothes-conscious New York's elegant Le Cirque, so he took along a silk foulard which he could wear if a tie was requested. As expected, owner Michel Crouzillat, a friend of Brandy's, gave him a long look, perhaps thinking of turning him away. Friend or no friend, Le Cirque was the most elegant restaurant in the city.

At that moment a lady sitting not far away recognized him, said hello, and beckoned him over. It was Barbara Walters, who had interviewed him the week before for the show "20/20" concerning a story about presidents' brothers. (Brandy had talked about Sam Johnson.) "Colonel Brandstetter," she said, "where in the world are you headed this time?"

Brandy glanced at Michel, who simply nodded him in. It was one of those satisfying little moments. Brandy stopped at Barbara's table and chatted for a minute. She jotted her phone number down on a slip of paper he had in his pocket from the Helmsley Plaza, and Brandy went on to meet with Nicolás Sánchez Osorio, his long-time friend from Mexico. The first stop, Sánchez Osorio explained, was Marrakech in Morocco. He planned a few days of touring and photographing the new styles with his beautiful models for *Vogue*. After that, they would take a flight to Capetown. Brandy could go his way into the wine country while Sánchez Osorio traveled his own way with his models. The group would get together again in Sun City, in Bophutswana.

The plan sounded good to Brandy, leaving him time to tour on his own. Furthermore, a visit to Morocco would be interesting, if for no other reason than one might dig up a little local information about the Polisario rebels in the southern province of Morocco, taken over two years before from Mauritania. The Polisario rebels were aided by Algeria and by Kadhafi in Libya. A side trip from Marrakech to the southern port of Agadir, near the former Spanish territory, might produce some information concerning the state of things in that troubled quarter of Africa. Sánchez Osorio had already selected the luxury hotels in Morocco, and Brandy looked forward to the trip.

In Marrakech, Brandy and Sánchez Osorio's group stayed at the Mamaounia Hotel. Later, Brandy rented a car with a driver for a trip to the Karamaides Mountains to the southeast of Marrakech. While shopping and sightseeing on 7 May, Brandy unexpectedly met a former Moroccan diplomat, M. M'Jid, who remembered him well from a stay at Casa Tranquilidad. Together they strolled through the bazaar, observing the copper and brass workers and admiring the craft. Ambassador M'Jid and Brandy stopped at an outdoor cafe for lunch, but during the meal the Moroccan diplomat excused himself rather mysteriously and returned after a few moments. They chatted about old times over a leisurely coffee. Brandy soon realized the reason for the delay. As they left, they went back to the metal craftsmen and M'Jid presented Brandy with a newly made, hand-wrought copper plaque with "House of Peace" written in Arabic script. Brandy thanked him and the plaque was shipped home, a treasured memento that was later mounted in the wall next to the gate at Casa Tranquilidad.

The group then drove to the village of Oukeïmedan on the slopes of Djébel Toubkal, where they stayed at the Grand Hôtel du Toubkal, with a view of the mountain. Brandy, as always, collected brochures, maps, hotel flyers, menus, matchbooks, business cards, receipts, and local tourist materials. The documents not only substantiated his trip, but would also serve to prompt his memory when narrating his visit. After a day of sightseeing at Oukeïmedan, the group left for Agadir.

The Moroccan government had advised tourists not to drive at night in the southern region. Nevertheless, Brandy and Sánchez Osorio drove through the mountains to Agadir, on the southern coast of Morocco, close to the western Sahara province where the Polisario rebels operated. There, on 10 May 1981, Brandy heard a radio address by Prime Minister Calvo Sotelo accusing foreign states of fomenting unrest in Spain. This speech referred to a spate of assassinations of military men and civil guard leaders over the prior week. An attempted coup had taken place in Madrid two-and-a-half months before, when Lieutenant Colonel Antonio Tejero Molina, a leader of the ultra-right, led a group of civil guard members in capturing the parliament with pistols and other small arms. They were arrested only after a long standoff. The killings and demonstrations of early May were directed against Molina and his supporters, it seemed. What was going on? Were the Franco Falangists going to make a comeback? Did the incident represent a threat to the democratic regime under King Juan Carlos, which had ruled Spain since Franco's death in 1975? Would Spain's move to join NATO be endangered?

Brandy hurriedly made arrangements with Sánchez Osorio to catch up with him in South Africa. Meanwhile, he wanted to be where the action was.

He took a short flight from Agadir to Casablanca, and then to Madrid, arriving on the evening of 10 May. He checked into the Hotel Villa Magna on the Paseo de la Castellana in Madrid, and searched his memory and his address book for a contact to explain what was going on. The ideal person was a woman whom he had met playing backgammon at Casa Tranquilidad as his guest, Maika Pérez e Cobas. She put him in touch with some of the political figures behind the incident in the parliamentary chamber. Brandy arranged some secluded meetings and discussed the political situation, since the determination about which side the armored division would support was unclear. He then phoned General Johnny Johnson in San Antonio, former military attaché in Mexico City who later served with the ACSI. General Johnson contacted the Pentagon, and in turn they called the U.S. Embassy in Madrid and gave a heads-up to the military attaché, Colonel Donald Mahlberg. Brandy met with Mahlberg and gave him a full briefing on what he had learned. He then flew on to Lisbon, stopped for lunch at the Solmar Restaurant for some Portuguese specialties, and flew on to South Africa to overtake Sánchez Osorio in Johannesburg.

On 15 May, after a brief visit with Sánchez Osorio, Brandy was on his own. He began to buy books, newspapers, magazines, and brochures, studying alone in a hotel. On the 19th, he flew to see Dr. Jack Penn in Capetown. He had no idea what to expect and was pleasantly surprised. Penn was a cultured and humane gentleman, full of political ideas and capable of a long-range view. He was working on a new book, gathering together short articles he had written and developing new ideas, in collaboration with others, about the place of South Africa in the modern world.

Brandy learned a great deal more about the background of Dr. Penn. Penn had operated on World War II casualties, particularly fliers whose faces were badly burned during aircraft crashes. He was attached to British forces and became professionally successful with facial restorations. He had developed a distinguished reputation and upon returning to South Africa, became the most prominent reconstructive surgeon there, with a specialty in rebuilding facial nerves. Penn built a hospital in Johannesburg, and worked for racial integration by offering black nurses positions in the white hospital. He was one of the first physicians to make such efforts and later began recruiting black interns. Penn then became a member of the Presidential Council, where he advocated his dream to integrate in a practical manner, step by careful step. Gradually, he believed, the country was following that ideal. Blacks were moving ahead in education, and the constabulary included both commissioned and non-commissioned young black officers.

Penn asked Brandy to see him again when he finished his tour of South Africa, and Brandy promised to comply. It was almost another commission. While in Cape Town, Brandy drove to the wine district near Stellenbosch, and stayed at the Mount Wilson Hotel. Sánchez Osorio routed to his room a whole folder of clippings and winery brochures he had collected and used in writing and illustrating articles for *El Hogar* in Mexico. Brandy returned to Cape Town, and then, with a list of hotels, set out along the coastal drive towards Durban on a trip of information gathering.

The first night out, 25 May 1981, he checked into Beacon Island Hotel at Plettenberg Bay, where reservations had been called ahead by

Brandy visits the Gold Mine Museum in Johannesburg, South Africa. Photo by Gold Mine Museum.

Sol Kerzener of the Sun Hotel chain. As he attempted to park the car, after registering, he suddenly discovered he had no brakes and that the accelerator was stuck, racing the engine. As he struggled with the gearshift to brake the vehicle, he realized the car might run off the cliff at the edge of the parking lot. He quickly ran it into the steep embankment, wrecking the car but saving his life. Brandy was shaken, and when the incident was reported to the police inspectors, they suggested to him that the brake line was cut and the engine rigged. He wondered if the perpetrators were enemies of Dr. Penn who felt he was talking to the wrong person, or perhaps they were anti-American agents? There was no way to find out, so he shook off his concerns. He stayed a second night at the hotel under a doctor's care and then moved on, putting the brake "accident" out of his mind.

Brandy rented another car with a driver to travel to Elizabeth. He then took a short shuttle flight, catching up with his itinerary in Durban

on Friday, 29 May 1981, the weekend of the celebration of the foundation of the South African Republic twenty years earlier. The anniversary
date was 1 June, but the celebration had already begun. The hotels were
full, and Brandy was happy to obtain even the smallest of rooms. Finding a select table in the hotel restaurant seemed a challenge, even after
he dropped Kerzener's name with one of the headwaiters. He was
promptly shown to a table, but was squeezed between celebrating South
Africans on every side.

The couple next to him noticed he was alone and apologized for
the rowdy singing of their compatriots by explaining their happy celebration and sharing a bottle of wine. Brandy took up the conversation,
soon discovering that his genial host, in mufti, was Lieutenant General
N. J. Nieuwoudt, surgeon general of the South African army.

The general asked if Brandy had met anyone in South Africa.

"Well, I do know Sol Kerzener," he said, "and Dr. Jack Penn. I just
saw him in Cape Town."

"How about that!" Nieuwoudt said. "Penn used to serve with me in
the South African army."

As they chatted, Nieuwoudt soon found out that Brandy had served
in World War II under Ridgway, who had written the preface to Penn's
book. "Look," said the surgeon general, "there is someone you will want
to meet, right over there." He pointed to a distinguished gentleman
across the dining room, a man with a military bearing. "That," said the
medical officer, "is Lieutenant General Peter Vander Westhuizen, head
of army intelligence in South Africa."

Brandy's ears perked up. Indeed, he would be interested. The army
medical officer introduced him to Vander Westhuizen, and after a few
words of exchange, the general asked Brandy to meet him in the hotel
bar after the other guests had departed.

Brandy waited, and soon was joined by Vander Westhuizen. The two
immediately hit it off. Brandy invited the general up to his small room
for a drink, and the conversation lasted into the night. Six hours later,
the two had consumed two bottles of cognac and had become close
friends. The conversation ranged over progress in civil rights, accom-
modation and peace, military security, and Communist influence. Vander
Westhuizen told Brandy that if there was anything he wanted, he only

needed to call headquarters in Pretoria. He gave him his private telephone number, and told him to visit later on his trip. Brandy promised to keep in touch, and in fact, from time to time on the rest of his journey, he would phone in to give his location and itinerary to Vander Westhuizen's assistant.

Brandy then continued in his rented car, driving up through Natal. Along the way he met a young Zulu, an Oxford graduate, who accompanied him as a guide and translator. He showed Brandy the sights in his Zulu homeland that included a stay at a chief's kraal. Brandy learned a great deal about the Zulus, their strong family orientation and loyalty to the clan. Continuing on his journey, Brandy stayed in three guesthouses near Kruger Park.

For a period in early June, Brandy made four separate trips into the thousand-square-mile game preserve of the park that stretches along the northeast frontier between the Republic of South Africa and neighboring Mozambique. Brandy carefully took notes on his trips into the park, placing on a large map each stop, showing driving times, sights, wildlife spotted, gates, fences, and other features. Four rhinos here, giraffe along this section, elephants in a group, leopards near the south-

Brandy watches Zulu women dance in a chief's kraal.

ern boundary. The zone along the boundary with Mozambique, he noted, was prohibited for travel. In fact, it was clear that with the park closed from 6:00 P.M. to 6:00 A.M. every day, and all vehicles checked for weapons to enforce game preservation, the park served as an ideal military barrier to penetration by hostile guerilla groups or weapons smugglers. Mozambique, as a "front-line," black-ruled nation, did in fact harbor militant forces seeking to overturn the white-ruled South African government.

As Brandy stayed in the nearby resorts, he was able to obtain reservations ahead by mentioning that he knew Kerzener. At one hotel, the management passed on to Brandy, perhaps inadvertently, a whole sheaf of telexes to and from the Sabi River Bungalows and Pine Lake Inn, that reflected the discussion of his status as a VIP and a friend of Kerzener.

After the visits to Kruger Park, Brandy drove to Pretoria, where he had a long conference with Vander Westhuizen and his deputies, including an admiral. As a mark of the government's sense of security, Vander Westhuizen and others flew to the Angolan frontier in southwest Africa to tour some of the front-line areas there. Brandy, when invited by the general to join the group, was impressed with the gesture. While in Pretoria, he also stopped at a mining museum and gathered bundles of materials regarding the mineral situation in the country.

After Pretoria, Brandy drove on to Bophutswana to catch up with Sánchez Osorio's group, joining them in Sun City. Like Las Vegas, Sun City thrived as an international gambling and hotel mecca. There, Brandy made other contacts, meeting the black officials of the Bophutswana government. He was impressed by the fact that in this racially integrated *bantustan*, the South African government retained two cabinet posts with white officers—defense and foreign policy—but that the rest of the government was operated very successfully by black African politicians. He met J. Moletsane, the chief of tourism, and talked with him as hotelier and traveler about conditions.

Brandy met Peter Wagner, the general manager of the whole Sun City complex, and Peter Iwand, the general manager of the hotel, comparing notes concerning the operation of a successful resort. John Burns, a journalist, encountered Brandy and assumed that he must be working for the CIA. Brandy truthfully denied the allegation, and indicated that he worked entirely for himself. He said that he approached his travels with no vested interest, because he was on no one's payroll. Burns sensed there was more to the story, but Brandy was adamant. He was entirely on his own. By contrast, he noted, journalists could claim no such independence and had to report only what would please their editors. Brandy, on the other hand, could travel and observe, completely self-funded, without worrying about how anyone would react to his observations. He was not sure that the point was well taken, but he had made it. Burns was a good observer, and Brandy thought he might be an important person to contact in the future for local information.

While staying at Sun City, Brandy met Sol Kerzener again and thanked him for his help in arranging rooms around the country. Through Kerzener, he ran into Mickey Ruden, whom he had seen a few weeks before in Los Angeles at the Portonova party. Ruden, there to arrange an upcoming appearance by Frank Sinatra, explained that if Brandy extended his stay, he could be there when Sinatra came to perform. Brandy made his apologies and returned to Johannesburg.

Brandy next called Dr. Penn, who flew up from Cape Town. Penn brought along a large packet of materials for Brandy to take back to the United States, including the collection of his manuscripts that he was compiling as a proposed book. The materials Brandy had gathered were getting voluminous, especially since he tried to maintain three identical sets. One, at first for General Ridgway, Brandy would eventually forward to defense intelligence. A second was for President Nixon, and a third for Gordon McLendon. Each set occupied two trunks, making a total of six.

As Brandy reviewed Penn's position in light of his extended visit around the country, he found he agreed with the doctor. South Africa was a beautiful country, modern, integrating, with a democratic government. Unfortunately, it received a bad press in the United States and all over the western world. How should the problem be attacked? Not only was good press needed, but also needed were opinion-makers willing to learn the truth about the country and disseminate it. Brandy promised himself he would help.

On 9 July he flew out, arriving the next morning in New York at 5:45 A.M. He waited until 7:45 and called Nick Ruwe, explaining that President Nixon had asked him to stop by as soon as he got in. Ruwe checked and called him back. "You have an appointment: tomorrow, Saturday, 11 July, at 4:00 P.M. in his New York City residence."

On Saturday, Brandy loaded two trunks, a complete set of the materials, into a taxi. He arrived at the town house ten minutes early, then ordered the taxi to circle the block until it was exactly 4:00 P.M. He wondered if the Secret Service men posted outside Nixon's residence worried about the cab with two trunks bulging from the rear that kept passing the building. Sure enough, when he stopped the car in front of the building, they accosted him and his trunks.

Nixon came to the door and greeted him, waving him past the security. He had driven to the city especially to meet Brandy, and was eager for his report. Brandy brought the trunks in and opened them up, sorting out the maps, clippings, and brochures, while telling the story of his trip. It was pure human intelligence. He related what he had learned: Jack Penn's position, the security at the frontier in Kruger Park, Vander Westhuizen's staff and their self confidence, the attitude of the people on the street, the way blacks and whites worked together, the newspapers and the range of editorials, the open discussion of politics, mineral production, synthetic oil production from coal by SASOL, and nuclear power. The discussion took over two hours, with Brandy and Nixon sitting together on the floor, surrounded by the papers. Nixon's questions were pointed, intelligent, and penetrating. Brandy was impressed. So was Nixon.

"This is great, what you've done, Brandy," he said.

Brandy then took a set of the material to Ridgway, before bringing it to the defense establishment. He spent the next few weeks being debriefed and working to arrange introductions. He persuaded Dr. Penn to fly to Washington and meet with his contacts in the intelligence community. From Dr. Penn's visit, plans evolved to have General Vander Westhuizen fly to Washington for a planned meeting with Jeanne Kirkpatrick, Reagan's appointee as U.S. ambassador to the United Nations. Somehow, word of the planned meeting leaked out and the liberal press had a field day.

Brandy worked with other contacts in the conservative community, hoping to improve the image of South Africa. George C. Pagonis, a shipping financier who wanted to use his fortune to influence political affairs, arranged to circulate news items to hundreds of opinion makers about South Africa's place in strategic minerals. Brandy talked to Brigadier Phillipe Shalkwyck at the South African embassy about means of getting their information out. Several of Brandy's former "Big Brothers" from the ACSI and the Defense Intelligence Agency were contacted; a few, in retirement, assisted in spreading some favorable publicity about South Africa's efforts at reform.

Brandy never knew if it made any difference, but his diligence in discovering and personally reporting ordinary details revealed his method. He did not need to travel under a "cover," since he truly traveled with a number of separate purposes at the same time. He did not need introductions, or need to travel officially, because with his knowledge of key people and a judicious mentioning of their names, he could instantly move into any circle that might be of interest. As a trained interrogator and observer, fluent in German, French, Magyar, English, and Spanish, his ordinary tourist travels to parks and museums would uncover rich collections of information. Since he was in no one's employment, he could honestly deny that he was on a mission. Everything he learned was openly given to him.

27

Searching for Tranquility

After building the villa, Casa Tranquilidad, and the chapel and cross above it, Brandy rarely had an extended period to relax and enjoy life. After the tragic deaths of the Trouyets and their interment in the crypts of the chapel, he faced continual challenges. Some were imposed, others he sought out. In 1975, the two younger surviving sons of the Trouyet family, Francisco and Roberto, and the executors of the estate, had decided to sell Las Brisas. The new management informed Brandy that his services as general manager were terminated. Later on, he entered a difficult and lengthy lawsuit to recover his retirement funds for which he personally had paid cash. Although he won three times in the labor court of Acapulco, where he was known, he finally lost the case on appeal to a higher court in Toluca, Mexico, due to the financial influence of Francisco and Roberto Trouyet.

The young Trouyets also removed Brandy from the board of trustees of the chapel, which he had not only conceived and built, but for which he had also paid the construction expenses. As a consequence, he raised his own private chapel in the corner of the garden at Casa Tranquilidad. He recalled his schoolboy days at Freistadt, Austria, after World War I. A nearby castle had been converted into a prisoner-of-war location for high-ranking Russian officers; in the grounds of the castle, the prisoners had constructed a small chapel for Russian Orthodox worship. The students at Freistadt had used that chapel, and Brandy had often visited there for private meditation. He constructed the small chapel in the corner of his garden along the same lines as the Freistadt chapel; he rescued from a trash heap an abandoned statue of the Virgin Mary which dated back to 1680, and had it restored for his chapel.

Over the years, visiting clergy would sometimes conduct masses there. In 1983 Mexican Archbishop Corripio Ahumada and his bishops all visited Casa Tranquilidad for eight days. While there, they conducted masses in the tiny chapel. Brandy has never forgotten the sounds of the Gregorian chant sung by Archbishop Corripio and the bishops in his private chapel. The resonance of the rounded roof with its perfect acoustics, similar to some cathedrals, left an inspiring imprint in his mind.

The search for tranquility, however, was always offset over the decades by Brandy's willingness to take on challenges, and by his burning creative energy which generated challenges if none came by accident. The turmoil of his life and adventures kept tranquility a distant goal.

Brandy's private chapel was constructed on the grounds of Casa Tranquilidad.

He kept in touch with dozens of the contacts he had made at Las Brisas. Among the friends he was particularly close to were the following: Phillipe de Vosjoli; Mike Howard from Lyndon Johnson's Secret Service staff; Nick Ruwe of Richard Nixon's staff, who became ambassador to Iceland; neighbor Clement Stone; Admiral Fritz Harlfinger of the U.S. Navy and DIA; General Johnny Johnson; British Ambassador Peter Hope; Assistant Director of the FBI Deke DeLoach; American astronauts Frank Borman, Joe Allen, Johnny Young, Buzz Aldrin, and others; and with various former "Big Brothers" and intelligence community members. He also kept in close contact with Matthew Ridgway, writing and phoning often, and frequently visiting the general at his home. And, of course, his closest friend was Gordon McLendon, with whom he communicated continuously. Each was a good friend; each generated new opportunities for challenging ventures and missions.

In 1973, before Brandy left Las Brisas, over two thousand American prisoners of war, many of them navy and air force pilots, were released from the Hanoi Hilton in North Vietnam. Brandy invited some of the

Deke De Loach, assistant director of the FBI, at an American Legion Convention.

officers who had been imprisoned to be his personal guests at Las Brisas. The Defense Department selected the officers who visited. Casitas, jeeps, and food were provided on a complimentary basis, similar to the arrangement he had made with the astronauts. The former POWs arrived with their wives, paying only the daily service charge to the employee gratuity fund. Dozens of former POWs took up the offer; Brandy met many of them and learned details of their incarceration in North Vietnamese prisons. He was shocked and appalled that the Geneva Convention had been repeatedly violated, in that the prisoners were chained to their pallets for days on end and suffered many other indignities and privations.

One of the former POW officers, J. M. McGrath, sat quietly by the pool at Casa Tranquilidad, illustrating on paper his recollections of the prisoner experience. Brandy suggested, with McGrath's permission, that he would like to publish the drawings of the prisoners' tortures in Vietnam and mail them to Senators and Congressmen, so they could see for themselves what some Americans had suffered. Gordon McClendon would finance and publish the book. Another POW, Admiral James Stockdale, who later served as H. Ross Perot's vice presidential running mate, recommended that the U.S. Navy publish the book, and he saw that it happened. The first book printed was sent to Brandy, inscribed by McGrath.

The lack of popular American sympathy for the POW conditions in the mid-1970s brought home to Frank how much needed to be done to build up American loyalty, in the wake of the disillusionment and cynicism of the post-Vietnam War period. The free lodgings at Las Brisas were Brandy's way of saying thank you for the patriotism and suffering of the former POWs.

During the mid-1970s, Brandy became more active in the American Legion, always paying his own way to attend the conventions. He became a member of the National Public Relations Committee of the Legion, whose director was Deke DeLoach, and met with a small group of Legion members who were self-supporting, nicknamed the "Iron Pants Gang." The small group stayed up one night, planning further steps to build respect for the country in the next generation. In the morning they held an early Mass, officiated by a Legionnaire chaplain who was one of the group. At times, a Jewish banker would officiate as altar boy. One of the ideas the small group developed, with Deke DeLoach, was the concept of the "Freedom Train." This train took George Washington's personal copy of the Constitution, a facsimile of the Declaration of Independence, and many other documents and artifacts on a tour of the United States, in celebration of the national bicentenary, bringing to the younger generation a knowledge of the nation's heritage and history. Brandy received a special plaque from the American Legion for this work. During this same period, Brandy urged his friend Edgar Bronfman to fund the production of the Broadway musical, *1776!* He continued to work on other fronts to address his concern for the decline of American patriotism and for the lack of knowledge of American history.

Brandy also participated in an association organized by David Atlee Phillips for ex-CIA officers. Phillips served as chief of the CIA's Caribbean and Latin American division before his retirement in 1975. He became distressed at the exposés of CIA officers, many stemming from the activities of Senator Frank Church's committee and the work of investigative reporters following the Watergate scandals. Phillips hoped to provide money that could serve as a legal defense fund for such officers, especially if they were libeled in the press and needed to file suit to restore their names. The organization could also conduct, as an outside group, public relations efforts to improve the image of the service as a whole. Brandy urged Phillips to expand his group to include not only former CIA officials, but also officers from other intelligence services, such as the army, navy, and air force. Accordingly, Phillips, with the approval of other CIA members, organized the Association of Former Intelligence Officers (AFIO). It was Brandy's responsibility to recruit the nucleus of former heads in the intelligence community, now retired, to represent the army, navy, and air force. This he did by recruiting Vice Admiral Fritz Harlfinger, U.S. Navy, ret., and Lieutenant General John Davis, U.S. Army, ret., formerly of the ACSI and deputy director of the National Security Agency (NSA). Brandy was offered a directorship, but he turned it down because of his comparatively low rank as a colonel. The organization needed leaders with significant Washington experience, with "Beltway" knowledge. He preferred to remain in the background. At his request, retired officers from other intelligence services, such as former members of the FBI, State, NSA, and others augumented the influence of the AFIO. Brandy remained an active member, quietly providing financial support and arranging contributions from several wealthy Americans such as Gordon McLendon and former guests of Las Brisas with whom he was in contact.

Often, those guests at Las Brisas became members of Brandy's extended network of interesting and thought-provoking friends. One such guest was Walter Dornberger, the German general who commanded Peenemünde during World War II, and had overseen the research, development, and deployment of both the V-1 and V-2 weapons. Brandy remembered well his questioning of German POWs in order to target Dornberger's Crossbow V-1 sites. Brandy's fluent German and his memory of the same events from the other side led to fascinating conversations. Dornberger, after being incarcerated by the British, moved to the United States and worked for several years in the defense industry advising von Braun and NASA. Brandy met Dornberger at the liftoff of Apollo 11 at the Cape. The general had retired to Mexico, living a comfortable life in the scenic lakeside town of Chapala, just south of Guadalajara.

During one of his birthday parties at Chapala, attended by many friends, Dornberger invited Brandy to visit. As he joined the banquet, Brandy realized that all of the guests, except for himself and one other, were former German scientists of the V-2 command. Dornberger proceeded around the table, introducing everyone. The other American, Dornberger explained, was a former CIC colonel, Jack Gallagher. Gallagher had been Dornberger's bodyguard during his early travels around the United States and Europe as he recruited German scientists for NASA. "Some bodyguard!" Dornberger explained. "His orders were, should it look like the KGB was going to succeed in kidnapping me, to shoot me dead!" Everyone roared with laughter and Brandy, unaccustomed to German humor and with some shock, made an effort to join in. When the introductions got around to Brandy, Dornberger explained, "And this is Colonel Frank Brandstetter. He is just an old, good friend."

Dornberger presented Brandy with several mementos of his time at Peenemünde, including some ancient cannonballs that were fired from

General Walter Dornberger, father of the German rocket program, visits his close friend Brandy at Casa Tranquilidad in 1976.

the Swedish ship *Vasa* and a small model of the famous multiple rocket launcher, the *Nebelwerfer*. Later, when Dornberger passed away, his widow sent the general's personal library, correspondence files, and mementos given him at West Point and elsewhere to Brandy. She knew that Brandy was an avid collector of such materials and would cherish and preserve them. He dutifully added them to his space collection.

Men and women who had worked with Brandy at Las Brisas became part of another wide network of contacts across Mexico as they dispersed to other jobs. With Brandy's supervision and recommendation to Deke DeLoach, Carlos Solana, his chief of security, had participated with a small group of Mexican security men in training at the FBI's facility in Quantico, Virginia, to become the first "SWAT" team in Mexico. Solana later moved to Monterrey, in the state of Neuvo Leon, with his entire team. In Monterrey he worked closely with the state government in fighting crime, corruption, and the penetration of the university by revolutionary agents. He continued to build a core of Mexican security agents dedicated to fighting Communism and corruption. Across Mexico, "alumni" from the training at Las Brisas went on to take positions in hotels, government, the tourist industry, the airlines, and other private businesses. Brandy constantly ran into them and exchanged correspondence with many.

Some of the contacts were international and some were highly placed in the Mexican government. Al Kaplan, who had served as Brandy's public relations man in the 1970s through his own company, moved on to be national director of tourism for the United States-Mexico Chamber of Commerce, with an office in New York City. On one occasion, when Kaplan visited Brandy in Acapulco, the two went to a small restaurant, Cocula, near the Villa-Vera Hotel where Kaplan was staying, to talk over old times. The bistro was managed by a former Las Brisas employee, and Brandy had frequented it years before with Vice Admiral Rodrigo del Peon Alvarez and other officers from the Mexican naval base. Kaplan had often worked with the legal attachés at embassies, and like Brandy, had voluntarily provided bits and pieces of human intelligence. The two had many old war stories to trade and recall. As they sat over a snack with tequila and beer, a man walked in with two men on either side. Four carried walkie-talkies, obviously serving as guards to the gentleman in the middle, apparently a Mexican government official of some sort.

Kaplan and Brandy stayed on, chatting quietly into the middle of the night, not paying much attention to the group at a nearby table. As Brandy was paying his bill to leave, the Mexican official left his bodyguards and came over.

"Colonel Brandy," he said. "It is many years ago that you were of great assistance to me." He gave Brandy an *abrazo*—a Mexican bear hug—nearly cracking Brandy's ribs.

Brandy looked closely, but did not recognize him.

"Please," he said, "refresh my memory."

The official explained that, years earlier, he had been in charge of the Mexican Army Intelligence Services, supervising the security surrounding Henry Kissinger when he had visited Acapulco and lunched at Casa Tranquilidad. During the security check, Brandy had pointed out one area, high on the retaining walls above the home, which had escaped the protective ring. Guards were placed there. As it happened, a plot to kill Kissinger was later uncovered. A group of assassins was arrested while waiting at the Acapulco airport for Kissinger's departure to Mexico City to meet the president of Mexico.

Brandy recalled the event. It was in 1978, when he had argued with

Kissinger over the Panama Canal Treaty. But Brandy could still not place the Mexican gentleman. The officer continued.

"You remember—I was a young captain in the Mexican Army's Security Service. I mentioned I had no wheels, and you turned around and gave me the keys to your jeep, saying, 'Captain, the jeep is yours, for the good of the service.' I still have it on my small ranch; I keep it for sentimental reasons!"

Brandy was flabbergasted. He had completely forgotten the jeep incident. They chatted further. The officer explained he was an avid reader and admirer of Vernon Walters, who was deputy director of Central Intelligence from 1972 to 1976, and Brandy explained that he knew Walters and had served with him. When Walters had been at Camp Ritchie in the French section, Brandy had been in the German section. It had only been a few years since Brandy had visited Walters at his office at the United Nations. Finally, Brandy drew the officer aside from the bodyguards, Kaplan, and the owner of Cocula.

"Tell me," he asked in a low voice. "What are you doing now—what is your current job, that you need four bodyguards?" He assumed it was still a low-profile position.

Brandy and Henry Kissinger confer with American Legion dignitaries.

It turned out that the young army captain he had assisted years before was now the nationally prominent General Acosta Chaparro, chief
of the Mexican Army Intelligence Services in Mexico City. Brandy had
not recognized him from his pictures in the newspapers.

Brandy's personal life had gone through several chaotic changes in
the late 1970s and early 1980s. Barbara became increasingly mentally ill
in the late 1970s, and stayed at the home he bought in Dallas to be
more comfortable. In 1978, at the behest of her sister, she filed for divorce, which was finalized on 8 May 1978. With the divorce, Barbara's
sister would inherit Barbara's share of her father's estate, instead of
Brandy. Barbara passed away on 14 May 1980.

After the divorce, Brandy married again. He had met Marianne
Porzelt at one of the backgammon tournaments organized at his home.
She was a strikingly attractive lady some twenty-four years younger than
himself, "a helluva backgammon player," and an Austrian by birth. They
were married 26 December 1978; the best men were Gordon McLendon
and the ex-President of Mexico, Miguel Alemán. Baron and Baroness
Portonova and many others from the international set attended the
wedding. The marriage was difficult; after two years, Brandy and

Frank, Marianne, and Gordon McLendon (far right) celebrate at the
Brandstetters' wedding in 1978.

Marianne separated. She loved skiing and St. Tropez, with its parties and yachts. Brandy sought quiet and tranquility. The divorce was finalized on 11 November 1983.

None of the employment difficulties, personal crises, business ventures, intelligence endeavors, network of contacts, or trips to points of crisis around the world were the sort of activities to bring him tranquility and peace. These he had sought in the building of the Chapel of Peace and the private chapel in the small courtyard next to his bedroom at Casa Tranquilidad. The search for emotional experience as the gateway to knowledge went on.

In 1992, on Brandy's eightieth birthday, Bart McLendon, the son of Gordon McLendon, organized a massive birthday party for him at Rancho Cielo, the ranch property near Dallas that he owned. Over five hundred guests attended from all over the world. The group included astronauts, politicians, military and hotel contacts, and a wide variety of writers and former government officials. A former German Luftwaffe ace attended as well. His old friend from the Cuba days, Al Kaplan,

Bart McLendon and Brandy visit the Rose Bowl for Super Bowl XXVII.

prepared a lengthy poem, "A Kernal of Truth." It was full of puns and allusions which served as an outline of his life, and at the same time, in the tradition of the Friar's Club Roast, gently ribbed Brandy on some of his adventures, characteristics, and personality traits.

The birthday party gave him pause, with people reminiscing about his extensive life. It made him want to think about the past. Yet he had never looked back; he always moved forward. The past was past, and only the now, the present, mattered. Tomorrow was in the hands of God. The effort was at once painful and bittersweet. After collecting his thoughts, he was persuaded by a close personal friend to organize his papers, work with his friends to get his biography written, and distill his philosophy of life.

Looking back to the years of his childhood and his path through the history of the twentieth century, he tried to capture, in a peaceful interlude, the *view from the hill.*

28

The View from the Hill

The breeze blows gently across the patio of Casa de la Tranquilidad during a typical fall evening. Music and laughter softly fill the night air from the nearby terraces. Frank M. Brandstetter looks out across the bay at the thousands of flickering lights that illuminate the Acapulco night. It is the late 1990s, approaching the millenium, and time for a recounting of an amazing life. The guests who visit Casa de la Tranquilidad are fewer now; most are close friends who have known Brandy for many years. The trips around the world continue, but most are planned for the purpose of revisiting the sites that he holds important to his life.

Some things, however, have not changed. The ideals, the philosophy of life, the values learned from important teachers, such as Matthew Ridgway and Carlos Trouyet, are ingrained in him. The memories come flooding back to Frank Brandstetter on these warm, tropical evenings in Acapulco. He remembers the world events he has experienced and outstanding individuals he has known.

In the summer of 1998, Brandy revisited the sites of his early military education and World War II experiences and relived some of the emotions and deep feelings of those memorable times. Brandy returned to the military academy in Köszeg, Hungary where, in 1924, his training was focused on character development and independent thinking. He was pleased to discover that the school was still being used, now as a teaching and rehabilitation institute for disabled Hungarian children. At Maria Theresianum school in Vienna, which he also revisited, Brandy had learned the discipline and endurance that was the foundation of the Austro-Hungarian empire.

Military schools trained him for the rigors of war, but nothing could have prepared Frank for the horrors of the German concentration camps. As part of Ridgway's command that liberated Wöbbelin camp, Frank witnessed the cruelty and depravity of Hitler's Reich. When Frank arranged for the burial site in the center of the nearby town of Hagenow, he hoped it would serve as a continuous reminder of the abhorrent activities that took place there. Upon returning to Hagenow, Frank found the cemetery still intact and well kept. Also, a large inscription in a stone wall outside the cemetery, honoring those who died at Wöbbelin, had been added.

Another stop on Brandy's 1998 European trip, Copenhagen, reminded him of the peculiar accidents of war. As Brandy dined at the D'Angleterre Hotel he recalled the incident which could have resulted in the capture of General Ridgway and his staff at the war's end. The general was not informed of the precarious nature of the situation until the anniversary of the event in 1985. Brandy, his dinner guests Dr. Dominic Monetta, Vice Admiral Al Burkhalter, and others decided to call General Ridgway and tell him, albeit thirty years later, how they deceived the Germans during the "occupation" of Copenhagen. The general appreciated the clever maneuver and was amused by the story.

Just as Ridgway played a central role in Frank's World War II experiences, the general also influenced his outlook on life. Frank identifies Ridgway as one of four men who were responsible for teaching him essential values. Other role models during various stages of Frank's life were his father, Ferenc, Barbara's father, Hartley Peart, and business partner Carlos Trouyet.

Brandy credits General Ridgway with instilling several specific qualities into his personality. The general insisted on a "can-do" attitude in his staff; when anyone visibly hesitated, he was off the staff. That attitude of accomplishment radiated out from the immediate staff to the airborne troops.

Ridgway also held loyalty central, and Brandy made that one concept his motto. This meant not only loyalty to country and flag, but to individuals and friends. The disappointments he had suffered from a few individuals, including some whom he had trusted in his business dealings, hurt not only because of the loss of funds or the breaking of legal and moral commitments, but even more so because of the sense of betrayal.

Brandy often said his mind was opened by Matthew Ridgway, the disciplinarian with a kind heart. Ridgway demonstrated this trait when he sent a copy of his own Congressional Gold Medal as a gift to Brandy on his eightieth birthday. The rare medal is granted for distinguished services rendered; its first recipient was George Washington. Brandy cherished Ridgway's attached note that stated the gift was for "services shared."

Frank considered General Ridgway his surrogate father because Ferenc Brandstetter, his actual father, had disappeared from his life at an early age. Ferenc, however, did contribute some valuable advice that Frank followed throughout his life. His father taught Frank that the military, politics, and religion were all separate entities that should not be combined.

Another major influence was his father-in-law, Hartley Peart, a leading San Francisco attorney. Peart assisted Frank with his knowledge of the intricacies of the business world and his connections with the corporate elite. Although Frank appreciated his father-in-law's attempts to secure him positions, he declined direct help in this regard. He applied the knowledge imparted by Peart to his subsequent business ventures.

These ventures included many in Mexico, where he met Don Carlos Trouyet, the last of the influential mentors Frank credits with his development. Trouyet became his closest business associate and taught him the ethics and responsibilities of financial success. Frank admired the Mexican financier because he had amassed a fortune by earning all of it, and not inheriting a cent. Don Carlos actively invested in projects that would create jobs for the Mexican people and develop the Mexican economy. Some of these ventures were risky, but Trouyet felt the ultimate goal was worth the gamble. Other traits Don Carlos exemplified were self-reliance and simplicity of manner.

Frank incorporated various concepts, ideals, and values of these men into his general philosophy of life. Also, his decades of experience and reading have culminated into a unique outlook on life. Contemporary thinkers and authors continue to enhance Frank's intellectual development. For example, the works of Clement Stone, the organizer and writer of the philosophy of Positive Mental Attitude or "PMA," and the inheritor of an institute for personal success, reinforced his ideas about self-enrichment.

Frank has found further support for some of his thinking in the writings of J. E. Knight, author of *Ramtha: A State of Mind*, and those of Edgar Cayce, along with a variety of other eclectic thinkers who have pulled together ideas from eastern religions and western thought. Finnish philosopher Esa Saarinen offers ideas on freedom, teaching, and modern communication that parallel Frank's attitudes and life experiences. Saarinen considers Frank the embodiment of his teachings, describing him as a "warrior of freedom" in an inscription to his work *Erektio*, and writes that Frank ''follows everything this book, a very personal book, is all about.''

As visitors sort their gin rummy hands and sip their drinks in the warm tropical night, the worlds of hotel hospitality, military affairs, and international intrigue are at once far-distant, yet hauntingly evoked.

The conversation turns with Brandy's recollections, his adventures and experiences, the winding course of his life through the web of twentieth-century history.

The principles by which he lived—loyalty to country, faith in God, service to others—run through the episodes with presidents and princes, ambassadors and authors, the powerful and the helpless. In the quiet night, the narratives of refugees from the turmoil of civil strife, wars and revolutions, the tales of families torn by tragedy, are immediate and real. Through all, Brandy's ideals were tested, re-affirmed, renewed.

Now he believes it is time to pass these ideals on to the youth of the world. Only through education at every level can future generations acquire these lessons of life. If Brandy's experiences can serve as a guide for today's youth, then all was worthwhile.

He feels like an Olympic runner eager to hand over to another the torch of responsibility and humanity that he always tried to carry before him. In the quiet Acapulco evening, he appreciates the tranquility of Las Brisas, the cool evening breezes and the crystal stars blinking across the velvet sky. Although it's late, he has a lot of living to do before passing on the torch.

During the summer of 1998, Brandy revisited European sites that he held important to his memory. Here he stands next to the stone inscription commemorating the dead at Wöbbelin concentration camp on his revisit to the area in 1998.

Brandy points across the Elbe, the location of a bridge built for a May 1945 crossing of American troops.

Fifty-three years after the fact, Brandy pauses at a bridge near Lübz in northern Germany, the farthest point he reached in advance of the 82nd Airborne in May 1945. At this bridge, Brandy persuaded a German commanding officer of an armored column to discard his weapons and continue toward the American line.

Frank in front of the Maria Teresanium Akademie in Vienna.

The Hotel D'Angleterre restaurant in Copenhagen, where Brandy spent anxious moments awaiting the arrival of British troops in 1945.

Frank was a frequent visitor to General Ridgway's home in Pittsburgh.

Ferenc Brandstetter provided invaluable advice to his son, Frank, at an early age.

Hartley Peart, Frank's father-in-law, was a prominent San Francisco attorney who assisted his son-in-law with the complexities of the corporate world.

Don Carlos Trouyet, second from right, with Dr. Denton Cooley, heart surgeon, and his wife, and Brandy. At Las Brisas in 1968.

SOURCE NOTES

Frank M. Brandstetter has always kept documents relating to his personal life. At the time of the writing of this biographical memoir, the authors worked with Brandstetter's personal collection from his home, Casa de la Tranquilidad, Club Residencial, Acapulco, Mexico. Documents in the collection include letters of recommendation, general correspondence, letters of commendation or award, invitations, military orders and records, letters pertaining to hotel work, reports authored by Brandstetter on diplomatic and business matters, lists of guests and notables visiting Acapulco, photographs, drawings of architectural projects, a library of about seven thousand volumes, clippings from magazines, newspapers, and other periodicals, and collections of artifacts. His collection of Space memorabilia, including some 160 books previously in the collection of General Dornberger, had been carefully documented and described for possible sale by a collection specialist, Mr. Colin Franklin, and was retained at Casa Tranquilidad.

In addition, Brandstetter had already made an effort to formalize his recollections of the past by writing out his memories of various events and by taping narratives. In addition, he wrote answers to queries which we developed. He not only prepared extensive reports, but he provided, identified, and pulled from the files, original documents to substantiate his commentary.

At the conclusion of the writing of this biographical memoir, Brandstetter made arrangements for the transfer of his documentary collection to the Archives of the University of North Texas in Denton, Texas. At the time of writing, the collection of documents, memorabilia, and memoir material had been roughly organized and subjected to the first archival review for preservation; for this reason, we did not cite letters to box or folder. Specific citations in this text to the source in a specific item in the unprocessed collection by box or folder description would not carry over to the archives' more formal organization. For these reasons, we have indicated specific items in these Source Notes in such a way that they could be located, if desired, after the collection is arranged professionally. For convenience of notation, we have indicated the presence of such documents in the "FMB Collection." It is anticipated that when fully archived, the final finding aid will allow an even better cross checking of the materials. As

351

indicated in the following notes, many parts of this collection are rich and detailed, and will provide interested researchers with further information.

Many facts in the Brandstetter story can be documented or substantiated from printed sources. Where a clipping or book in the Brandstetter Collection, or a source we find in the course of outside research, serves to confirm or provide further detail, we have indicated the published source below. We have mentioned such items more generally available in library sources following standard bibliographic style in the Source Notes. In the course of organizing the files, we developed a preliminary folder list and binder title list of the approximately fifty cubic feet of documents which served to aid us in locating materials pertinent to particular passages.

Brandstetter taped over twenty-five hours of interviews with the authors. The tapes and transcripts of these materials will be included with the FMB Collection. An earlier tape between Brandstetter and Dominic Paolucci is also included. In addition, both authors took extensive notes during unrecorded conversations with Brandstetter.

Brandstetter's respect and admiration for General Matthew Ridgway prevented him from contradicting small errors of fact that appeared in Ridgway's memoir, as told to Harold Martin, *Soldier*, (New York: Harper and Brothers, 1956) and others that appeared in Clay Blair's *Ridgway's Paratroopers: The American Airborne in World War II* (Garden City, New York: Dial Press, 1985). The outlines of the events presented in those books were largely correct, and many had been documented from the general's memory and his own notes. Brandy, out of respect, simply kept his file of documents and made personal notes of several relatively minor historical discrepancies and previously overlooked details. In the chapter by chapter Source Notes which follow, we have attempted to make particular reference to documents which provide such corrective detail.

The regard of Brandstetter and Ridgway was mutual. Ridgway inscribed a copy of Blair's *Ridgway's Paratroopers* for Brandstetter's library as follows: "Few, very few American patriots have served our country with the courage, vision, and selfless integrity of my dear friend Frank Brandstetter for many years in war and in peace, M. B. Ridgway, General, U.S. Army, Retired, 24 Jan. 86."

Much of Brandstetter's career as a G-2 officer and as a reservist with the staff of the army's Assistant Chief of Staff-Intelligence (ACSI) was confidential, and for that reason, documentation on a number of his activities was inappropriate, or where permissible, difficult to obtain. In

1988, several of his friends sought to secure official recognition for his decades of undercover work, and the FMB Collection contains a number of letters written at that time. Some of these letters provide a few sketchy details of his work, as discussed in the text of Chapter 22. We have limited our coverage in this book to declassified or never-classified incidents, sources and contacts whose exposure represents no threat to national security.

Chapter 1

At the time of the writing of this work, partial inventories of the Brandstetter artifact, library, and document collections were available. A professional inventory and description of the "Dornberger Collection," prepared by Colin Franklin in 1985, described the artifacts and documents in that group. In addition, within the general Brandstetter document collection there was an inventory of ships' plaques left by the officers of visiting warships, a partial list of the books in the library, and several other partial inventories. Other material derives from direct observation by the authors and from organization of the document collection.

Chapter 2

This chapter was based upon taped interviews with Brandstetter, upon memoir material prepared by him and upon photograph collections in the FMB Collection. Description of the Austro-Hungarian Empire and Hungarian politics and geography are derived from: Priscilla Robertson, *Revolutions of 1848: A Social History* (Princeton: Princeton University Press, 1952); Robert A. Kann, *A History of the Habsburg Monarchy* (Berkeley: University of California Press, 1974); Oscar Jaszi, *The Dissolution of the Habsburg Monarchy* (Chicago: University of Chicago Press, 1929); and Joseph Held, *The Columbia History of Eastern Europe in the Twentieth Century* (New York: Columbia University Press, 1992).

In response to queries, Brandstetter prepared a detailed collection of material regarding Köszeg, his travels as a child, and his father's politics during the 1920s. The FMB Collection contains a set of school records, albums of photos from childhood and school years, and other ephemera from the years prior to 1928.

Chapter 3

Most of the detail in this chapter was based upon interviews with Brandstetter. Dates of employment were confirmed by reference to a file of

"To Whom it May Concern" letters of reference from employers in the 1930s, supplemented by military personnel records in the FMB Collection and several published works by and about the people he met.

The textbook by Louis Toth and Ernest Horvarth was *Hotel Accounting* (New York: Ronald Press Co., 1928). The fourth edition was issued by John Wiley and Sons in 1978. The text served as a sophisticated introduction to all aspects of hotel management and financial control, showing that Toth was perhaps the best mentor that an aspiring hotel manager might have encountered in the 1930s. Dr. Geza Takaro published a set of his sermons in Hungarian in 1931.

Details of the Sikorsky company were confirmed in Frank J. Delear, *Igor Sikorsky: His Three Careers in Aviation* (Dodd Mead & Company, New York, 1969); the Rentschler quotation is from p.141.

The description of Laurel-in-the-Pines derives from Paul Axel-Lute, *Lakewood-in-the-Pines: A History of Lakewood, New Jersey* (South Orange, New Jersey, 1986).

Chapter 4

A good source on hotel crises in New York during the Depression is Ward Morehouse, *The Waldorf-Astoria: America's Gilded Dream* (New York: M. Evans, 1991). Secondary material for background on J. Edgar Hoover, Clyde Tolson, and Walter Winchell is extensive. An early journalistic account of Walter Winchell, which gives many details of his life in New York and Miami, and confirms his stays at the Roney Plaza, is St. Clair McKelway, *Gossip: The Life and Times of Walter Winchell* (New York: The Viking Press, 1940). The work confirms Brandstetter's memory that the Roney Plaza was Winchell's residence in Miami, p.40.

The details of the life of Zanvyl Krieger were confirmed from *Who's Who in America*, 1974. Krieger later became assistant attorney general in Maryland, a member of the board of U.S. Surgical Company and active in organized professional sports in Maryland. In 1992, he donated fifty million dollars to his undergraduate alma mater, Johns Hopkins University (*New York Times*, 21 December 1992).

Brandstetter's information about Briarcliff Lodge was supplemented by reference to Mary Cheever, *The Changing Landscape: A History of Briarcliff Manor-Scarborough* (Briarcliff Manor Historical Society, 1990) and *Our Village: Briarcliff Manor, New York, 1902 to 1952* (Historical Committee of Briarcliff Manor, 1952). Brandstetter listed Gilbert Temple as a reference in later years. Temple's wife was one of the daughters of the founder, Dr. Matthew Reaser.

The departure of Baron Louis Rothschild from Vienna is described in Virginia Cowles, *The Rothschilds: A Family of Fortune* (New York: Knopf, 1973), p.232. The details of the stripping of the Rothschild household are recounted by William Shirer in *The Rise and Fall of the Third Reich* (New York: Simon and Schuster, 1960), p.351. Shirer witnessed the looting. Brandstetter was present at the St. Moritz in April 1939. Since Louis was the only Rothschild fleeing Vienna at the time, we conclude that he was the Rothschild Brandstetter remembered at the St. Moritz.

Other pertinent papers in the FMB Collection included partnership documents with Dr. Eugene Hegy and with Wachter and Palmer regarding the Champlain Hotel. Other documents collected concern re-immigration in 1937.

The attendees at the military attaché dinner were listed in the local Plattsburg newspaper dated 19 August 1939. A photo of the officers' hats on the hotel rack appeared in *Life* in the 4 September 1939 issue, p.27. The luncheon menu can be found in the FMB Collection. Thomas Dewey's luncheon meeting of August is in the *New York Times*, 29 August 1939, p.15; it is also noted in a retrospective of the week the war broke out in *Life*, 18 September 1939, p.76.

The story of the closing of the Lake Champlain Hotel is based on an interview with Brandstetter in *Travel Scene* (The Official Airline Guide) 15 March 1977, which includes details of the meeting with Bronfman of Seagram's.

Chapter 5

The major source for material on Brandstetter's years in military training consists of interviews, supplemented and confirmed by military records in the FMB Collection. Vernon Walters, *Silent Missions* (Garden City, New York: Doubleday, 1978), presents an account of Camp Ritchie that is extremely close to Brandstetter's memory of the facility.

Chapter 6

Brandstetter maintained a full file of materials on the Devizes Plot, including copies of the dispatches by McDermott, reports from officers at the scene later declassified, and related correspondence. *New York Times* coverage, 11 May 1945, was very cursory, as was a short treatment in a British magazine years later: "German POWs in England," *After the Battle,* 1977, Issue 17, p. 49, for the reasons mentioned in the text.

Charles Whiting's *The March on London* (London: Leo Cooper, 1996), supports this presentation of the Devizes Plot. For a differing interpretation, see Roderick De Normann's *For Führer and Fatherland* (Phoenix Mill, England: Sutton Publishing, 1996).

Other aspects of the chapter derive from interviews, confirmed from military record files in the FMB Collection.

Chapter 7

David Niven described the organization of the Phantoms in his autobiography *The Moon's a Balloon* (New York: G. P. Putnam, 1972) and later provided Brandstetter with an inscribed copy. For activities in World War II Europe see Clay Blair's *Ridgway's Paratroopers* and Harold Martin's *Soldier: The Memoirs of Matthew B. Ridgway* (New York: Harpers, 1956). In his memoirs, Ridgway recalled several specifics of the surrender attempt, including sending Brandstetter across the lines, but incorrectly indicated the date of the memo as 15 April and suggested that there were two visits, rather than the three actual visits. Brandstetter's photocopy of the English version of the surrender offer with the allusion to Robert E. Lee is clearly dated 16 April. Clay Blair, in *Ridgway's Paratroopers,* also presented a version of the events which suggested two separate missions to Model's HQ, perhaps based on a misunderstanding of Brandstetter's first visit to the industrialists.

Ridgway's memoirs included an edited version of the speech delivered by Cain at the burial service in Hagenow. Multiple copies of the complete printed version are in the FMB Collection, from which the transcription in the text is taken. The differences between the text in Ridgway's memoir and the printed copy suggest that Martin (Ridgway's amanuensis), had access to a more generic draft of the speech, possibly one that was prepared for delivery at all three of the towns, to duplicate the procedure at Hagenow.

In answer to queries, Brandy recorded his impressions of his first encounters with General Ridgway and Ridgway's methods of command. Although Clay Blair, who wrote a thorough treatment of Ridgway in *Paratroopers,* had telephoned Brandstetter and asked him to supply material (the phone note request of 2 February 1984 is in the Blair papers at the Carlisle Military History Archives), Brandstetter declined, not wanting to offer any details which would contradict Ridgway's own account in his memoir. He prepared a lengthy memo in May 1994, providing corrections to various aspects of the treatment by Clay Blair.

One discrepancy in the pontoon bridge story occurred when Blair claimed that Don Faith, an aide to Ridgway, was on the bridge with Ridgway and prepared the report which earned Ridgway the Silver Star. At that time, Brandy allowed that detail to go uncorrected because the general was still living. Brandstetter's own 1994 memorandum detailing the pontoon bridge account is in the FMB Collection.

Chapter 8

Ridgway's memoir, *Soldier*, provides some background for the 1945–46 shift to the Pacific Theater, to Caserta, and to the U.N. conference in London. Details were fleshed out by an interview with Brandstetter.

In addition to interview material, the FMB Collection has a file of social page clippings regarding his marriage in San Francisco, a file on the inspection of the frontier with Austria including reports from the CIC agent, maps and descriptions of the trip south of Trieste into Yugoslav territory (with notes on the briefing regarding the WWI battle), and a full report on the trip to Vienna and Bratislava. Colonel Emil Pratt provided Brandstetter with a biography in Slovak (in the file), which was then translated and incorporated in the report to Ridgway.

There were two copies of the memorandum delivered to Anton Dostler. Details of Ridgway's heart attack are derived from an interview and query responses, as are descriptions of Brandstetter's trip from London to New York. Dr. Homer Dupuy, who attended Ridgway at Trieste and Caserta, and traveled with Brandstetter to Bratislava, later established a well-known heart surgery practice in New Orleans, and was still living there in the early 1990s. A memo of Brandstetter's visit with Dupuy, dated 30 July 1994, is in the files.

Chapter 9

The basic sources for the material in this chapter are oral history interviews and answers to authors' queries by Brandstetter. The FMB Collection has memoranda and letters from his work with the Santa Barbara Biltmore Hotel and with the Orinda Country Club. Brandstetter published an extensive article on wine merchandising at the Orinda Country Club in the professional magazine *Club Management: The National Magazine for*

Executives of Town and Country Clubs, April 1949, that provides details on his management at Orinda.

The FMB Collection has a section of materials on the Continental Trailways operations, at that time a Santa Fe RR subsidiary. Included is a news clipping from the *Wall Street Journal*, dated 11 May 1954, that provides some background on both the corporation and the restaurant operation.

The FMB Collection contains copies of Army Reserve records, as well as notes and drafts which Brandstetter prepared for the emergency civil defense reports he developed while working at the Presidio. Specific dates of his assignments and other details regarding the Reserve tasks were drawn from these Army Reserve documents.

Chapter 10

Brandstetter's memory of the Jamaican venture with William Palmer was painful, and thus the oral history material regarding this episode was brief. The files contain some advertising material on the Sans Souci Hotel, clippings regarding his stay in Kingston, and several copies of the record of the court case against Palmer.

Material regarding the Murchison plans derived from an interview.

Chapter 11

Brandstetter's adventures in Cuba have been retold in several interview-based news and magazine stories. The FMB Collection contains two large scrapbooks of clippings from Chicago, Miami, and New York papers covering the 1958 and 1959 events in Cuba. In particular, these clippings fleshed out the story: *Wall Street Journal*, 23 December 1958 and 5 January 1959; *Chicago Tribune*, 2 January 1959 and 4 January 1959; *Miami Herald*, 3 January 1959.

The scrapbooks also contain press releases, flyers, correspondence, and other clippings, all pertinent to the stay in 1958. Brandstetter filled in some of the anecdotal material, especially regarding Manual Ray and the operation of the hotel in conversations and interviews.

The correspondence with ACSI is in the FMB Collection military files.

Chapter 12

Brandstetter's standoff with the rebels was recounted in a column by Frank Farrell, *New York World Telegram and Sun*, 9 January 1959, and as noted in the text, in Philippe Thyraud de Vosjoli, *Lamia* (Boston: Little Brown, 1970), p. 282. De Vosjoli dedicated the book to Brandstetter on the frontispiece. Brandstetter retained the sign-up list for the first caravan out of Havana, containing de Vosjoli and his wife's signatures. Other items from the clipping albums include: *Chicago Tribune*, 9 January 1959, 10 January 1959, and 11 January 1959. David Atlee Phillips, *The Night Watch* (New York: Atheneum, 1977) details the night of 31 December 1958 to 1 January 1959.

Letters thanking Brandy for his actions include, among others, those from: Jules DuBois, Clay Gowran, John Thompson, all of the *Chicago Tribune* (cable to Conrad Hilton) 6 January 1959; E. M. Schloss, 8 January 1959; Nat. E. Geismar, 8 January 1959; Richard Heller (to Robert Caverly) 9 January 1959; Curtice Rosser, 12 January 1959; Ernest Dumler (to Conrad Hilton) 16 January 1959; Reply of Henry Crown to a letter from John Thompson of the *Chicago Tribune*, 19 January 1959; Jack Paar, 3 February 1959.

The albums also contain Castro's invitation to tourists, a carbon of a letter from the Miami AAA 12 January 1959, and an annotated mimeographed report from the Havana Hilton regarding the extra services of buffet and lodging during the first week of January 1959. The narrative is compiled from the letters, clippings, and interview material.

Chapter 13

The FMB Collection contains a brief corporate prospectus from Continental Leasing. Details regarding the visit to Hilton Continental in Mexico City and the conversation with Henry Crown derive from interviews and conversations with Brandstetter.

Chapter 14

Most of the detail regarding hotel management is based upon interviews and discussions Brandstetter had with the authors. Many magazine clippings and reprints in the FMB Collection, also based on interviews, reflected similar information regarding the Juan March days at Las Brisas, the absence of uniforms, the no-tip policy, the role of Ron Urbanek, and other details of management.

Chapter 15

Several cubic feet of Special Attention notices and VIP files in the FMB Collection gave more than ample data on the types of visitors. Correspondence in these files detailed many of the anecdotes, supplemented by material from oral history interviews. Most of the Space memorabilia collection and its documentation were not made part of the FMB Collection, but several items reflecting the presence of the astronauts and their treatment were in the file. Reflecting astronauts' visits to Acapulco is a memoir by Jim Lovell and Jeffrey Kluger, *Lost Moon* (New York: Houghton-Mifflin, 1994) that mentions FMB on p. 38.

The oral interview notes on the visit of Tito were substantiated by a photo album in the collection.

Several items of correspondence by and about Derek Gore and Peter Hope described the story of the consulate that was also discussed on tape. As noted in the text, with dates and issues cited there, a range of articles in travel magazines gave rich detail.

The oral history interviews contained details of the humorous anecdotes and some of the public relations efforts. A copy of the Graham Kerr cookbook in the files prompted the oral account of the underwater filming of the marzipan scene.

Chapter 16

Much of the detail of the construction of both Casa Tranquilidad and the chapel are richly documented in plans, photo albums, and correspondence files in the FMB Collection. Dedication documents regarding the chapel contained the sermons and commentaries referred to, as well as other material lauding FMB for his work in bringing the chapel to completion. Interview material and personal observation by the authors added to the detail regarding Casa Tranquilidad.

Chapter 17

In addition to oral history materials, several documents substantiate and expand the various aspects of the Leon Uris/Philippe Thyraud de Vosjoli story. *Lamia* (Boston: Little Brown, 1970) by de Vosjoli, and *Topaz* (New York: McGraw-Hill, 1967) by Leon Uris convey parallel, but significantly different stories.

The FMB Collection has extensive clippings and correspondence, as noted in the body of the text. Pertinent clippings include: *New York Times,* 16 April 1968; *Washington Daily Times,* 10 February 1972; *Washington Post,* 11 February 1972; *Miami Herald,* 13 February 1972; *New York Times,* 10 February 1972; a review in *Miami Herald,* 6 December 1970 by John McDermott; and the *Washington Post,* 23 December 1971.

Specific letters cited to and from Brandstetter are all in the FMB Collection in the de Vosjoli folders.

The *Life* magazine coverage was extensive. The account was published in the regular edition of 16 April 1968 and in the International or "Atlantic" edition, volume 44, number 8, 29 April 1968, in an article titled "The French Spy Scandal." The cover of *Life* depicted the same photograph of de Vosjoli that was later used on the dust jacket for *Lamia*. The coverage was published in a special section within the Atlantic edition, on separately numbered "SP" pages, and included a long memoir by de Vosjoli: "So Much has been Swept Under the Rug," on pages SP4 through SP9; page SP10 contained an article by John Barry, of the London Sunday *Times*, "Broad Impact of 'Martel' everywhere but France." Details of the French bureaucracy's reaction to de Vosjoli are drawn from these accounts and from *Lamia*.

For details of the Golytsin revelations in the American intelligence community, see John Ranelagh, *The Agency: The Rise and Decline of the CIA* (New York: Simon and Schuster, 1987), 565–66, and David Wise, *Molehunt: The Secret Search for Traitors that Shattered the CIA* (New York: Random House, 1992), p. 104ff. Wise provides a fully detailed analysis of the impact of Golytsin's revelations and accusations.

Reference to the abortive publication of *Topaz* by Harper are from the oral history interviews. The library collection of FMB contained the proof copy.

Chapter 18

This chapter derives largely from interviews with Brandstetter, revealed by documentation in the Brandstetter Collection on OPERATION BONNY DATE, correspondence with Mike Howard of the Secret Service, and with a collection of thank-you notes from LBJ's wife and daughter. Lady Bird Johnson's *White House Diary* (New York: Holt, Rinehart and Winston, 1970), Sam Houston Johnson's *My Brother, Lyndon* (New York: Cowles Book Co., 1970), and Lyndon Baines Johnson, *The Vantage Point* (New York: Holt, Rinehart and Winston, 1971)—all memoirs—help confirm a few personal details of the family.

The FMB collection contains a rich folder of materials on OPERATION BONNY DATE, and one of the photo albums gives dramatic pictures of the helicopter and troop operations.

Chapter 19

There are about two cubic feet of materials in the collection dealing with navy visits. The episodes detailed in this chapter are culled from a review of the correspondence, given flavor by information from the oral history interviews. On the whole, the visits were not given much publicity, but several clippings in the collection confirm the "s.o.p." of the visits, as does the correspondence.

Chapter 20

The letter from HRH Charles thanking FMB helped substantiate this story, which was largely based on two separate interviews made at different periods (1988 and 1994) detailing the visit. In addition, the FMB Collection contains several photos of the meeting in the reception line, and the invitation to the embassy reception.

Chapter 21

These anecdotes were based largely on documents in the FMB Collection. There is one cubic foot of material on Playa Encantada, two folders on El Tapatio, and two others on Acolman. Grapetree Bay is represented with a cubic foot of material and there are scattered folders on the other ventures. Some notes by FMB on the Russian planning and a few anecdotes on tape helped piece together the ventures. Albums, scrapbooks, and a picture and ephemera collection of brochures, menus, flyers, and clippings provided further detail.

Chapter 22

The FMB Collection contains extensive correspondence by General Stillwell as he sought foundation for the case. Materials on the de Vosjoli case and notes by FMB on the meeting with Fitch helped establish the basis. Charles Raw, *Do You Sincerely Want to be Rich?* (New York: Viking Press, 1971), and Arthur Herzog, *Vesco: From Wall Street to Castro's Cuba* (New York: Doubleday, 1987) helped provide background.

Stillwell inscribed a picture of himself as follows to Brandstetter: "To Brandy, A rare human being who commands my admiration and respect by reason of his steadfast adherence to principle, his strategic perspectives, and tactical effectiveness, his resolute courage in all manner of crises. In short, a 'winner' that I am proud to have as friend. Dick Stillwell." Another note from Stillwell in the Brandstetter collection reads: "16.1.88 Dear

Brandy—No student of the ancient wargame ever learned more from a master instructor or with a lesser tuition! A million thanks! May all things good be your constant lot in the Year of the Dragon (and the XXIV Olympiad.) Respectfully, Dick."

Among the letters supporting Stillwell in his search for documentation was one dated 18 April 1988 from Tom Polgar, who had served with the CIA for eighteen years. Polgar remarked on Brandstetter's "extensive knowledge of Mexican economic and political conditions" and his "vast net of interlocking contacts capable of providing insight on developments relating to the stability of Mexico and on matters bearing on U.S.-Mexican relations."

Other letters in the files from William Webster and from Al Burkhalter also spoke to Brandstetter's service.

There are two letters from J. Edgar Hoover thanking FMB for his assistance in rounding up the two fugitives.

Chapter 23

Oral history interviews on the Moe Morton case were detailed in a full copy of the transcript of the hearings of the Illinois Racing Commission. Background can be found in works on organized crime. Specifics of the Gelli case appeared in Claire Sterling, *Time of the Assassins* (New York: Holt, Rinehart, and Winston, 1984) and in David Yallup, *In God's Name* (New York: Bantam, 1984). Richard Hammer, *The Vatican Connection* (New York: Holt, Rinehart, and Winston, 1982) also provides good background. The film, *Godfather III*, gave a fictionalized account of the Ambrosiano scandals.

Chapter 24

The FMB Collection contains two cubic feet of materials regarding Seagrams, together with three photo albums. There was a thick folder regarding the visit with Allen Drury to the Bohemian Grove. One album contains news clippings in Spanish and original photos regarding Seagrams de Mexico in 1966; the second contains photos of the various public relations activities, with clippings in Spanish and English, regarding the golf tournament, the fair in Taxco, and the yacht regatta; the third contains details of the January 1976 backgammon tournament at Las Brisas, with photos taken of the layout of the tables and the guests as they played.

The two cubic feet of Seagrams folders contain extensive details regarding the problems with the Hacienda and with the SEC (including a *Wall Street Journal* clipping, 11 September 1978, regarding that investigation), and extensive correspondence between FMB and various Seagrams' executives on planning, business activities, and reports of reforms. Also included are his itineraries to the London board meetings, planned and executed itineraries for both SDM and SOSCO, and extensive public relations materials, including clippings of the Osorio articles. Several copies of the brochure he designed, together with the original sketch for the brochure, are in the files. Background material on Seagrams includes: the *Annual Report*, 1975; a commemorative photo brochure by *Seagrams Spotlight Magazine* on Sam Bronfman; a report titled "Tequila Operations;" and other business reports given to FMB as part of his background reading.

FMB prepared an extensive and detailed chronology of the events during his stay at SDM, coupled with substantiating copies of letters and memoranda, which helped unravel the unfolding crises and problems.

Pertinent clippings include: *Travel Scene* 15 March 1977; *Impact* (newsletter of the Wine and Spirits Executive), 1 June 1978; *Time Magazine*, 16 May 1994; *Business Week*, 1 June 1987; *Mexico City News*, 13 September 1976; and *Daily News* (New York) 13 November 1974. Several copies of pertinent issues of Osorio's *Novissimo* provide details of the tournaments and other public events.

Oral history interview tapes expanded on the personal anecdotes of FMB encounters with Sam and Edgar Bronfman and conveyed FMB judgments about the enterprises.

Chapter 25

The stories of these visits were told in oral history interviews. Clippings and collections from Corsica, together with a marked-up map of the island and photo collections, help provide more detail than given on tape. Several clippings from French magazines and newspapers taken during the stay helped provide background on the local political situation. FMB's notes on the Greek trip helped establish dates of visits, combined with comments from the oral interviews.

FMB provided the authors with a rough draft set of notes on the Argentine trip, which, when coupled with photographs, became the basis of the account. Information on the Malvinas-Falkland War and the dispute over the Beagle Channel Islands was confirmed from Richard Natkiel and Anthony Preston, *Atlas of Maritime History* (New York: Gallery Books, 1987).

Chapter 26

Brandstetter's oral history was supported by a thorough collection of materials, amounting to two cubic feet, including itineraries; receipts; business cards; hotel, travel, and museum brochures; maps with notations including a very detailed account of the trips to Kruger Park; copies of materials from Jack Penn; newsclippings from South African newspapers; notes and comments by FMB; and a miscellaneous collection of ephemera and scraps, some of which proved quite interesting and were used to expand or confirm the story provided by interview. For example, menus and business cards confirmed the side trip to Spain and the meetings there. Corrected itineraries and maps confirmed the interrupted trip at Plettenberg. The file of inter-hotel telexes confirmed the efforts of the Sun chain to treat FMB as a visiting VIP. There was a note from Barbara Walters, which FMB picked up at the Le Cirque, written on Helmsley Plaza stationery with her phone number.

The oral history taped account for this trip was quite extensive and gave a clear description of the Nixon meeting, the trip itself, and encounters with officials in South Africa. The reporting channel to the American defense community was made no more explicit than conveyed in the text, although the post-trip meetings with Nixon, Ridgway, and Defense Intelligence are reflected in the correspondence files in this section of the FMB Collection.

The collection contained several copies of Jack Penn's *The Right to Look Human*.

Chapter 27

This summary of events derives from the oral history tapes, with dates confirmed from the documents in the collection. There are extensive folders on the Grey Eagles, on the formation of the AFIO, and many papers relating to such friends and acquaintances as McLendon, Kaplan, Clement Stone, and others. FMB's various activities through the 1980s included support for Danny Graham in the High Frontier initiative, that later became the Strategic Defense Initiative, and the support of a number of politically conservative causes through both the American Legion and contacts in academic circles. The files contain some materials on these subjects which may be useful to students of the era.

Chapter 28

 This summary of the influences on FMB's life derives, to a great extent, from several long sets of notes he prepared for the authors, representing his own attempt to condense his views. In addition, a number of the elements in this chapter are derived from extensive interviews at Casa Tranquilidad. Well-thumbed copies of the works by Clement Stone and J. E. Knight are in Brandstetter's library.

INDEX